Central ✔ KT-140-110

U.S.A.

Joe Allens
327 W 46th St
between 8th/9th.
Jimmy's Metro Deli
790 8th Ave W. 48th S

How to use our guide

These 256 pages cover the highlights of the U.S.A., grouped under eight regional headings. Although far from exhaustive, our selection of sights will enable you to make the best of your trip.

 The **sights** to see are contained between pages 37 and 194. Those most highly recommended are pinpointed by the Berlitz symbol.

The **Where to Go** section p. 35 will help you to plan your visit according to the time available.

For **general background** see the sections America and the Americans p. 8, Facts and Figures p. 15, and History p. 16.

Entertainment and **activities** (including eating out) are described between pages 195 and 215.

The **practical information,** hints and tips you will need before or during your trip begin on page 216.

The **map section** at the back of the book (pp. 240–251) will help you find your way round and locate the principal sights.

Text: Jack Altman
Staff editor: Christina Jackson
Layout: Doris Haldemann
Cartography: Falk Verlag, Hamburg

We wish to express our thanks to all the local tourist offices around the U.S.A. and the U.S. Rangers in the national parks. We are particularly grateful to Mrs. Darryl Kestler and to Anne Merewood for their help.

Printed in Switzerland by Weber S.A., Bienne.

11th edition (reprinted with corrections 1996)

CONTENTS

CONTENTS

Although we make every effort to ensure the accuracy of all the information in this book, changes occur incessantly. We cannot therefore take responsibility for facts, prices, addresses and circumstances that are constantly subject to alteration. Our guides are updated on a regular basis as we reprint. We are always grateful to readers, however, who let us know of errors, changes or serious omissions.

Photos: pp. 169, 175, 178, 179, 182, 186/187, 191, 211, Claude Huber; pp. cover, 38, 39, 43, 53 Jean Mohr; pp. 8, 11, 13, 16, 33, 54, 56, 76, 77, 91, 96, 122, 132, 133, 138, 156, 193, 200, 204, 210, Georg Stärk; pp. 9, 22, 49, 64, 67, 70, 71, 80, 87, 90, 100, 129, 137, 147, 149, 157, 171 KEY-color/ZEFA; pp. 61, 153, 166 KEY-color; pp. 17, 27, 34, 141, 201 Maximilien Bruggmann; p. 194 Kurt Ammann; pp. 107, 110, 115 Jacques Bétant; p. 117 Martin Gostelow; p. 103 Philadelphia Convention & Visitors Bureau; p. 144 Denver & Colorado Convention & Visitors Bureau; p. 197 Keystone Photo, Colorado.

For those planning long stays in New York, Washington D.C., Boston, Florida, California, Los Angeles or Hawaii, our regional guides provide information on those destinations in greater depth. Berlitz Travel Guides are available at most bookshops, newsstands and airport terminals.

AMERICA AND THE AMERICANS

It's significant that, in spite of the honourable competing claims of Canada, Mexico, Brazil or Argentina, when Anglophones talk of "America", they mean the United States. This cannot just be imputed to a political or economic domi- nance or a cultural or other form of "imperialism". It's simply a tribute to the way the world's popular imagination has been captured by the adventure that has taken a pion- eering people from the green fields of Massachusetts to the deserts and mountains of California—and up to the moon and back.

"America" is part of our global dream and the United States has

embodied it with an infinitely varied continent that challenges the senses of the first-time visitor and remains a constant source of excitement for those who have lived there all their lives.

The old civilizations of Europe and Asia have it seems always needed to come to the United States to recharge their batteries. For the U.S.A. is still an apparently inexhaustible reservoir of energy, whether in its primary forms derived from oil in Texas and Alaska or uranium in Colorado and Utah, or the other, far more exhilarating energy of ideas, in the computer world of Silicon Valley, California, the movie industry in Hollywood, the business world of Wall Street,

American ways of life

the Washington "think tanks", or the cosmic explorations of Houston and Cape Canaveral.

But nobody knows better than the Americans that all work and no play would make Jack, Giovanni or Hans a dull boy, and so the United States is also blue jeans, tee shirts, fast food, surfboards and soft-wheeled roller skates. Other countries proudly display their glorious past in museums, cathedrals, temples and palaces. America joyfully displays its exuberant present—in the street and on the beach. Other countries talk of their culture, America talks of its way of life. Visitors to the United States are catching up with their own century.

And just when Europeans might hazard a patronizing observation on America's cultural life, they'll be made to eat their words by any one of half a dozen world-class symphony orchestras in Chicago, New York, Los Angeles, Philadelphia, Cleveland, Washington or Boston (an American half-dozen quite naturally has seven in it). Or by the endlessly innovative painting and sculpture of Manhattan, the great museums of New York, Washington and Chicago, and, nationwide, an architecture forever seeking surprising solutions—often superb, occasionally horrendous, but never timid—to the problems of housing in our overcrowded age.

Yet Americans, clearly the spoilt children of creation when it came to distributing the bounty of the earth, have at their disposal a huge diversity of landscapes to which they can run from that overcrowding. Luckily for them—and for foreign visitors—man's environmental reawakening came just in time to preserve much of the beauty of the continent's wide open spaces. For sailors and fishermen there are the wild Atlantic coast of Maine and its Pacific counterpart in northern California, Oregon and Washington. Or the calmer waters of Long Island Sound, Chesapeake Bay or the lazy beaches of Florida and southern California. In between, the Great Lakes of the Midwest might qualify as seas anywhere else in the world.

Stretching right across the country are the great national parks and nature reserves, luring people to paddle around the swamps of Florida's Everglades or hike and climb in the White Mountains of New Hampshire, the Great Smokies of North Carolina and Tennessee and the Rockies of Colorado. The vast parks of the West, with the geysers, waterfalls and evergreen forest of Wyoming's Yellowstone, the rainbow canyons of Utah's Zion, the massive granite and red-

New York, New York!

woods of California's Yosemite or Sequoia and of course Arizona's Grand Canyon, offer humbling sanctuaries in which to meditate on the natural beauty that is perhaps the soul of this industrial giant of America. Even the deserts—the Petrified Forest south-east of the Grand Canyon, or Death Valley in California's Mojave—grant you an enriching respite from civilization.

But civilization American-style is too much sheer fun to stay away from for too long. Each of the major cities offers its own adventure. The street life of New York is a carnival — endless movement, colour, noise and smell—sometimes hair-raising, always stimulating. Boston, Washington and Philadelphia are the metropolitan pillars of United States' history, proud and dignified, though never taking themselves too seriously. New Orleans offers an unashamedly theatrical view of a bygone elegance and decadence, part Gallic, part Deep South, all tongue-in-cheek. Santa Fe is somehow its grand Spanish counterpart, quieter, more romantic. Nothing quiet or romantic about big, boisterous Chicago in America's heartland, but the town never fails to surprise visitors with the beauty of its lake-front architecture. Dallas and Houston are the bumptious concrete realizations of the Texan dream, ranchers gone urban. And

crazy Los Angeles and lovely, non-conformist San Francisco are the last extravagant statements of America's push to the West. Big and small, America's cities—they may occasionally call themselves towns, but never villages—can be enjoyed both as playgrounds and as workshops displaying all the good and bad aspects of our century's urban development.

And when you're tired of coping with the real world, you can sneak off to the fantasy realms of Disney World and Disneyland and Magic Mountain and Knott's Berry Farm and all the other "theme parks" that have mushroomed around the country. Here the thrills and excitement and joys and fears are carefully calculated not to create too much stress. Good clean family fun. Chil-

American football—war with a smile

dren have a very important place in American life, and Americans have long understood that all of us, some of the time and more often than we care to admit, are children.

Americans love to play. Their own versions of old European

13

AMERICA AND THE AMERICANS

sports—baseball (which American encyclopedias reluctantly admit is "doubtless derived" from English cricket and rounders) and what they call football, which looks to European eyes like something Roman gladiators would have invented—are marvellously exuberant spectacles. And in addition to the myriad spectator sports there's the endless flow of fads that spring up around the beaches of Florida, California or Hawaii—surfing, roller-skating, hula-hooping—they come and go with the airy grace of a Frisbee. Where else in the world would the gruelling torture of marathon running be turned into a carnival for the whole family in towns like New York or Boston?

Americans, Americans—in a country as vast and varied as the United States, it's hazardous to claim that you know what you're talking about when you use the word "Americans". White Anglo-Saxon Protestants? Irish Catholics? Hispanics, Poles, Italians, Germans, Greeks, Scandinavians, Russians, Jews, Czechs, Africans, Chinese, Japanese, Vietnamese or Sioux, Navajo, Cherokee and Cheyenne? Or, for that matter, New Yorkers and New Englanders, Southerners and Texans, Midwesterners and hill-billies, and again, to confound all generalizations, Californians? It's worth making out this

long and far from exhaustive list just to be able to contemplate the incredible diversity of these people we call Americans.

And then you suddenly realize you have the answer. There is the valid definition of Americans. They are this people of boundless variety. Somehow people from every corner of the earth have landed up living together, by no means always peacefully, but this is the only place where that has happened on such a scale and, for all the revolution and civil war and riots, with such astounding success. Perhaps the greatest adventure of your whole American journey will be to encounter as many as you can of the different people making up these United States: the cool New Englanders, pushy New Yorkers, bluff and hearty Texans, earnest midwestern farmers—and their exact opposites, for no generalization stands up to more than five minutes' scrutiny in this place. But at least it can be said that they have not coalesced into one dull, homogeneous nation of look-alikes, talk-alikes and laugh-alikes. Martin Luther King, Jr., was right to contest the image of America as a melting pot. He said it was in fact a good bowl of vegetable soup in which you could taste the carrots, potatoes, leeks and peas, all separately, and together.

FACTS AND FIGURES

Geography: With an area of approximately 3,615,000 square miles (including Alaska and Hawaii), the U.S. is the fourth largest country in the world, or nearly 40 times bigger than the U.K. Mainland U.S.A. (excluding Alaska), called the 48 conterminous states, stretches for 3,000 miles from the Atlantic to the Pacific and for some 1,200 miles from the Canadian border to the Gulf of Mexico. Hawaii, the 50th state, is situated in the Pacific Ocean, some 2,500 miles to the south-west. The conterminous states consist, roughly, of the highland region of Appalachia in the east, the Rocky Mountains in the west and the Great Plains in the centre.

Highest point: Mount McKinley (Alaska), 20,320 feet.
Lowest point: Death Valley (California), 282 feet below sea level.

Population: 250,000,000 of which 83% are Whites, 12% Blacks, 1% Indians and 4% of other races. The density is 64 people per square mile. 73% live in urban areas.

Capital: Washington, District of Columbia (pop. 638,000).

Major cities: New York (7,353,000), Los Angeles (3,353,000), Chicago (2,978,000), Philadelphia (1,647,000), Houston (1,698,000), San Diego (1,070,000), Detroit (1,306,000), Dallas (987,000).

Government: The U.S. is a federal republic (consisting of 50 states and 1 federal district), with a two-party system (Democrats and Republicans). The government is based on the Constitution of 1787. The president is elected for a period of 4 years, and can be re-elected once. The Congress is composed of the Senate (with 2 senators per state) and House of Representatives (435 members). Each state has its own semi-autonomous government (and local laws) headed by a popularly elected governor.

Religion: 55% Protestant, 37% Roman Catholic, 4% Jewish, 3% Orthodox (Eastern churches), 1% miscellaneous.

HISTORY

A European visiting an Indian village near the Grand Canyon was asked by one of the residents how long he'd been in America. "A month", he replied. "That's nice", said the Indian. "We've been here all the time".

If not all the time, for at least 25,000, maybe as much as 40,000,

years, when mammoth and bison left Siberia in search of new pastures across a now submerged land bridge over the Bering Strait. Mongolian hunters, the Indians' ancestors, followed into what is now Alaska.

Over the centuries, some of them made their way down the Pacific coast and east across the continent. Between 500 B.C. and A.D. 500 the Hopi and Zuni had settled down in farming communities in the adobe-walled *pueblos* (villages) of New Mexico and Arizona. By 1500 the only truly nomadic Indians were the Plains Indians, roaming between the Rockies and the Mississippi River forests. Tribes living along the east coast were skilled farmers, growing beans, squash, maize and tobacco. But they had no wheel, either for wagon or pottery, no metal tools, and no horses. Their only beasts of burden were dogs.

The Europeans Arrive

Although the claim that the 6th-century Irish monk, St. Brendan, got there first is considered a nice piece of blarney, historians do accept that Norsemen living in Greenland made their way across to Newfoundland between 1001 and 1015. But they disappeared again without trace.

Not so the Spanish. It was 10 o'clock at night on October 11,

1492, when their Genoese captain, Christopher Columbus, stood with his watchman looking at a pale light on the western horizon. It turned out to be on an island in the Bahamas, just 380 miles from Miami Beach.

Five years later, another Genoese-born sailor, John Cabot, set foot in Newfoundland, stopping just long enough to stake the fateful English claim to North America for his master, Henry VII. But it was the name of a third Italian explorer, Amerigo Vespucci, that was used by a German mapmaker and stuck to both northern and southern continents.

The first European contact with the future United States mainland came in 1513 when Spanish explorer

Cliff Palace at Mesa Verde

Juan Ponce de León was searching for the fabled Fountain of Youth. He stumbled, appropriately enough, on the coast of Florida, where elderly Americans still come from the chilly north and midwest to warm their tired bones. In 1565, the Spaniards built a fort in St. Augustine, the first permanent settlement in North America.

Other areas touched by Spanish exploration were New Mexico, the Grand Canyon in Arizona, Texas, and the Mississippi River. At their height, the Spanish brought to the New World an irresistible mixture of courage, brutality and civilization. If the Indians succumbed in the confrontation, it was due not only to their vulnerability to the strange European diseases and superior weaponry, but also—perhaps primarily—to their lack of unity. Each tribe had a name that was a variation of "We the People", considering all other tribes as potential enemies. Europeans were hailed as "Men from the Sky"—heaven-sent allies against their rivals. It took several generations for the Indians to unite in common cause and by then it was too late.

The British finally got into the colony business in 1607. After cursory examination of California (by Sir Francis Drake) and some unsuccessful efforts on the east coast (by Sir Walter Raleigh), they established their first settlement at Jamestown, Virginia.

Then on November 11, 1620, 102 Separatists landed on Cape Cod, Massachusetts, aboard the *Mayflower*. The seeds of American democracy were contained in a remarkable covenant drawn up by these "Pilgrims"—the Mayflower Compact which provided that laws accepted by the majority would be binding on all. They founded a community at Plymouth Bay, learning from friendly Indians how to fish and plant maize. Half the pilgrims died that first hard winter. The following October, after a good harvest, the survivors and 90 Wampanoag Indians held a three-day feast of wild turkey and waterfowl—their first Thanksgiving.

Between 1630 and 1646 many Puritans arrived in New England under the charter of the Massachusetts Bay Company, and groups from the "old country" stayed intact to form the new townships. Local affairs were decided and local officials elected at town meetings of the landowners. But all were not satisfied with the way things were run. Clashes between conservative elders and opponents of the religious oligarchy led to new community experiments a little further west—in Rhode Island and Connecticut. America was already on the move.

In 1626, the Manhattan Indians sold their island to the Dutch West India Company for the legendary sum of $24 and New Amsterdam sprang up as a classic seaman's town of taverns and seedy hangouts for smugglers and illicit traders. The clergy of the Dutch Reformed Church and the few wealthy businessmen with houses there found it was none too safe to walk around Manhattan late at night. Apart from a few farms or *bouweries,* the Dutch didn't invest much in their American property, concentrating their energies on the East Indies. Smart New Englanders moved down to Westchester and Long Island and the British began putting pressure on the Dutch to move out. In 1664, with the British fleet hovering in the harbour, the Dutch governor, Peter Stuyvesant, let New Amsterdam become New York without a shot being fired in protest. A few Dutch families remained, including the Roosevelts.

Meanwhile the French, who had been up in Quebec since 1608 converting Indians into Christians and beavers into pelts, were extending their fur trade with expeditions down the Mississippi River. They founded Louisiana in 1682.

In the same year, William Penn set up a colony in Philadelphia. This energetic Quaker from London had inherited a useful fortune and established the proprietary province of Pennsylvania as a haven of free enterprise and religious tolerance. The Swedes, Finns and Dutch already settled there were now joined by farmers from Britain, France and Germany. The American adventure of ethnic coexistence was under way.

Things were slightly less peaceful back in Massachusetts. The Reverend Cotton Mather was stirring up hysteria arising from the horrendous Salem "witch hunts". Children told stories of broomstick-flights, witches' sabbaths, flying saucers and sexual relations with the devil. Trials led to the hanging of five men and 14 women by the summer of 1692. The fear of godlessness spreading through New England brought about a religious revival in the 1730s, known as the "Great Awakening", with hellfire-and-brimstone preachers roaring from their pulpits.

Towards Revolution

As the British Empire expanded in the middle of the 18th century, London demanded that the American colonies contribute more to its upkeep and defence. While accepting London's authority in foreign affairs, the colonists assumed they would enjoy the same freedoms and privileges as other Englishmen. But between 1764 and 1767 a series of special taxes (on newspapers and legal documents) and duties (on imported sugar, silk, linen, Madeira wine, paint, lead, paper and tea) made them realize they weren't just Englishmen abroad. A South Carolina leader, Christopher Gadsden, drew the inevitable conclusion: "There ought to be no New England men, no New Yorkers known on the continent, but all of us Americans".

Groups known as "Sons of Liberty" formed in New York, Charleston and Boston and attacked the royal tax collectors' houses and burned their furniture. In Boston, the propagandist and agitator Samuel Adams led dances around the Liberty Tree, an elm from which unpopular officials were hanged in effigy. As unrest mounted, the British sent two regiments to Boston. In March 1770, a mob snowballed guards in front of the Boston Customs House. The attack grew fiercer and the British were ordered to fire, killing four Bostonians.

Most of the offending duties were repealed, and there followed three years of peace and prosperity. But the duty on tea remained. While Charleston, Philadelphia and New York staged boycotts, Sam Adams' Sons of Liberty (disguised as Mohawk Indians) boarded three British ships in Boston Harbor and dumped the cargo into the sea. The momentous Boston Tea Party of 1773 moved George III to say: "The colonies must either submit or triumph". The Americans agreed.

Britain stepped up its repressive measures and the American colonies called their First Continental Congress in Philadelphia in September 1774 to coordinate opposition. Once again, Massachusetts took the lead, declaring itself a "free state" and preparing to resist any British offensive with weapons and ammunition stored at Concord. The British moved 12,000 troops to Boston and, in April 1775, a contingent marched out to deal with the rebels. As any American schoolchild can recite, the patriots' messenger, Paul Revere, rode "through every Middlesex village and farm" to warn of the British advance on Concord. The first resistance took place at Lexington, but it was on the bridge at Concord that "embattled farmers" faced the British and "fired the shot heard round the world".

With a Virginian colonel, George Washington, as Commander-in-Chief of the newly constituted Continental Army, the Revolutionary War's first staged battle at Bunker Hill outside Boston resulted in a technical victory for the British with enormous casualties of 1,000 out of 2,200 troops.

But despite the Second Continental Congress's push for independence—led by Massachusetts' John Hancock, Virginia's Thomas Jefferson and Pennsylvania's Benjamin Franklin—many were still reluctant to sever the ties with Britain. In January 1776, the officers' mess at Washington's headquarters was still proposing a toast to George III. "Loyalists" were a considerable faction—big landowners in Virginia and Maryland and small farmers in New York and the Carolinas, even a number of merchants in Massachusetts.

Within a few months, though, the situation had changed. Success at Bunker Hill and the forced evacuation of Boston by the British, as well as a good deal of fervent propaganda in favour of independence brought the representatives around. They moved: "That these United Colonies are, and of right ought to be, Free and Independent States". Two days later, July 4, 1776, the Declaration of Independence was signed, proclaiming the aim of the United States of America's government to be the protection of "life, liberty and the pursuit of happiness".

But the war dragged on for seven more years, with a citizenry not at all keen on protracted warfare. The Americans liked the excitement of victory, vigorous skirmishes and then back to the farm, not this morale-sapping exhaustion of strategic attrition. After the Battle of Long Island in August 1776, the British took control of New York for the rest of the war. Philadelphia fell in September 1777, leaving Washington and his depleted forces to shiver out the winter in nearby Valley Forge.

However, rather than press his advantage after taking Fort Ticonderoga on his way down from Canada, General "Gentleman Jack" Burgoyne preferred to wait for his silver plate, champagne and 30 wagons of personal baggage. The result was defeat for his German mercenaries at Bennington and his own humiliating surrender at Saratoga. Now the British were ready to negotiate a conciliatory peace, but the Americans chose to exploit their new military alliance with France for total victory.

At first, French help, under the ineffectual leadership of Admiral d'Estaing, proved less than helpful. The British assumed control of the Atlantic coast, gaining victories at Savannah and Charleston. Then American troops forged north to Virginia, picking off British outposts along the way. There, French support paid off in a combined action with Washington in which 15,000 men won the decisive Battle of Yorktown. On October 17, 1781, Lord Cornwallis's British soldiers surrendered.

The epic of the Far West re-enacted

After two years of tedious negotiations led by Ben Franklin, the Peace of Paris ended the war on September 3, 1783.

The New Republic Expands Westwards

New York was the first capital of the new United States of America and it was on a balcony overlooking Wall Street on April 30, 1789, that George Washington was inaugurated as president. Endowed with great character, he made up for his lack of political talent by surrounding himself with men who possessed it in abundance, among them, Thomas Jefferson as secretary of state and Alexander Hamilton at the treasury. His vice

president was John Adams—cousin of Sam, the troublemaker.

In the Republic's early years, Hamilton, a brilliant administrator, favoured a governing class of merchants, industrialists and bankers in the authoritarian European model, while Jefferson was eager to break with traditions that he felt had made Europeans "either hammer or anvil". As champion of a new democracy, Jefferson was disturbed by an obstacle to it on his own doorstep. The United States' first census of 1790 showed a population of nearly 4 million of whom 700,000 were black slaves. Himself a slave-owner on his Virginia farm, Jefferson expressed hopes for "a total emancipation", fearing otherwise the direst trouble for the Union of the states.

23

Jefferson was elected president in 1801, the first to be inaugurated in the new capital at Washington, on the Potomac River. Apart from the White House and the Capitol, there was little more than a collection of ramshackle boarding houses where many senators and congressmen had to bed down on the floor.

One of the major triumphs of the Jefferson presidency was the Louisiana Purchase of 1803. The French territory stretched from the Mississippi to the Rocky Mountains, 828,000 square miles that more than doubled the size of the country. Preoccupied with an insurrection in Haiti and his war with the British, Napoleon was happy to sell for $15 million. The next year, Captain Meriwether Lewis and Lieutenant William Clark set out from St. Louis to explore the uncharted West up to the Pacific Ocean.

The expedition was intended not only to lay American claim to the Oregon territory but also to size up the Indian situation in the northwest. Many suspected that the British were encouraging the Indians to resist American western expansion. This and disputes over free trade rights during Britain's naval blockade of Napoleon led, under President James Madison, to another war with the British, from 1812 to 1814. The U.S. invaded Canada, killing the great Indian leader Tecumseh and burning parliamentary houses in York (later Toronto) as well as surrounding villages. The British retaliated at Fort Niagara and Buffalo. Washington was attacked, the White House set on fire.

General Andrew Jackson made the reputation that was to win him the presidency 15 years later with ferocious assaults on the Indians in Tennessee and Florida, and on the British at New Orleans—a tragic battle that left 2,000 British dead or wounded for the loss of only 13 Americans, although a peace treaty had been signed in Belgium two weeks before.

With Jackson turning his attention back to Florida, Spain hurriedly sold off its lands east of the Mississippi and its claim to the Oregon country for a flat $5 million. While participating enthusiastically in the great powers' expansionist spirit of the 19th century, President James Monroe proclaimed his well-known doctrine warning Europeans to keep their hands off North and South America: "We should consider any attempt on their part to extend their system to any portion of this hemisphere as dangerous to our peace and security".

The Jacksonian era from 1829 to 1840 covered not only the presidency of crusty old Andrew Jackson but also that of his protégé Martin Van Buren. After years of gentlemanly rule by the Republic's founding fathers, this new generation of populist Democrats took power with no political programme beyond a general pride in their log-cabin origins and prowess in battle.

Jackson's was the spirit that pushed the American frontier to the west. Trappers and furhunters led the new pioneers from the Missouri River to the Rockies during the 1830s. Then, in canvas-covered wagons known as "prairie schooners", thousands of backwoodsmen set out for the Oregon country in the 40s. America's drive to the Pacific was widely proclaimed to be the nation's "manifest destiny".

Other Americans moved beyond the United States frontiers to Mexican-owned Texas. By 1836 they were 20,000 strong, outnumbering the Mexicans there by 4 to 1. They liked Mexican horsemanship, saddles and trappings, but rebelled against the authoritarian government. After fierce fighting in retaliation for the Mexican massacre of Americans at the Alamo, the Americans made Texas an independent "Lone Star Republic". In 1845 it was annexed to the U.S.

The tough, expansionist president, James Polk, blustered his way into war with Mexico for California and the south-west in 1848, ultimately winning California, Utah, Nevada and parts of Arizona, New Mexico, Wyoming and Colorado. For all this, the U.S. paid $15 million, a bargain that turned into a bonanza with the discovery of gold in California.

Americans against Americans

Throughout the era of western expansion, the slavery issue festered. Slaves made up 40 per cent of the southern states' population. As long as cotton was "king", representing two-thirds of U.S. exports, the South felt it could justify working slaves on the plantations. But the cost of their upkeep was prohibitive, outweighing the cotton profits when settlement of the Great Plains opened up a new market for the north-east, making it less dependent on southern trade. But the economic factor proved secondary to the social status conferred in the South on slave owners. When rebellions broke out in South Carolina and Virginia, repression was ruthless and strict curfews were placed on all Blacks. Owners organized night patrols, and teaching slaves to read or write was strictly forbidden.

In the North, the abolitionist movement grew to 200,000 by 1840. Since slave owners could legally reclaim fugitives in the northern states, an "Underground Railroad" was organized to help escaped slaves up into Canada. By the 1850s, any lingering moral considerations the South may have had were blurred by the purely political issue of states' rights. The slave states insisted on the right to decide their own affairs without the interference of the federal government.

A new Republican Party was founded in 1854 on an anti-slavery platform and, by the 1860 presidential elections, was firmly identified with the North. The Democrats split on the issue of whether the new western territories should be obliged to permit slavery, and southern states fielded their own candidate in addition to the Democrats' official nominee. The Republicans chose a man of reassuringly simple personality who could get enough support in the new midwestern states to guarantee victory over the divided Democrats. The homespun Illinois attorney, honest Abraham Lincoln, did the trick.

When South Carolina immediately led Mississippi, Alabama, Florida, Georgia, Louisiana and Texas into secession from the Union, the stated reason was unambiguous: the North had "united in the election of a man whose opinions and purposes are hostile to slavery". In fact, Lincoln's aims were not that simple. As he wrote to a New York editor: "My paramount object in this struggle is to save the Union and not either to save or

destroy slavery". But he had said earlier: "I believe this government cannot endure permanently half *slave* and half *free*".

In February 1861, the Confederate States of America elected as their president Jefferson Davis, an aristocratic ex-soldier from Kentucky. Arkansas, Tennessee, Virginia and North Carolina joined the Confederacy, but Kentucky, after

some hesitation, did not. Nor did Missouri, Maryland or Delaware. Virginia's great military leader, General Robert E. Lee, was more ambivalent than the politicians. "I can contemplate no greater calamity for the country", he wrote in January 1861, "than a dissolution of the Union. Still, a Union that can only be maintained by swords and bayonets and in which strife and

Washington, Jefferson, T. Roosevelt and Lincoln carved into Mt. Rushmore

civil war are to take the place of brotherly love or kindness, has no charm for me". This troubled, noble hero promptly emancipated his slaves but joined the Southern cause.

April 12, 1861 marked the start of the Civil War, when local South

27

Carolina troops opened fire on the U.S. military base of Fort Sumter. The rest of the four-year war was a horror. Grand moments of heroism in the great pitched battles of Antietam (Maryland), Gettysburg (Pennsylvania), Fredericksburg (Virginia), Shiloh (Tennessee) and Vicksburg (Mississippi) were mere punctuation marks, however glorious, in the miserable, cold, wet, disease-ridden guerrilla warfare that characterized most of the campaign. In this war of Americans against Americans, dysentery, typhoid, malaria and consumption killed more than twice as many as did bullets and bayonets.

The South, with its proud military tradition, had superior officers and training, but the North, with an overwhelming supremacy in heavy industry, railways and arms manufacture, inexorably triumphed despite its frequently incompetent military leadership. While Lee brought a certain classical elegance and Thomas "Stonewall" Jackson a fatalistic sense of realism to Southern generalship, the North's heroes —Ulysses Grant and William Sherman—demonstrated relentless willpower and sheer brute force.

After Grant occupied the Confederate capital of Richmond, Virginia, Lee submitted the South's surrender at Appomattox on April 9, 1865. Just five days later, Lincoln was assassinated at Ford's Theater in Washington, by Confederate sympathizer John Wilkes Booth. This well-known actor leapt onto the stage after shooting the president, shouting "*Sic semper tyrannis!* The South is avenged!"

Reconstruction

But the revenge was not sweet for the South. Ravaged by the war, its major cities reduced to rubble, Georgia in utter ruin from Atlanta to Savannah, the South found its economy was shattered, its banks insolvent and the cotton crop of 1860 not matched again till 1879. As the planter-aristocracy moved out, either to towns in the North and West or abroad to England, Mexico or Brazil, the poor white farmers took over. The North had prospered, the war having profited a new class of millionaires—Armour in meatpacking, Rockefeller in oil, Remington in guns (later typewriters), Marshall Field in merchandising. Over 800,000 immigrants streamed into the North during the war and over 3 million more followed in the next ten years.

The Blacks, 4 million freed by the Union's victory, faced more hardships. After the first euphoria they woke to the embittered South's new "black codes" under which they could not vote, testify against Whites, bear arms or frequent public places reserved for Whites. In Washington, federal mismanagement could not make good on the "40 acres and a mule" which had been promised each slave. The most positive achievement of the Freedmen's Bureau was to set up new hospitals and schools. Black activist Booker T. Washington wrote of the wholesale rush to the classrooms: "Few were too young and none too old to make the attempt to learn. The great ambition of the older people was to try to learn to read the Bible before they died". But many Blacks also faced greater violence than they'd ever known as slaves, and the Ku Klux Klan, founded in Tennessee in 1866, spread political terror throughout the South.

The federal government's Reconstruction Acts replaced recalcitrant southern state governments with northerners and Blacks, backed by federal troops, to guarantee "equal protection of the laws". While many northerners went south with the noble intention of protecting civil liberties, there were many more "carpetbaggers", aided by southern "scalawags", who exploited the situation for their private profit. Blacks participated in southern government but never had a controlling say, despite their overwhelming majorities in South Carolina, Mississippi and Louisiana.

The Reconstruction governments were often incompetent or corrupt but not more so than before or after. They did introduce tax reform, poor-relief and free public schooling, but white prejudice and hostility were unrelenting. By 1876 the nation was tired of the black civil rights issue, and a "soft" Republican, Rutherford Hayes, defeated tough, reform-minded Samuel Tilden in the presidential election. Enforcement Acts were nullified and for the next three generations southern Blacks were left in a limbo between slavery and freedom.

The World Stage

By 1914, America had established itself as the world's leading industrial power. Railways, steel, coal, oil and the vast agricultural resources of the Great Plains brought wealth such as the planet had never before witnessed.

From 1860 to 1920 the population more than tripled from 31 to 106 million. This was the period of massive immigration: four million British, four million Irish, six million Germans, over two million Scandinavians, and Italians, Poles, Czechs, Austrians, Hungarians, Serbs and Russian Jews. Northern Europeans went west, to the farmlands; southern and eastern Europeans and the Irish stuck to the big eastern and midwestern cities. Jews went into the garment industry, Finns into the mines, Portuguese into textiles. The Chinese worked in the mines and on the railways— and suffered from anti-Oriental laws when white Americans became scared for their jobs.

The trade union movement—or organized labour as it is known— proved less political than in Europe. Rather than question the virtues of the capitalist system, it preferred to demand its fair share of the profits. This proved hard enough, and the strikes, lock-outs and pitched battles between company militia and workers were as violent as anything in the revolutionary "old country".

In keeping with the imperial spirit of the times, America bought Alaska from the Russians in 1867 and gradually absorbed Hawaii by negotiating trading and military privileges with these strategically vital Pacific islands. In the Caribbean, the U.S. proved itself adept at classical gunboat diplomacy. In the 1898 war against the Spanish, America ended up with Puerto Rico and Guam (in the Pacific), military occupation of the Philippines and the role of godfather to Cuba's independence.

As the old nations were engaged on the battlefields of Europe, America was clearly ready for the world stage. Woodrow Wilson, son of a southern Presbyterian minister and president of Princeton University, brought a decidedly moral and didactic flavour to the role. After helping the Allies to victory over Germany, the American President presented at the Versailles peace negotiations an elaborate plan for democracy, international peacekeeping through a League of-Nations, and clemency towards the defeated. He ran into the anti-German jingoism of the British and the open cynicism of France's Georges Clemenceau: "Mr. Wilson bores me with his Fourteen Points; why, God Almighty has only ten!"

Boom and Crash

Following the Russian Revolution, America succumbed to a Red Scare. The New York state legislature expelled five socialist members because their politics were felt to be "absolutely inimical to the best interest of the State of New York and of the United States". In 1927, Bartolomeo Vanzetti and Nicola Sacco, two Italian-born anarchists charged with murdering a shoe-factory paymaster in Massachusetts, were executed. Many held that the jury was swayed more by its fear of anarchic politics than by its conviction of criminal responsibility.

But the '20s were also when the good times rolled: jazz, radio, silent movies, and cars—26 million by the end of the decade. Materialism was respectable. As President Calvin Coolidge put it: "The business of America is business"—and it was enjoying a boom.

The growth of the big cities with their—to Anglo-Saxon Protestant eyes—exotic immigrant populations, brought a threat to the old American rural and small-town principles. Prohibition of alcohol in 1920 was justified with the argument that "Our nation can only be saved by turning the pure stream of country sentiment and township morals to flush out the cesspools of cities and thus save civilization from pollution". Far from upholding the old morality, Prohibition promoted gangland crime and even drove federal enforcement agents into league with Al Capone's bootleggers.

In 1928, Herbert Hoover, very much the candidate of that American business, a great humanitarian in World War I with a mining engineer's efficiency, arrived in the White House with high hopes: "We shall soon with the help of God be in sight of the day when poverty will be banished from this nation". The next year came the Great Crash of the New York Stock Exchange and America slumped into the Depression. Between 1929 and 1932, 5,000 banks closed down.

By 1933, one third of the population were either unemployed or members of families in which the breadwinner was out of work. People went hungry while fruit, vegetables and grain were in abundance. Houses were unheated while coal piled up in mountains. America was stunned by the failure of its classic virtues of business leadership, organization and efficiency.

In 1933, Franklin D. Roosevelt embarked on a whirlwind "Hundred Days" of economic and social measures to conquer the catastrophe. With a canny sense of public relations, the president confided in the people with radio "fireside chats", and immediately cheered them up a little by legalizing wine and beer while Prohibition was dismantled federally and handed over to state legislation.

FDR's "New Deal" proliferated with new initials: NRA (National Industrial Recovery Act) to regenerate industry and improve working conditions; PWA (Public Works Administration) to create jobs with such projects as the Chicago subway, express highways in Virginia and new ships for the Navy; WPA (Works Progress Administration) to build parks and schools and encourage artists, writers, actors and musicians; and the TVA (Tennessee Valley Authority), a regional reconstruction experiment that attracted worldwide attention to its dams for flood control, electric power generation, resettlement of small farmers and rural public health programmes. The New Deal did beat back the disaster of the Depression, but economic recession did not end till World War II.

From World War II Onwards

After Woodrow Wilson's internationalist adventures, much of America preferred the small comforts of isolation, coupled with a pacifist reaction in general. Even FDR said in 1936: "We shun political commitments which might entangle us in foreign wars". But the neutralist policy was revoked after Hitler's 1940 *Blitzkrieg* against Belgium, France and the Netherlands. Congress appropriated $37 million for U.S. arms and aid to its allies—but still resisted military conscription. The Japanese raid on Pearl Harbor, on December 7, 1941, ended all hesitation.

The United States gave unstintingly in manpower and money to the Allied war effort against Germany and Japan. At the same time the war gave a huge boost to American industry. Meat, fuel and tyres were rationed, but the general standards of living remained high throughout the war.

Roosevelt was re-elected to an unprecedented fourth term in 1944.

As a *Chicago Daily News* writer commented: "If he was good enough for my pappy and grandpappy, he is good enough for me". After a long struggle against infantile paralysis, FDR died in April 1945, before the final victory. It was left to Harry Truman to make the momentous decision to use the atom bomb that ended the war against Japan.

In some ways, events after World War II followed the pattern of those after World War I—a Red Scare sparked by the Cold War and underlined by the McCarthyite-witch-hunts; an era of happy materialism under Eisenhower; rock music in place of jazz; illegal marijuana in place of bootleg alcohol; boom prosperity alternating with recessions.

But two outstanding events set these years apart. In the 1960s, under Martin Luther King's inspired and inspiring leadership, black Americans finally obtained the emancipation promised them a century earlier, or at least as much of it as mere legislation can guarantee. At the end of that decade, Christopher Columbus's New World adventure achieved a new dimension when men took off from this continent to go to the moon. In the end, the business of America is *not* business, it's making dreams come true.

WHERE TO GO

Confronting your journey to the United States, you have to make some rather painful decisions. If this is likely to be a once-in-a-life-time trip, you may want to get a feel for the whole country or at least a representative slice of it. Essential to this is a sense of the sheer size of America, in which case you may want to take in both the East and West coasts with some of the grand wide open spaces and natural wonders in between. This is an entirely feasible and financially reasonable proposition with the many special airline tickets that permit multiple destinations, often with almost unlimited mileage. But to "do" America this way, without exhausting yourself, you'll need at least a month.

If, however, this is to be just one of many trips to the U.S., or if you don't have much time, it might be better to concentrate on one or two major regions. Don't forget, any one of these regions might embrace a whole European country, if not two or three.

First-time visitors with just two weeks available could, of course, begin with New York. Without it, they can't claim to have seen Amer-

Dramatic rock formations at Bryce Canyon

ica. Manhattan itself will do for a start. In this car-dominated nation, you should realize that a car in Manhattan is worse than useless. Elsewhere, however, you'll find a car an important asset for excursions. In cities like Los Angeles or the big towns of Texas, you just can't do without a car.

For cross-country trips, Greyhound-Trailways visit all important points on the continent. Trains are less practical, except along the East Coast. Obviously flying is the best choice for long distances, much cheaper and simpler than in Europe. On the "shuttles" between New York and Washington, for instance, it's like taking a bus. But do try the bus or car if you can, to get a taste of America's immensity.

From New York the most convenient regions to include in a two-week stay are the Mid-Atlantic (Washington D.C. and Philadelphia) for the historically minded, and/or New England (Boston and the resorts of Massachusetts and Rhode Island) for those who would like to mix history with relaxation. Or, the Florida part of the South for those who want nothing but fun in the Disney and other theme parks round Orlando, or on the endless beaches.

Another possibility for the two-week holiday is to combine New York with an excursion further afield, either clear across the continent to California, or to one of the country's natural wonders such as the Grand Canyon or Yellowstone. New York, especially in summer, is an exhilarating but also exhausting experience, so you'll need to pace yourself for the rest of the trip.

For the month-long stay, your itinerary might include New York–Boston–Washington, then directly to California, making your way back east via Yellowstone or Grand Canyon; then perhaps San Antonio or Santa Fe for a taste of Spanish America; a distinctive big city like New Orleans or Chicago, then rest up on a beach in Florida till your plane carries you home. If you want to see a lot of America in your four weeks, resist the temptation to start with California. You may be so seduced by it that you'll forget to look at the rest of the country.

The combinations are endless, but remember that Americans themselves like the good life to be both exciting and relaxed. If you want to survive your holiday, follow their example of enjoying both the big city and the parks and handy resorts. Even a town like Chicago has sandy beaches on the lake; New Orleans has its restful bayou country; New York, its Long Island; Boston, its Cape Cod, and most of Los Angeles is beach anyway.

NEW YORK CITY

Perhaps more than any other place on earth, New York is a city people feel they know before they get there. Films and magazine photos have so stamped it into the popular consciousness that you believe you already possess its ferocious mystique of movement and noise, that you're already familiar with the gigantic chasms of skyscrapers, the underworld steam puffing through the manhole-covers and the milling crowds of people.

Then, one day, you go. And it's more than you ever dreamed. Coming in from JFK airport, as you approach Manhattan, the city's skyscrapers loom higher, more impressively than in any film. In the flesh, the crowds on Madison, Fifth and Sixth avenues are a drama of colour you could never conceive of in the abstract. Right in there among the city's Irish, Italians, Chinese, Jews, Germans, Puerto Ricans and Blacks, not to forget the white Anglo-Saxon Protestants, you'll plunge into one of the last travel adventures of our time. Every other place has been discovered, New York is new every time.

While you can't know America without first seeing New York, don't mistake New York for the rest of the U.S.A. Both New Yorkers and non-New Yorkers insist on that with equal vehemence. Facing east, it has always had a taste for Europe. Founded as New Amsterdam by the Dutch in 1626, the city numbered 1,500 inhabitants speaking 18 different languages by 1644. From their earliest years, New Yorkers' loyalties have been divided between America and Europe. On the day George Washington left to take

---

New York in Figures
The dimensions of New York are more than mere figures can express but here are a few to play with anyway:

The five boroughs (Manhattan, Brooklyn, Queens, the Bronx and Staten Island) have a total population of 8 million. With the surrounding suburbs, this figure rises to 12 million, and if the outlying satellite cities are included, the total attains a phenomenal 16 million inhabitants.

New York City covers an area of 300 square miles. It has 6,400 miles of streets and 18 miles of beaches. There are 1,100 parks, squares and playgrounds with a total area of 37,000 acres; 120 museums; 400 galleries; more than 30 department stores; 400 theatres; about 100 skyscrapers; 3,500 churches; 25,000 restaurants; 100,000 first-class hotel rooms and 12,000 taxis.

About 4 million people ride the subway every day. Some 2½ million catch a bus. The number of shops is well up in the thousands. Roughly 17 million people visit New York each year, 2½ million of them from overseas.

---

command of the Continental Army, half the town went to cheer him off. The other half was down at the harbour welcoming the British governor returning from London.

MANHATTAN

This island, 13 miles long and 2 miles wide, encompasses almost everything you will want to see or visit. The other four boroughs, mostly residential, have their own special flavours, but for locals and tourists, New York *is* Manhattan.

As intimidating as it may seem at first glance, Manhattan is, in fact, a very easy place to get around. It divides up simply into three parts: Uptown, Midtown and Downtown (which, unlike in other cities, is the

lower rather than the central part of town). Uptown is north of 59th Street, Midtown speaks for itself and Downtown is the area south of 34th Street.

The backbone of the island is Fifth Avenue; all areas to the west of it as far as the Hudson are known as the West Side, while the East Side covers the area between Fifth Avenue and the East River. Fifth Avenue begins at Washington Square down in Greenwich Village. There and in the Wall Street area, streets still have the names and irregular lines of the colonial era. Otherwise, the roads intersect at right angles and the streets have numbers rather than names. Avenues (First to Twelfth) run

Rockefeller Plaza in summer

north–south, streets (1st to 220th) run east–west. Some avenues have names—York, Lexington, Madison and Park (attempts to rename Sixth the Avenue of the Americas seem doomed). Broadway, obeying no rules, runs more or less diagonally.

With the so-called grid system of rectangular blocks, you pinpoint a place not by street-number but by the nearest intersection of street and avenue; e.g. the Whitney Museum is at Madison and 75th, one block east and seven blocks south of the Metropolitan (Fifth and 82nd).

Midtown

Chances are your hotel will be located in Midtown so that you can cover the area on foot. At any rate, this is the centre, the place to begin.

☑ Rockefeller Center

This soaring cluster of towers between Fifth and Sixth Avenues, from 48th to 51st Street, is the undisputed magnetic core of New York City. Without any one of them being an architectural masterpiece, this ensemble of Indiana limestone buildings achieves a power and harmony that attract thousands of office workers, shoppers, street-vendors, and your better class of roustabout all day long.

The place breathes prosperity. John D. Rockefeller, Jr. originally leased the site from Columbia University in 1928 to rescue it from the infamy of Prohibition speakeasy saloons. They quickly disappeared under the first skyscrapers of a booming business and communications centre, linked by an underground pedestrian concourse, which includes over 200 shops and restaurants.

You immediately sense the cheerful genius of the place with the fountains and flower beds of the **Channel Gardens** that slope down from Fifth Avenue south of 50th Street to the sunken plaza. Akin to the English Channel, the gardens separate the Maison Française on the left and the British Empire Building on the right. At the end is the **Rockefeller Plaza,** parasoled garden café in summer and ice-skating rink in winter. Watched over by a statue of Prometheus, the plaza is dominated by the Center's tallest tower, the **RCA Building,** home of NBC Television. Take its elevator to the 65th floor for a ticket to the **Observation Roof's** great view of Manhattan, five floors higher. Alternatively, try a drink or a meal at the elegant Rainbow Room (also on the 65th floor) and see Manhattan light up at night.

At one time, Rockefeller Center was supposed to be built around a new Metropolitan Opera House. Instead, we got **Radio City Music Hall,** one of the world's most marvellous cinema-cum-variety-palaces —a brilliant 1930s pick-me-up for the Depression blues. Try to see a show there, with the Rockettes, America's most famous troupe of dancing girls, kicking their legs to the Radio City's own symphony orchestra and wonderful Wurlitzer organ, the world's biggest, as you might expect. (Or at least take one of the backstage tours organized seven days a week.) The shimmering chandeliers and mirrors of the lobby would have impressed King Louis XIV. The auditorium, seating over 6,000, is ornamented with fantastic semicircular bands of light. Can you imagine, they nearly tore it down in the 1970s but, as the *New York Times* said in support of the public outcry: "If Radio City Music Hall really closes, it will be a little like closing New York". Finally, they kept both open.

Fifth Avenue

Fifth Avenue—at least the stretch between 34th Street and Central Park—is synonymous with luxury, to sample or to look. If you can't afford to stay at the Plaza Hotel by the Park or to dance, like novelist Scott Fitzgerald's wife, Zelda, in its famous fountain, you can bask in the understated opulence of the diamond-studded windows of Tiffany's jewellery shop—or Cartier's or Van Cleef & Arpels'. Or stroll

around the smarter department stores like Saks Fifth Avenue, Bergdorf Goodman or (just around the corner on 57th Street) Henri Bendel; or try the leather-shops of Mark Cross and Gucci and the high fashion of French and Italian boutiques cashing in on New York's affluent sophistication.

A stunning addition to the Fifth Avenue scene is **Trump Tower** at 56th Street. Inside you will find the ultimate atrium, a cool, airy space, six storeys high, exquisitely finished in rich rose-coloured marble and gleaming brass. An appropriate collection of exclusive and expensive shops surrounds the courtyard.

Amid all this sometimes overripe elegance, turn off a moment at West 47th Street—**"Diamond Row"**—centre of the diamond trade, where black-coated Hassidic Jews from Eastern Europe hurry back and forth with a glitter in their paper bags, under the benign protection of uniformed and plainclothes police.

The valiant effort of **St. Patrick's Cathedral** (between 50th and 51st) to imitate Cologne's Gothic cathedral is a little lost today among the skyscrapers of Rockefeller Center and the Olympic Tower next door. The 1879 building comes into its own for many New Yorkers on the occasion of the spirited Irish Catholic parade on St. Patrick's Day

(March 17) when the Cardinal comes out to greet the marchers.

Times Square and Broadway

The august *New York Times* publishes, it says, "All the News that's Fit to Print" and the old Times Tower gave its name to that bizarre mixture of chic and sleaze—Times Square (on the north side of 42nd Street between Broadway and Seventh Avenue). Times Square in fact encompasses the area from 42nd to 47th Street, between Sixth and Eighth avenues. It's the heart of the theatre district with many first-run cinemas, and is also headquarters for the city's nastiest strip joints and sex shops. Excellent restaurants rub shoulders with the seamiest bars. Sleek limousines deposit ladies in evening dress, just down the street from prostitutes, drunks and dope-dealers, all serenaded by street-entertainers similarly varying from the sophisticated talents of an out-of-work jazz musician to the crummy twanging of someone who stole a guitar.

But New Yorkers make a neat distinction to cope with the incongruous intermingling. Though one and the same area, the pornography and drugs are "at Times Square" while the art and good food are "on Broadway". At all events, the area is generally too depressing by day —go at night when you can't see the garbage and when the neon lights earn Broadway the nickname "the Great White Way".

If the Times Square/Broadway atmosphere gets to be too much for you, take time out in the snug armchairs of the lobby or Blue Bar of one of the greatest monuments of Manhattan's 1920s, the Algonquin Hotel (44th, between 5th and 6th). Partake of the rarefied ambience of New York literati—or at least overhear people repeating the great lines of *New Yorker* magazine wits Martin Amis, Calvin Trillan and Sandy Frazier.

42nd Street

Another haven of peace, as well as an architectural delight, is the **New York Public Library** (5th Avenue between 40th and 42nd). The building is a masterpiece of Beaux-Arts, a 1911 American reinterpretation of the French design school's neoclassical style at its gentlest and restrained best. Set back at the end of a wide, gradually rising stairway, the noble facade's three arches with their coupled Corinthian columns around the entrance invite you in off the street for an hour's tranquility. In this most public of public libraries, relax with a book in the great reading room, admire the changing exhibitions in Gottesman

Manhattan – mineral and vegetables

Hall or laze outside on the steps, where you are well protected by E.C. Potter's giant lions.

East on 42nd Street, at the end of Park Avenue, **Grand Central Station,** terminus of the Vanderbilt railway empire, is as much a legend as it is a building. Like the library, its Beaux-Arts pedigree is utterly impeccable (although it took a U.S. Supreme Court decision to save it from destruction). Over the great clock of the façade, the sculpture of the eagle among various standing and reclining Roman deities apparently symbolizes America's special relationship with the gods. Completed in 1920, the station's 123 rail lines built on two levels, 66 above and 57 below, move half a million people in and out of the city every day, jaded commuters from the suburbs and wide-eyed newcomers from the great beyond. Watch them at rush hour in the vast barrel-vaulted **main concourse.** Fateful Zodiac formations painted in the blue heavens of the ceiling hover over these adventurers.

The Met Life Building over the station infuriated art critics, but the neighbourhood has some other impressive skyscrapers. A superb example of Art Deco can be seen in the stainless-steel swordfish pinnacle of the **Chrysler Building** (Lexington and 42nd). Of course, its glazed enamel, white-brick silhou-

ette is best viewed at a distance, but from the upper floors of nearby hotels you get a close-up of the weird gargoyles inspired by various radiator caps for Chrysler cars. **Citicorp Center** (Lexington between 53rd and 54th) brings an outstanding touch to the skyline with its dramatically sloping silver roof. At ground level, its urban consciousness is emphasized by a lively three-storey "market" of shops and restaurants around a skylit central courtyard as well as, by the same architect, Hugh Stubbins, the free-standing, polygonal **St. Peter's Lutheran Church.** By no means overwhelmed by its skyscraper environment, the church contains a lovely chapel decorated by sculptor Louise Nevelson.

Undoubtedly the best of the sleek office-blocks on Park Avenue is the **Seagram Building** (between 52nd and 53rd). Designed by Mies van der Rohe and Philip Johnson, the pure lines of this bronze-tinted glass skyscraper are considered the ultimate refinement of Mies' International Style. The lobby is decorated by Picasso's stage-backdrop for *Le Tricorne*.

The United Nations (*First Avenue, between 42nd and 48th*)
John D. Rockefeller, Jr., donated the 17-acre site to persuade U.N. members to make their headquar-

ters in New York. A disparate team of international architects, including the Swiss-French master, Le Corbusier, somehow managed to put up buildings in the early '50s with considerably more unity and harmony than are ever achieved inside by the diplomats. The Secretariat is housed in the tower, the General Assembly in the lower block with the concave roof. The complex, including the Dag Hammarskjöld Library, memorial to the late secretary-general, and the Conference Building, is best seen as a whole from the East River on a boat ride around Manhattan.

At the information desk in the lobby (45th and First), you can get tickets for the General Assembly, when it's in session, and guided tours of the whole U.N. complex. Member states have donated parts of the complex—the three Council Rooms, for instance, being the gifts of Norway, Denmark and Sweden, while Britain provided the Barbara Hepworth Sculpture in the Plaza pool (the pool itself was a donation from American schoolchildren).

For a pleasant view of the skyscrapers along U.N. Plaza, buy a sandwich to eat in the garden, or have your lunch (passholders only; reservations at the lobby information desk) in the Delegates' Dining Room overlooking the East River. You can get very reasonably priced craftwork from all over the world at the U.N. gift shop. The post office here sells U.N. stamps only (not American) for letters and cards posted inside the complex.

Empire State Building

Situated on the corner of Fifth Avenue and 34th Street, the Empire State Building is open to the public from 9.30 a.m. until midnight. Although Chicago's Sears Tower is currently the "world's tallest" title-holder, King Kong still prefers the Empire State. Follow him, but take the elevator—there are 1,860 stairs.

Everything about the Empire State Building is huge: 102 storeys; 60,000 tons of steel; 3,500 miles of telephone wires and cables; 60 miles of pipes; the building occupies 11/2 million cubic yards and King Kong had to climb 1,472 feet. Built in 1931, most of its office space was empty in the early Depression years and it paid its taxes with income from the sightseers.

In order to get your ticket to the **Observation Deck,** go down first to the basement—arrows point the way. Next to the ticket office you'll find the Guinness World Records Exhibit. The museum features life-size displays of world-record holders, videos, a data bank on sports, space, science and music superlatives, as well as a ten-foot sculpture of New York landmarks.

The elevator takes you to the 80th floor in under a minute, then you catch the "local" to the 86th. A heated shelter protects you in winter, otherwise the outside terrace offers a fantastic **view,** often of ships 40 miles out at sea. For those who want to go all the way, a third elevator goes to the observation deck on the 102nd floor, at the base of a 204-foot-high communications tower and antenna, from which television and FM radio stations transmit programmes to the metropolitan area.

Downstairs again on 34th Street, you're in a great popular shopping area; stroll over to 32nd Street and Seventh Avenue, where you'll see the enormous **Madison Square Garden,** Manhattan's most famous sports arena.

Downtown

Wall Street Area

Here at the southern end of Manhattan, the skyscrapers assert all their power, closing in on each other across narrow canyons to form ramparts for this almost awe-inspiring capital of capitalism known as Wall Street. Appropriately it was conceived in 1653 as a protection for America's first great financial bargain—a wooden stockade to keep the Indians from invading the island they had sold to the Dutch for $24 (60 guilders) 30 years earlier. Today no address anywhere holds greater prestige.

The beating heart of the Financial District is the **New York Stock Exchange,** reverentially designed as a Roman temple. The entrance at 20 Broad Street leads into the visitors' gallery, open during most of the Exchange's trading hours (weekdays 9.15 a.m. to 4 p.m.). There you can watch the mad transactions on the trading floor that send the sacred Dow Jones Average up and down. A film and permanent exhibition relate the history and workings of the Stock Exchange. The famous ticker-tape is on display, although these days it's been displaced by electronic screens. (The traditional ticker-tape parades for returning war heroes and astronauts have to be fed now with the "top secret" confetti of automatic shredding machines.)

From the temple of the money lenders it's but a short step to the Episcopalian **Trinity Church** (dating from 1846) at the Broadway end of Wall Street. This first, and for many, most successful of America's Gothic Revival churches offers tired office workers—and sightseers—a moment's peace in the cemetery garden. Alexander Hamilton, first secretary of the treasury, is buried here.

During the brief period that New York was the United States' first capital, the **Federal Hall** (corner of Wall and Nassau streets, demolished in 1812 and rebuilt in 1842) was the home of Congress and the place where George Washington took the oath as president on April 30, 1789. His bronze statue stands outside. The other landmark dating from the inception of the Republic is **Fraunces Tavern,** located at the corner of Pearl and Broad streets. It was here that Washington took leave of his officers at the end of the Revolutionary War, six years before his inauguration. The black tavern-owner, Samuel Fraunces, later became Washington's steward in the White House. The present building is an approximate reconstruction of the original.

To the north of Trinity Church, the twin towers of the **World Trade Center** (Church Street between Liberty and Vesey) are overpoweringly big. The great surprise as your eye travels 1,350 feet from top to bottom is in those slim Venetian-Gothic arches at the base. The buildings accumulate impressive figures: 43,600 windows, 198 elevators. A gigantic bronze fountain globe highlights the central square. The whole Center covers an area of 16 acres. A railway station and various subway stations occupy the basement levels, and the concourse (street) level is the site of a vast shopping centre. The **observation deck** is up on the 107th floor of Two World Trade Center looking out over the metropolis, New Jersey and the ocean. You can have that fabulous view during a meal at the Windows on the World restaurant, also on the 107th floor, in One World Trade Center. In February 1993 the center was hit by a terrorist bomb which caused chaos and fatalities; order was rapidly restored over the following months, and security has been tightened.

Statue of Liberty *(15-minute ferry ride from Battery Park)*
It is difficult to imagine a more eloquent symbol than the one this "Lady" of the Statue of Liberty offered those desperate refugees sailing to the New World at the end of the 19th century. Today few Americans or foreigners, however cynical about corny patriotism, can remain totally blasé about this monument, rising 305 feet from its pedestal base to the tip of the torch.

Start at the **American Museum of Immigration** in the base of the statue. This provides an excellent audio-visual introduction not only to the saga of all the ethnic groups coming to America, but also to the story of the American Indians already there and to the Blacks, who were scarcely willing passengers.

You can either pay to ride the elevator or climb the steps to the top of the pedestal. The ultimate feat is to continue up to the platform inside the Lady's crown. The **view** is certainly worth the effort.

The statue's proper name is "Liberty Illuminating the World", a French idea linking the French and American Revolutions. The $250,000 it cost was jointly, and privately, funded, the French paying for the statue and the Americans for the pedestal. The sculptor Frédéric-Auguste Bartholdi took 10 years to complete it, with Gustave Eiffel taking time off from his tower to provide the inner steel casing for the copper-plated figure. Once completed in Paris, it had to be taken apart and shipped over in 214 cases for its 1886 inauguration by President Grover Cleveland.

West of Liberty Island is **Ellis Island** where 12 million of those "huddled masses" passed through immigration checks between 1892 and 1924, where the medically suspect were marked with chalk on their lapels—H for heart, K for hernia, Sc for scalp, X for mental defects. Today, the "island of tears" has been declared a national monument, and has been restored and turned into a museum.

If you don't want to join the crowds on Liberty Island, but want a cooling boat ride as well as a

marvellous view of Manhattan, take the **Staten Island Ferry** (also from Battery Park)—take it anyway, it's the best bargain ride in town. For a superior view, stand forward on the second deck.

Lower East Side *(From Canal Street north to 7th Street)*
This is where the immigrants headed first. Most stayed just long enough to learn English and then headed uptown or out west to the continent beyond the Hudson River. It says something about their special ethnic solidarity that substantial groups of Chinese, Jews and Italians chose to settle here a little longer in their own enclaves. The Chinese are still here in strength, but the colours, sounds and smells of the other communities also linger on vividly enough for you to capture, in an easy afternoon's stroll, the old flavour.

If you take the subway (underground) to **Chinatown,** you won't go wrong: the Canal Street Station has signs in both Roman and Chinese characters. The telephone booths have pagoda roofs, tiny shops sell ivory and jade jewellery, grocers display snow peas, Chinese cabbage and winter melon, and countless restaurants vie for attention with their Cantonese, Shanghai and Szechwan specialities.

Well over 100,000 Chinese live in Chinatown, a loosely defined area centred around Canal Street, Mott Street and Chatham Square. The earliest arrivals came to the country during the California Gold Rush in the 19th-century; most of the immigrants today come directly from Hong Kong. To learn about the history and sites of the area, take the daily hour-long walking tour conducted by the New York Chinatown History Project (tel. 212 691-4785).

The Chinese from the rest of New York come here on weekends to do their grocery shopping and to

---

Invitation to Hope
The famous inscription on the pedestal of the Statue of Liberty was written by Emma Lazarus, a New York poet, in response to the Russian pogroms of the 1880s which drove so many Jews to cross the Atlantic. Her lines have since taken on a universal significance for all the world's oppressed:
> "Give me your tired, your poor,
> Your huddled masses yearning to breathe free,
> The wretched refuse of your teeming shore,
> Send these, the homeless, tempest-tossed, to me:
> I lift my lamp beside the golden door."

enjoy a meal out. The Canal Street supermarkets sell the finest China teas and pretty porcelain to drink it from. Take a look at the Chinese Museum (8 Mott Street) and the Buddhist Temple (64 Mott Street).

South of Mott Street, at 55 St. James Place, is New York's oldest "monument", the Shearith Israel cemetery, founded in 1683 by Portuguese Sephardic Jews from Brazil. But the **Jewish quarter,** settled principally by Eastern European Ashkenazi Jews, is on the northeast side of Chinatown, around the old Hester Street market. Walk along Delancey and Orchard Street and you'll see only a shadow of its heyday at the turn of the century, but such a lively shadow that you sense how hectic it once was. Dormant on the Sabbath from Friday evening to Saturday night, the place springs to life on Sundays, when Orthodox Jews in black hats and long black frock coats pick their way among Hispanic and black vendors. The clothes stores and delicatessens ring with accents inherited from the Jewish villages of Polish Galicia and the Ukraine. For a snack, try a bulging pastrami (seasoned smoked beef) sandwich and a cup of lemon tea in one of the kosher dairy restaurants.

Even tinier than its name suggests, **Little Italy** is centred on Mulberry Street a few blocks to the north-west—and shares its southern part with Chinatown. The Italian section is now principally a gastronomic hub, with expensive as well as moderately priced restaurants and espresso bars, high-quality caterers and, scattered among them, souvenir shops and the occasional grocery store specializing in homemade and imported Italian delicacies. The street is at its liveliest during the ten-day Feast of San Gennaro in September.

Greenwich Village and SoHo

The Village was once New York's artistic centre, home of such illustrious writers as Mark Twain, Edith Wharton, John Dos Passos and O'Henry and painters like Edward Hopper, Ben Shahn and Franz Kline. In the 1950s Villagers went off to listen to the jazz of Miles Davis and Charlie Parker at the Village Vanguard, in the 1960s to hear the first jokes of Woody Allen at the Bitter End cabaret.

Today you can recapture something of the feeling in the crazy second-hand clothing stores around Bleecker Street. At night the jazz cellars are as aromatic as ever and a few coffee houses still serve some very good espresso over which you read your weekly *Village Voice*. A bygone charm and quaintness is still to be found in MacDougal Alley and Washington Mews, the

New York's Best Bridges

Water-laced New York has 65 bridges to hold it together, 14 of them connecting the isle of Manhattan with the surrounding area:

The 1,595-foot Brooklyn Bridge created a sensation when it opened in 1883. But it was plagued by misfortune from the start. Its engineer, John Roebling, died in the early phases of the project as a result of an accident, and his son, Washington, who carried on the work, was paralysed by the bends contracted in the course of the job. And they were not the only casualties. Nonetheless the bridge with its wire webbing is a beautiful success and a favourite subject for photographers and Sunday painters.

The George Washington Bridge spans the Hudson between Manhattan and New Jersey. Designed by Swiss-born O.H. Ammann, its graceful lines show up best at night when the bridge is illuminated.

Newest on the New York horizon is one of the world's longest suspension structures, the 4,260-foot Verrazano-Narrows Bridge from Brooklyn to Staten Island, also the work of Ammann. It's named (give or take one z) after the Italian, Giovanni da Verrazzano, who discovered New York Bay in 1524, landing near the bridge's Staten Island base.

antique shops and, jarringly less authentic, in the candlelit bistros with checked tablecloths and French-sounding food.

Henry James lived for a few months on **Washington Square,** the title of one of his novels and heart of the New York University campus. His grandmother lived in one of the Greek Revival houses along the north side (no. 19), among the most elegant dwellings in New York. A gap in the middle gives you a view up Fifth Avenue from the **Washington Arch,** the work of architect Stanford White, commissioned in 1889 to mark the centenary of Washington's inauguration as president. The park has historically been a rendezvous for criminals—the old oak which was once a gallows for highwaymen today provides shelter for the Village's many drug dealers.

The area south of West Houston Street, **SoHo** (short for South of Houston), is following the pattern of Greenwich Village. Artists who couldn't afford the rents after the Village's commercialization moved south to the abandoned lofts and warehouse floors of the industrial district. The most successful artists were able to install kitchens, bathrooms and comfortable interiors. Others made do with bare walls and floors for the sake of the ample space and light. Through the curtainless windows you can admire either some affluent décors or some huge canvases and monumental sculpture in the making. With the success of the avant-garde galleries on West Broadway, especially number 420, where the old pillars of the Pop Art movement, Andy Warhol, Robert Rauschenberg and Roy Lichtenstein, displayed their works, rents soared. The interior decorators and gallery owners took over from the artists, many of whom moved out, heading south-west to the TriBeCa (*tri*angle *be*low *ca*nal) area.

Uptown

The Upper West Side—that is, west of Central Park—defies any label to its neighbourhoods other than "mixed". Intellectuals and artists live side by side with the shopkeepers and bus drivers of every ethnic and racial background. Street life manages to be both harmonious and lively.

Lincoln Center *(W. 62nd to W. 66th, between Columbus and Amsterdam)*
With most of the prestigious fine arts museums situated on the affluent Upper East Side, the Lincoln Center for the Performing Arts provided a good balance and a perfect fillip for the revival of the neighbourhood in the 1960s. Since

Daddy had to shelve his plan to put the Metropolitan Opera in the Rockefeller Center, John D. III led the drive to find it another home, along with the New York Philharmonic, the New York City Ballet and the Juilliard School of Music. The Center replaced a Puerto Rican neighbourhood of the kind immortalized by Leonard Bernstein's musical comedy *West Side Story*—

Bernstein moved on, too, after a stint with the Philharmonic.

As you go up the steps to the plaza on Columbus Avenue—especially at night with the central fountain bathed in ethereal light—you may find the effect a little too self-consciously "prestigious". New Yorkers do take their arts seriously. The undoubtedly important buildings around the plaza are over-

whelmingly monumental, starting on the left with the severe modern classicism of Philip Johnson's **New York State Theater,** home of the New York City Ballet and New York City Opera. Men can't help adjusting their ties and women straightening their dresses when entering the opulent foyer with its gilded-chain drapery and gold-velvet ceiling.

At the back of the plaza, Wallace K. Harrison's grand design for the **Metropolitan Opera House,** with its tall glass façade arched in travertine marble, red-carpeted lobby with dazzling crystal chandeliers, makes it almost an impudence to call it the "Met". You can see the Chagall from the plaza.

Originally completed in 1962, the Philharmonic or **Avery Fisher Hall,** on the right, had to be reconstructed several times over the next 14 years before achieving today's excellent acoustics and admired architectural simplicity. Beyond the Philharmonic, at the back of a handsome reflecting pool with sculpture by Henry Moore, is the **Vivian Beaumont Theater,** originally intended as the base for a New York repertory company. Designed by Eero Saarinen, it houses both a large round auditorium with a versatile movable stage at plaza level and the small Mitzi Newhouse Theater below. Behind the Vivian

Beaumont, the New York Public Library and Museum of the Performing Arts at Lincoln Center includes a film archive and a file on actors, film stars and directors.

A bridge across 65th Street connects the Center to the **Juilliard School,** world-famous music conservatory. On the ground floor, in its Alice Tully Hall, you can hear chamber music ensembles and afternoon concerts by the best Juilliard School pupils. (One-hour guided tours of Lincoln Center start at the concourse level of the "Met".)

Central Park

A vast green breathing space in the centre of Manhattan (half a mile wide and 2½ miles long), Central Park is sports field, playground and picnic spot for tens of thousands of city-dwellers. In the 1840s the poet William Cullen Bryant realized that New York needed more parks for its rapidly expanding population. He launched a campaign to persuade the city to buy the land—then wasteland beyond the city limits, inhabited by squatters. Landscape gardeners Frederick Law Olmsted and Calvert Vaux were called upon to design the park. It took 3,000 workers 16 years to complete it. Conceived in the English style, the park doesn't really look man-made—the Lake, the "forests", the paths and the meadows might have

55

been there since time immemorial. The 75,000 trees, flourishing despite the shortage of soil and the abundance of rocks, are home to countless half-tame squirrels.

By day it's perfectly safe to go walking in the park, but be wary of those around you. Avoid it at night, unless you're going to the outdoor summer theatre.

Starting from the south-east corner of the park, skirt the Pond to the small, modern **zoo**. Then call in at the **Dairy**, the Central Park Visitors' Center, for a calendar of park events. From here, head up the wide, tree-lined Mall to the ornamented **Bethesda Fountain and Terrace**. In summer, you can hire a rowing boat at the Loeb boathouse—to your right—for a trip on the pretty Lake stretching out below the terrace. To the east, at the oval **Conservatory Water**, permit holders sail their miniature boats next to statues of Hans Christian Andersen and Alice in Wonderland. On a hill level with the Metopolitan Museum of Art stands **Cleopatra's Needle**, a 3,000-year-old obelisk that was a gift from Egypt in the late 19th century.

A more recent addition to Central Park, **Strawberry Fields** (at Central Park West between West 71st and 74th streets), is Yoko Ono's horticultural memorial to her husband, John Lennon, who was shot in 1980 just across the street, in front of the Dakota apartment house (1 West 72nd Street).

The 1½ mile path around the Reservoir is especially popular among joggers. For active sports lovers, something is going on in the park every day, but most of all on Sundays in the summer. There are miles of bicycle and jogging paths, which are turned into cross-country ski runs in winter, along with tennis courts, an ice-skating rink and adventure playgrounds for children.

Free open-air concerts and operas are presented on the **Great Lawn** during the summer months, and in **Belvedere Castle**, there are exhibits and special events.

The **Delacorte Theater**, south of 81st Street on the west side of the park, has an excellent Shakespeare in the Park Festival (free: queue up ahead of time for tickets).

Harlem

"Won't go to Harlem in ermine and pearls", says the old song, but that's no reason not to go at all, as long as you take the proper precautions. Of course, this place can be dangerous, a large part of it is a slum and slums everywhere are dangerous. But it's also part of New York's reality, which you should not avoid. This is one time when a guided tour is highly recommended as the best way to do it.

A drive through Harlem is included in most sightseeing tours of Manhattan. There are also a couple of agencies run by black organizers who want to show their community to outsiders without concealing the worst features or overemphasizing the best. For addresses, contact the New York Convention & Visitors Bureau (tel. 397-8222) or the Harlem Visitors & Conventions Association.

Harlem stretches from the northern reaches of Central Park to 178th Street. In the 1950s, it was the home of a million Blacks from the southern states and the Caribbean. Today barely a quarter of a million remain. Optimists attribute this exodus to the new housing programmes and improvements in living standards. The pessimists say that dilapidation just drove people out to new ghettos such as the South Bronx, which has become another Harlem.

Originally founded by Dutch settlers, Harlem remained a village separate from the rest of Manhattan until the end of the 19th century, when middle-class Americans moved north away from the new immigrants of the Lower East Side. You can still make out the genteel façades of some of their houses. Black people started moving in around 1920, the beginning of the Jazz Age. After the South, New York was the "Promised Land".

Duke Ellington and Cab Calloway played the Cotton Club and the Apollo, drawing crowds of white people up to Harlem.

It's difficult to imagine how it was in those days. But signs of renewal are spreading. The famous Apollo Theater (West 125th Street between Frederick Douglass and Adam Clayton Powell Jr. boulevards) has come to life again as a combined cinema and concert hall, which is especially popular for its animated amateur night shows.

And some nice streets remain, particularly around Edgecombe Avenue, an area peopled by wealthy Blacks who could afford to move away but have stayed out of solidarity. One of New York's last remnants of the colonial Georgian architecture is the **Morris-Jumel Mansion,** a stately house set in a picturesque garden. Built in 1765 and used by George Washington as his headquarters at the beginning of the Revolutionary War, it was bought in 1810 by a French wine-merchant, Stephen Jumel. Jumel's widow, Eliza, a remarkable woman who claimed to have slept with both George Washington and Napoleon, married her second husband, Aaron Burr (who was third Vice President of the U.S.), in the house. Now it is a museum dedicated to American decorative arts from the 18th and 19th centuries.

The east side of Harlem is the domain of the Puerto Ricans—**Spanish Harlem.** Visit **El Museo del Barrio** (Fifth Avenue at 104th Street), a museum devoted to the art and culture of Latin America and, in summer, take in the atmosphere of La Marqueta, a colourful market on Park Avenue between 112th and 116th Streets.

Museums

With its 120 museums, New York performs a unique service to world civilization as a cultural bridge between the Old and New worlds. You could spend a lifetime in them.

Metropolitan Museum of Art (Fifth Avenue at 82nd Street). Indisputably one of the world's greatest museums, the Metropolitan consists of nearly 250 rooms with over 4,500 paintings and drawings, one million prints, 4,000 musical instruments and countless pieces of furniture and sculpture. Only a quarter of the collection is on display at any one time. Exhibits are ingeniously set out in their appropriate surroundings. Especially interesting are the American Wing, a glorious celebration of the architecture, decorative and fine arts of America; the Lehman collection of early Italian and French Impressionist painting; the primitive art in the Michael C. Rockefeller wing; the sections devoted to European painting from the 15th–20th century; and the Egyptian department.

Museum of Modern Art (W. 53rd Street between 5th and 6th avenues). MOMA to habitués, this private museum boosted by the Rockefeller family has more than 100,000 works of art from 1880 to the present, but only part of the collection is on view at any one time.

Guggenheim Museum (Fifth Avenue and 89th Street). Designed by Frank Lloyd Wright, the museum's architecture is as important as its contents. Late 19th- and 20th-century collection as well as works by Paul Klee, Kandinsky and Chagall. The annexe offers some fine Van Gogh, Gauguin and Modigliani and a superb group of Picassos.

Whitney Museum of American Art (Madison and 75th). Drawing on the great vigour of American 20th-century art, the museum has marvellously lit, imaginative and adventurous exhibitions.

Frick Collection (E. 70th Street and Fifth Avenue). Industrialist Henry Clay Frick's classical European paintings, furnishings and other treasures are presented in the opulent setting of his own home.

American Museum of Natural History (Central Park West at 79th Street). The largest of the world's natural history museums, with a remarkable collection of minerals and gems and important anthropological exhibitions devoted to Asia and North American Indians.

Cooper-Hewitt Museum (Fifth Avenue and 91st Street). America's largest collection of decorative art from the 15th to the 20th century.

Jewish Museum (Fifth Avenue at 92nd Street). Jewish ceremonial objects, archaeological remains from Israel and excellent avant-garde art shows.

Museum of the American Indian (1 Bowling Green, State and Whitehall Streets). The largest collection of Indian art and artefacts from North, Central and South America.

Museum of the City of New York (Fifth Avenue and 104th Street). Important for the town's exciting history. Great old toys.

Pierpont Morgan Library (Madison Avenue and 36th Street). Rare books, Old Master paintings, Florentine sculpture, etc., amassed by the American industrialist, J. Pierpont Morgan.

Intrepid Sea-Air-Space Museum (Pier 86, West 46th Street and 12th Avenue). Centred on the converted World War II aircraft carrier *Intrepid*, with planes on her deck and displays below.

International Center of Photography (Fifth Avenue and 94th Street). Library, exhibition galleries and laboratories.

EXCURSIONS

Atlantic City *(New Jersey)*
(From New York, Lincoln Tunnel and south on New Jersey Turnpike and Garden State Parkway)
Atlantic City has made its way into most American homes via the original version of Monopoly. Since the 1930s, when it was a fashionable

seaside resort, the streets of Atlantic City served as the "properties" to be bought, bartered or mortgaged on your path to riches or ruin. With its rebirth as a casino town, the name of Atlantic City's game today is variously roulette, blackjack, craps or baccarat, and riches are paid out in real dollars. Big-time and small-time gamblers pour in from all over the East Coast with the hope of hitting one of the jackpots pouring out of the one-armed-bandit slot machines. The rest of the development that was supposed to follow failed to materialize, leaving vast desolate spaces.

Niagara Falls *(New York State)*
An eight-hour drive from New York brings you to Niagara, where nature still manages to triumph

over tawdry commercialism. No amount of pushy pedlars or tacky honeymoon motels can diminish the awesome spectacle of that mass of white water plunging nearly 200 feet on its way from Lake Erie down towards Lake Ontario.

It's worth looking at the Falls from more than one perspective. Make your first vantage-point Goat Island, a nice mini-tram ride from Prospect Point. The island divides the waters of the Niagara River into the eastern **American Falls**—182 feet high, 1,076 feet wide—and the western **Horseshoe (Canadian) Falls**—176 feet high and 2,100 feet wide—with a smaller cascade known as Bridal Veil off to the side. On Goat Island you can choose between a helicopter tour over the whole falls area or an elevator ride down to where the white water crashes into the lower river bed. There you can walk behind the wall of cascading water and experience the cataract's overpowering roar. Tour operators provide protective clothing, but nothing is totally waterproof against Niagara.

Cable cars take you high above the rapids, three boats, all named *Maid of the Mist*, give you a safe view from the river. More adventurous, but not unsafe, is the raft trip through the rapids at the base of the falls. There are numerous observation towers and the best are on the Canadian side (no immigration or re-entry problems). The viewpoints of the Skylon and Minolta Towers are respectively 770 feet and 665 feet above the falls.

At night the Horseshoe Falls gleam in multicoloured illuminations with 4,000 million units of candlepower generated by the falls themselves. The United States and Canada have collaborated to exploit Niagara's tremendous power resources—2,190,000 kilowatts on the American side and 1,775,000 kilowatts on the Canadian side.

Four miles north on Route 104, go and visit the interesting **Niagara Power Project** to see how this energy is harnessed. A geological museum in Prospect Park describes how rock erosion will completely flatten out the falls in the next 30,000 to 40,000 years.

You might also like to make a side-trip to **Buffalo,** a charming city with a very lively cultural life. The Albright-Knox Art Gallery (1285 Elmwood Avenue) has some fine examples of American and European art of the 18th, 19th and 20th centuries. The gallery is set in the lovely **Delaware Park,** landscaped by Frederick Law Olmsted and includes a zoo with some obligatory Buffalo buffalo. The Buffalo Philharmonic Orchestra is first class and gives concerts at the Kleinhans Music Hall.

NEW ENGLAND

From north to south, New England comprises six states—Maine, New Hampshire, Vermont, Massachusetts, Rhode Island and Connecticut, with Massachusetts' Boston as the undisputed capital. Their combined area would scarcely cover any one state in the west, but their historical significance in the Republic's exciting beginnings and their present role in American political and cultural life are impressive.

And beyond the historic prestige of New England, there's a terrific holiday to be had along the rugged coastline and little fishing ports from the Canadian border down to Boston. You may prefer the glorious sandy beaches of Cape Cod, or the rolling hills of the Berkshires in western Massachusetts and the White Mountains of New Hampshire, and everywhere among the woods, the splendid trees that cover four-fifths of the New England landscape. Even that grand past is a pleasure to behold in the spotless Massachusetts villages of white clapboard houses and red-brick mansions clustered around their church on its impeccable green.

Crisp spring and drowsy summer are delightful times in New England, but the trees claim a special short season to themselves in the place where the expression "Indian summer" came into its own. After the first cool spell in autumn, there's a sudden new burst of sunshine, when warm days and cool evenings combine to create a spectacular explosion of colour in the leaves. People travel from New York and from all over the northeast to see the gold of the poplars and birches, the scarlet of the oaks, dogwoods and maples and the magic copper-orange of the mountain ash and hickories. The green leaves of Maine, New Hampshire and Vermont start turning in mid-September and a couple of weeks

---

Festivals

New England abounds in annual festivities—historic, social, sporting and cultural. Here are a representative few:

Patriot's Day (Monday closest to April 19): pageants in Lexington and Concord, Mass., commemorating outbreak of Revolutionary War, 1775; and the Boston Marathon, massive international event.

Berkshire Music Festival at Tanglewood (Lenox, Mass.), July–August; **Newport Music Festival,** July; **Jacob's Pillow Dance Festival** (Berkshires), July–August.

Pilgrim's Progress: costumed Sabbath procession at Plymouth, Mass., every Friday in August.

Thanksgiving Celebration at Plimoth Plantation, Mass. (last Thursday in November).

Autumn countryside in Vermont

later in Massachusetts, Rhode Island and Connecticut. This natural spectacle has become so institutionalized that you can telephone state tourist offices to find out where to see the best displays, which usually peak around mid-October. This is also a great time for the country fairs, communal flea markets and individual garage-

sales (see "Shopping" on p. 198) and pay-for-what-you-pick apples and pears in the orchards.

New England is packed with interesting and beautiful places to visit and deserves, in many people's eyes, a whole vacation to itself. But a first-time visitor to the United States can get a good feel for the region by concentrating for a start on Boston and on the surrounding Massachusetts country-

inside the narrow city limits but nearly of 4 million if you include all the townships of metropolitan Boston. Those small towns are how America began, and the big city, packing 70 colleges into the metropolitan area at the centre of the huge "brains industry", which is New England's greatest resource, is working on the country's future.

Apart from its transient student population, Boston comprises first (though no longer foremost) the Anglo-Saxon descendants of the original settlers, the very proper "Brahmins" who favour the elegant neighbourhood of Beacon Hill in the city's north-west, down to the Charles River. They now play a distinguished second fiddle to the Irish who have spread through the town since fleeing their 1845 potato famine to become labourers, then "lace-curtain" bourgeois and finally to see first the Fitzgeralds moving into City Hall and then the Kennedys into Washington and the White House. The Italians make up an equally lively community, based in the town's North End. The Black community, with a proud past in Boston as the first freed slaves, is largely centred on Roxbury and Dorchester.

side where America's Revolution began. With a side-trip to the nearby seaside playground of Newport, Rhode Island, you will have covered the historical, cultural and social heart of New England.

BOSTON *(Massachusetts)*

This city encompasses the essence of America's origins and the blossoming of its 20th century. It's a bustling place of 600,000 people

Boston is a good town to walk in. The narrow streets of the most interesting sections make driving diabolically difficult, and parking is almost impossible. So park your car outside the city and take the "T" underground to the city's heart, the **Boston Common.** Lying between Tremont, Boylston and Beacon streets is the green nucleus of the 50 acres which the Massachusetts Bay Company bought from a beleaguered hermit, the Reverend William Blackstone, in 1634. He was there already when the 900 Puritans arrived and sold out when he decided he couldn't take any more of their officious manners. As if to make his point for him, they subsequently established on the green—in addition to the usual grazing for livestock—a pillory and stocks, whipping post, sinners' cage and gallows. The first victim of the pillory was its carpenter, punished for charging too much for his labour. In the old Puritan days, it was the one public place where Bostonians were permitted to smoke tobacco. Today the Common is popular for baseball and touchfootball.

Immediately west of the Common is the **Public Garden,** reclaimed in the 19th century from the marshes south of the Charles River. The neat little beds of tulips and pansies made up the country's first botanical garden. The artificial pond in the centre provides gentle rides on board its whimsical, flat-bottomed swan boats in summer, and ice skating in winter.

The Visitors Information Center is on the Tremont Street side of the Common, a good place for maps and brochures and orientation for the 1½-mile **Freedom Trail** around the city's principal historical sights. The route is marked by a painted red line or by red bricks set in the pavement.

A good first stop is the tranquil-looking, white-steepled **Park Street Church,** built in 1809. But at one time this was called Brimstone Corner—as the church served as a gunpowder storehouse during the war of 1812. Just as explosive were the first anti-slavery speeches that were deli-vered from its pulpit in 1829 by abolitionist William Lloyd Garrison.

In the church's **Old Granary Burial Ground** lie the victims of the Boston Massacre (see p.20), as well as Paul Revere, Sam Adams and John Hancock. The last two signed the Declaration of Independence, but it was Hancock's name that was immortalized as synonymous with any more or less honourable signature in the phrase "put your `John Hancock' here". Children may be more interested in the tombstone of Mary Goose, said to be the original Mother Goose of the nursery rhymes.

Boston's Hancock Tower

King's Chapel (Tremont and School streets) was the colonies' first stone church (1754). Originally Anglican and then Unitarian, when the Church of England fell into disrepute after the Revolution, its dark granite walls and columned portico make an austere exterior. But the interior is more graceful, thanks to the canopied pulpit from an earlier church of 1719 and the red damask-lined box pews.

The **Old South Meeting House** (Washington and Milk streets), originally a Puritan church and now a museum of the Revolution, is best remembered as the assembly hall for Sam Adams' protests against the Massacre and the place where he planned the dastardly Tea Party. The British used it as a riding school during their occupation of Boston, burning the pews and pulpits for firewood, but the rest of the original woodwork is intact.

Further along Washington Street, the **Old State House** was the British Governor's Residence and it is still embellished by the lion and unicorn of the royal coat of arms (copies of the originals burnt on Independence Day 1776). It was on the Congress Street side of the building that the Massacre took place, a monument marking the spot where Crispus Attucks was shot, a black man and the first martyr of the Revolution.

Faneuil Hall (rhymes with "panel") has earned its name as the "cradle of liberty" with the speeches of two centuries of politicians from Sam Adams to John Kennedy, not to mention Susan B. Anthony, who rocked the cradle. She spoke out here against the slavery both of Blacks and of women— she even had the gall to try to vote in national elections, 46 years before it was legal. If you like

Indian Tea Time
On the night of December 16, 1773, Sam Adams led his Sons of Liberty in three companies of 50, all with coal dust on their faces disguised as Mohawk Indians, to board the Dartmouth, Eleanor and Beaver. The ships were moored to unload their brew at Griffin's Wharf. Armed with hatchets for tomahawks, the Boston "Mohawks" split open the tea-chests to make sure the contents would steep properly when hurled overboard. The party was attended by a merry crowd cheering from the docks. Sam's cousin, (later president) John Adams, immediately recognized that this was not a childish act of irresponsibility, but an invaluable moment of grand historic theatre. He wrote in his diary the next day: "The Destruction of the Tea is so bold, so daring, so firm, intrepid and inflexible, and it must have so important Consequences, and so lasting, that I cannot but consider it as an Epoch in History." He wasn't wrong.

weapons, take a look at the collection of the Ancient and Honorable Artillery Company. If you like pewter, you can buy handmade reproductions of old American pewter in the Heritage Shop. On the hall's dome is one of the city's most familiar landmarks, a grasshopper weathervane inspired by the one of London's Royal Exchange.

From Fan'l Hall, make your way via Union and Marshall streets under the Fitzgerald Expressway to **North End,** now the colourful centre of the Italian community—fresh pasta shops, aromatic grocery stores and pizza parlours amid charming old houses coiffed by roof-gardens. Resume the Freedom Trail here on North Square at the wooden-frame **Paul Revere House,** the oldest house in Boston, built soon after the disastrous city fire of 1676. The Revolutionary hero moved here in 1770, five years before he set off on his historic ride. Take a look inside at the Revere family's own furnishings.

The intrepid horseman's statue can be seen north of his house on Paul Revere Mall, with the fine **Old North Church** (1723) behind him. It was in the church tower, designed in the style of Christopher Wren and restored after being toppled in a 1954 hurricane, that two lanterns were hung to signal to Revere that the British were marching out. The

unusually tall pew-boxes were meant to keep out the winter draughts, the boxes built square to enable worshippers to sit around their communal footwarmer.

The Freedom Trail continues across Charlestown Bridge to the site of the Revolutionary War's first pitched battle at Bunker Hill, but you may feel that that's enough history for the time being, in which case, make your way back to Fan'l Hall. To the east of it is **Faneuil Hall Market-place,** a lively haven tucked among the administrative buildings of Government Center and the new skyscraper office-blocks. This lively centre of boutiques, galleries, restaurants and cafés is one of the country's most successful pieces of urban restoration. Three run-down granite market buildings, which formed part of the seedy dockland back in 1825 before the land to the east was reclaimed from the sea, have been rehabilitated as light, airy halls around a pedestrian mall shaded by locust trees (the wholesale markets have moved to the suburbs). Glass-enclosed arcades open up in summer as café terraces, lit in the evening by attractive clusters of fish-bowl lamps posted among the parasol tables.

The central domed building is Quincy Market, specializing in gourmet foods. South Market offers art galleries, jewellery and gift-stores while North Market has the fashion boutiques.

A major rehabilitation project was started in the city in the 1960s under the direction of architect I.M. Pei, who provided a modern complement to Boston's traditional historical image.

Charles River; Quincy Market

Part of that modern image is much in evidence at the **Government Center,** which is dominated by the two towers of the John F. Kennedy Federal Building as well as by the inverted concrete pyramid of **City Hall.** The Plaza's almost aggressively 20th-century stance has been offset and subdued by the use of traditional materials in the red-brick paving.

Recapture the city's old serenity on **Beacon Hill,** the noble neighbourhood of Boston's best, sandwiched between Government Center and the Common. Here among the cedars and chestnuts and gas-lanterns of **Mount Vernon Street** and Louisburg Square, where, as the saying goes, "the Lowells talk only to the Cabots and the Cabots talk only to God", you can admire the restrained glories of Boston's finest residential architecture. It was here in the heady years of the 1790s that Boston-born Charles Bulfinch, one of the principal designers of the U.S. Capitol in Washington and America's first native-born professional architect, developed his Federal-style houses. Their simple red-brick façades, with a marble strip separating the

71

storeys, plus a few classical details, are the very essence of Boston dignity. **Louisburg Square,** with its residents' fenced-off garden in the centre and the three-storey curved, bow-fronted houses, will remind some of Georgian London. Others, seeking something a touch more dashing in their houses, went in for the Doric-columned porches of Greek Revival. This can be seen in its most monumental form in Bulfinch's gold-domed **State House** (1798), off Beacon Street, a building that got him his Washington commissions (it has been a little fussed up by later additions).

Back Bay, west of the Public Garden, was quite literally a bay at the rear of Boston's 19th-century city centre until landfill turned it into a residential neighbourhood with a quintessentially Victorian character for the city's newly rich merchants. Now it is enlivened by some fairly chic boutiques and art galleries and is dominated by the towering Hancock and Prudential skyscrapers. Both offer excellent observation decks on their top floors, but the architecturally more satisfying of the two is I.M. Pei's elegant **John Hancock Tower,** sheathed in reflective glass (now cured of an alarming early tendency to pop out). The slanted, rhomboid form escapes the standard rectangular block with an intriguing V-incision at either end. There's a grand view from the 60th floor (half a minute in the lift) over Cambridge and Charlestown all the way to the New Hampshire mountains.

Trinity Church, on Copley Square, is a solid, late 19th-century monument of American homage to the European Middle Ages. Its architect, Henry Hobson Richardson, makes no bones about it being a "free rendering of the French Romanesque" of the 11th century. Experts have spotted elements of Provençal Arles in the west porch and Spanish Salamanca in the central tower, but they find the whole combination unique enough to be dubbed "Richardsonian Romanesque". The interior is worth a look for the rich polychrome décor of John La Farge—quite startling when the lights are turned on.

Museums

Museum of Fine Arts (465 Huntington Avenue) has one of the best collections in the country. American, European and Oriental works are well laid out according to departments. Don't miss I.M. Pei's West Wing.

Isabella Stewart Gardner Museum (280 The Fenway). Superb European collection in a building which recalls a Venetian *palazzo*.

Children's Museum (Museum Wharf). Among other things, children can blow giant bubbles, visit a Japanese house and climb through a multi-level maze. There's an indoor play area and a "supermarket" for smaller children.

The **Computer Museum,** which is housed in the same building as the Children's Museum, offers a fun, inter-active look at the history of computers, with many hands-on exhibits, as well as a two-storey, walk-through computer.

Beaver II, Tea Party Ship (Congress Street Bridge on Fort Point Channel) is a full-scale replica of one of the three British ships raided by the Bostonians to protest the duties on tea.

CAMBRIDGE
(Massachusetts)

There's more to Cambridge (separated from Boston merely by the Charles River) than **Harvard,** but mostly it's Harvard. Founded by the Massachusetts Bay Colony as America's first university in 1636, it is named in honour of a young churchman, John Harvard, who bequeathed it £780, half his worldly wealth, as well as his library of 320 books. Now it has an endowment of $2,500 million and about 100 libraries with over 10 million volumes. In 1965, Harvard merged with Radcliffe College for women (founded in 1894) and the combined institutions now number over 36,000 students. They have the use of 17 university departments, nine faculties, more than 50 laboratories, two astronomical stations and nine museums. Other American universities rival Harvard in individual departments but overall the oldest has remained the country's best, both in the breadth of its undergraduate courses and in its dedication to research.

At the western end of Massachusetts Avenue, **Harvard Square** makes a bustling introduction to the town, with its cafés, restaurants, bookshops and the "Coop" (short for "co-operative" but pronounced like a home for chickens) reputedly the country's biggest.

For orientation around the campus, start at the Information Center in the rather daunting modern block of Holyoke Center, just south of the square. The campus clusters mainly around **Harvard Yard.** Unlike much of the university architecture to be found elsewhere in the country, Harvard's, with its earlier foundation, avoids the "Collegiate Gothic" of spired towers that too often unimaginatively recall Oxford and the other Cambridge. Harvard went for red-brick, a more traditional New England style, that is still seen in **Massachusetts Hall** (1720) and **Harvard Hall** (1766), along with the good old clapboard of **Wadsworth House** (1726), formerly the home of college presidents. The one concession to Gothic Revival is Memorial Hall (1878), a Victorian structure commemorating Harvard's fallen in the Civil War.

In front of **University Hall** (1815), a classical granite edifice by the indefatigable Charles Bulfinch, notice a statue described as "John Harvard founder 1638". A shameless falsehood. Not only was the college founded two years earlier, but John Harvard was merely a benefactor, not the founder. The fellow portrayed is actually an undergraduate who posed 150 years after Harvard's death.

There are some lovely 18th-century houses along Brattle Street, west of Harvard Square, known as Tory Row after their Loyalist owners. At 105 is the **Longfellow National Historical Site,** home of Henry Wadsworth Longfellow, sometimes unkindly called the best bad poet in the world. Built in 1759, it served as Washington's headquarters during the siege of Boston. Longfellow lived here from 1837 to 1882, wrote *Hiawatha* and taught modern languages at Harvard.

The most noteworthy of the campus's modern buildings is the **Carpenter Center of Visual Arts** (on Quincy Street), designed by Le Corbusier, his only American building (if you discount his collab-orative effort on the United Nations Building in New York). With a characteristic touch, "Corb" moves the visitor up the outside of the building along an elevated ramp, from the studios to the art galleries at the top.

Harvard's arts department has its home in the **Fogg Art Museum** next door. It offers the public an impressive Oriental collection, including some fine Chinese jades and bronzes, and good representative European works, notably Italian paintings from the 14th century to the High Renaissance and the French Impressionists and Post-Impressionists.

The **Sackler Museum,** across the street, displays Chinese, Indian, Roman and Greek art in a striking building designed by Britain's James Stirling. Admirers of German art will find a rich 20th-century collection at the **Busch-Reisinger Museum** (29 Kirkland Street).

On Divinity Avenue, the University Museum houses four distinct museums. The most prestigious is the **Peabody Museum of Archaeology and Ethnology.** This has been enriched over the years by the expeditions around the Americas and voyages of exploration to Africa and the Pacific sponsored by the university.

The **Geological and Mineralogical Museum** has an exhibition of minerals, gems and meteorites and a dramatic model of a Hawaiian volcano. At the **Zoology Museum,** look out for the world's oldest egg (225 million years old) and the 25,000-year-old Harvard Mastodon from New Jersey.

The **Botanical Museum** is also known popularly as the Glass Flower Museum because of its unique collection of 784 flowers modelled life-size in glass at the Dresden workshop of Leopold Blaschka and his son Rudolf over a period of 60 years. Botanists vouch for the models' scientific accuracy; the rest of us can just gasp at their amazing beauty.

If you return to Boston via Harvard Bridge, stop off at **M.I.T.** With its solid research in the natural and social sciences, in engineering, architecture and urban planning, the Massachusetts Institute of Technology has created for itself the most prestigious academic initials in the world. Visitors enjoy looking round the **Hart Nautical Museum,** which makes clever use of models, prints and photos to display one thousand years of ship design. Two intriguing architectural oddities worth noting are the strangely warped-roofed **Kresge Auditorium** and the moated cylindrical brick **M.I.T. Chapel** with its aluminium bell tower; both are by the Finnish designer Eero Saarinen.

OTHER NEW ENGLAND HIGHLIGHTS

Lexington *(Massachusetts)*
(From Boston, take Interstate 93 to the Woburn exit west)
Almost engulfed by the expanding web of metropolitan Boston, Lexington still has the classical elements of the small New England country town. There's an immaculate **village green,** with on one side a tavern and on the other a church.

Revere for the Record
Thanks to Longfellow's exciting but frequently inaccurate poem, Paul Revere got all the glory for the ride to alert the fighting men of Lexington and Concord, but in fact he was, luckily, not alone. The British caught up with him soon after he reached Lexington and his co-riders William Dawes and Sam Prescott had to carry the news on to Concord without him. All the same, Revere's versatility and devotion to the American cause would have won him a prominent place in history. He rode with important Massachusetts legislative resolutions to the First Continental Congress in Philadelphia. As an accomplished engraver, he designed and printed the national currency during the war. An equally talented silversmith, he made the noble Liberty Bowl on show at Boston's Museum of Fine Arts. And, oh yes, he was also one of the "Mohawks" at the Boston Tea Party.

the Minutemen's leader, Captain-Parker. At the other, inscribed on a boulder of the **Revolutionary Monument,** are the Captain's heroic words: "Stand your ground; don't fire unless fired upon; but if they mean to have a war, let it begin here".

It did, at 5 a.m. on April 19, when the first of 700 British soldiers arrived. The British ordered the militia to disperse, but a shot rang out and the British opened fire. In the skirmish eight Minutemen died, and the wounded were taken to **Buckman Tavern,** which you can see today restored to its 18th-century glory. For those who spare a thought for the poor British—they did suffer 272 casualties before they got back to Boston from this fateful sortie—there are also guided tours of the 17th-century **Munroe Tavern,** which doubled as the British field hospital and headquarters.

This was the town into which Paul Revere rode on the evening of April 18, 1775, to warn colonial leaders John Hancock and Sam Adams that the British were coming. Their target: American arms and ammunition in nearby Concord. The tavern is Buckman Tavern, which served as rallying point for 77 Minutemen, rustic militia so-called because they had to be ready at a minute's notice. At one end of the village green is a **statue** of

Concord *(Massachusetts)*

Concord has successfully resisted the encroachments of the metropolis and would be worth a visit even without the Revolutionary associations. Its calm and serenity—still relatively unspoiled—made it a perfect haven for great thinkers like Ralph Waldo Emerson and Henry David Thoreau and for novelists Nathaniel Hawthorne and Louisa May Alcott.

But let's go back first to the excitement of the Revolution. From a hill above the Concord River north of town, about 100 Minutemen watched the British searching for the military supplies. Seeing fires starting in town and fearing the hidden ammunition might blow the whole place up, the militia descended to the river and met up with the British on **Old North Bridge.** A replica of the bridge has been built west of Monument Street, with a Visitor Center organizing guided tours. The **Minuteman statue** of Daniel Chester French marks the spot, as Emerson wrote in his *Concord Hymn:* "Here once the embattled farmers stood / and fired the shot heard round the

Montpelier, Vermont

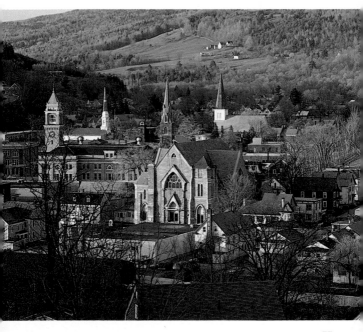

77

world." The farmers' stand was enough to drive the British off.

But Concord, named after a peace treaty between early settlers and the Indians, regained its more natural, unbellicose role during the 19th century. In the **Ralph Waldo Emerson House** (28 Cambridge Turnpike), you'll find memorabilia of the philosopher-poet who lived in Concord from his birth in 1803 to 1882. The local countryside reinforced the mystical love of nature expressed in his philosophy.

Across Cambridge Turnpike at the **Museum of the Concord Antiquarian Society,** you can enjoy the genteel trappings of the old Concord life—with the Chippendale and Queen Anne furniture and the solid, more austere colonial style. The museum has a replica of Emerson's study and some of Henry David Thoreau's belongings from his **Walden Pond** cabin. (The 64-acre pond is still there, 1½ miles south of town off Walden Street, and is open for swimming in the summer months.)

At **Orchard House** (399 Lexington Road), you can see where Louisa May Alcott wrote her eternal bestseller, *Little Women* (1868), the story of her own New England childhood. Her royalties enabled her penniless philosopher-father, Bronson Alcott, Concord's school superintendent, to pursue his own

brand of transcendentalism in his School of Philosophy, still operating on a hillside above the house.

At Sleepy Hollow Cemetery on "Author's Ridge" you can see the graves of Emerson, the Alcotts, and Nathaniel Hawthorne, who made his home for a time at the Old Manse (on Monument Street near the Old North Bridge).

Salem *(Massachusetts)*
(North on Route 1 and 1A from Boston)

The name Salem, from the Hebrew word "Shalom", meaning peace, is somewhat ironic considering the town's violent history. Salem is known primarily as the site of the USA's most infamous witchcraft trials; it's also famed for its more glorious maritime past.

In 1692, a negro slave's tales of sorcery had a strong effect on two impressionable young Puritan girls. Their exaggerated gossip soon led to mass hysteria, witch hunts, and the hanging of 19 "witches". For the best retelling of this gory story, visit the multi-media exhibit at the **Witch Museum** sited on Washington Square. **Witch House** on Essex Street was once the home of hanging judge Jonathan Corwin, where suspects were cross-examined.

With the witchcraft era behind it, Salem soon became a prosperous seaport and home to America's first millionaires. Down at Derby Wharf, **Salem Maritime National Historic Site** tells the story of Salem's great seafaring days; the old **Customs House** across the street can also be visited. Ship owners made a fortune out of the China trade, and many of their spoils—from Burma, India, Indonesia, China, Japan and Korea—are now on display at the **Peabody and Essex Museum**, the oldest continously operating museum in America. The same museum also protects several splendid houses on Essex Street.

At number 128 is the **Gardner-Pingree House** (1805) by Salem architect Samuel McIntire—an outstanding example of the Federal style. Note the simple elegance of the rose brick facade topped by a white wood balustrade and the superb woodwork of the interior. The Peirce-Nichols house (1782) at 80 Federal Street is also by McIntire.

Salem is also known as the birthplace and home of 19th century novelist Nathaniel Hawthorne, who worked at the Customs House. His **House of the Seven Gables**, at 54 Turner Street on the waterfront, is an interesting place to visit.

Besides being a historic treasure, Salem, with its green common, pedestrianized centre and restored waterfront (visit the shops and restaurants on pretty Pickering Wharf) is a lovely place to wander.

Cape Cod *(Massachusetts) (Interstate 93 out of Boston, Route 3 to the Cape)*

The beaches, sand dunes and marshlands of Cape Cod's east coast are both invigorating and relaxing. It was a surprise to no one when, in 1961, President Kennedy made the coast a protected area—the **Cape Cod National Seashore.** It had, after all, been his family's holiday home for years.

He did the rest of us a favour, too, because the Rangers of the National Park Service have done a superb job of protecting the fauna, flora and fragile geological formations for the permanent benefit of cyclists, hikers and bathers. The 27,000 acres of parkland include more than 50 miles of beach between Chatham and Provincetown.

A good place to start is the **Nauset Area's** Salt Pond Visitor Center, where Rangers will brief you on the area's history, the Indians and the local ecology, and provide brochures about the trails to the seashore and the regulations to observe for its protection. A bicycle trail takes you east to Coast Guard Beach or you can walk the Nauset Marsh Trail around the ponds and through a red maple swamp.

The Marconi Area contains a few relics of the transatlantic radio station established here in 1901 by the Italian inventor, Guglielmo

Marconi. Erosion of the shore has toppled most of the station into the ocean and your walk along the Atlantic White Cedar Swamp Trail will show you how brushwood and beach grass help resist the continued onslaught of the sea. The varied flora include midget scrub oaks as well as the swampland cedars.

One of the best panoramic views of the dunes is from a hillock north-west of Pilgrim Lake in the **Pilgrim Heights** area. The Pilgrim Spring Trail takes you to a spot where in 1620 the people of the *Mayflower* drank their first American fresh water, according to local legend.

At the north-west tip of the Cape, you can tour the dunes in four-wheel-drive vehicles around **Race**

Rocky coastline in Maine

Point and **Herring Cove,** two great swimming beaches. (A special permit may be obtained from the Rangers at the Province Lands Visitor Center.) The driving is not at all easy and you may prefer one of the guided tours organized from nearby Provincetown. The drivers are very knowledgeable and speak with great feeling for the natural environment, its erosion and enrichment. The best time to go, if you can't make it at dawn, is just before sunset when the light on the dunes and swaying beach grasses and brushwood is a pure joy.

The harbour of **Provincetown** or P-town was the first port of call for the *Mayflower* Pilgrims after a voyage of extreme hardship, but soon they decided to continue on to Plymouth. P-town was subsequently settled by a more impudent band—whalers, smugglers and bohemian artists—injecting a whiff of brimstone into the sober New England puritanism. Modelled like an Italian bell tower, the **Pilgrim Memorial Monument** pays due tribute to the *Mayflower* people and the view of Cape Cod from its observation deck is well worth the climb. The nearby **Provincetown Museum** is a celebration of the town's seafaring past. Note the fine examples of scrimshaw carving.

MacMillan's Wharf is the centre of the fishing fleet's activities and the spot to hire a boat, set off on a harbour cruise or take part in a whalewatching expedition. From May to September, both humpback and sperm whales are particularly abundant in the area. Reservations for expeditions in July and August are strongly recommended.

Artists congregate around the Provincetown Art Association (on the corner of Bangs and Commercial streets), and continuing the town's traditions of avant-garde theatre is the P-town Theater Company. Eugene O'Neill started out here and, if you don't spot his ghost or that of Tennessee Williams, you may at least see Norman Mailer walking on the street with another Great American Novel on his mind.

At the southernmost tip of Cape Cod, Woods Hole ferries take you across to Martha's Vineyard (45-minute crossing) and Nantucket (3 hours)—two island resorts which are very popular with discerning New Englanders and New Yorkers. There are no wild grapes growing on **Martha's Vineyard** any more, but the local artists drink plenty of wine. You can get around the island by shuttle-bus or rent a bicycle or moped. The beaches are excellent, Katama on the south shore being especially prized by surfers. For a lovely view, go west of Katama up onto the **Gay Head Cliffs,** which consist of layers of coloured clay—

red, orange, grey, blue and ochre. The local Indians turn it into pottery. Equally brightly coloured are the charming gingerbread cottages of **Oak Bluffs**, while the grander houses of **Edgartown** are made of sparkling white clapboard.

Nantucket Island is just right for the family. The beaches on the north side of the island—Jetties and Children's—are washed by the warm waters of the Gulf Stream, and offer easy swimming. Hardier swimmers go to Cisco and Surfside for the big breakers of the south shore. Nantucket town, beautifully preserved on the cobbled **Main Street,** has a proud whaling history (ending abruptly in the second half of the 19th century when Pennsylvania oil replaced whale blubber). At the **Whaling Museum** (Broad Street) is all the sailor's paraphernalia of the whaling industry. If you're taken by the impressive exhibition of scrimshaw, you may want to buy some in the waterfront shops on **Straight Wharf,** at the end of Main Street, a delightful place to hang around the yachts.

Plymouth *(Massachusetts)*

On your way from Boston to Cape Cod stop off on Route 3 to pay homage to the site of New England's founding. A boulder on the edge of the harbour is said to be the legendary **Plymouth Rock** onto which the first *Mayflower* Pilgrim stepped in 1620. Today, the sacred boulder is protected by monumental granite pillars. Few countries in the Western world celebrate the historic sites of their beginnings with more reverence. North of the Rock, at State Pier, is *Mayflower II,* a replica which sailed from England in 1957. Just south of the town is **Plimoth Plantation,** reproducing the Pilgrims' first village of 1627: thatchroofed, clapboard cottages with 16th-and 17th-century English furniture, barns and stables, as well as actors in 17th century costume, and rare breeds of cattle and sheep. Nearby is a 17th-century Wampanoag Indian Summer Encampment.

The Berkshires

(Massachusetts) (Interstate 90 from Boston or Interstate 87 from New York)

The rolling foothills of the Taconic and Hoosac mountains offer wonderful opportunities in the summer to combine music, dance and theatre with hiking and fishing. The Berkshires are the place for watching the autumn foliage and there's skiing in winter. Dotted among the hills are the grand 19th-century estates that provided summer homes for wealthy New Yorkers and Bostonians and are now resort hotels and rest-homes.

Since 1934, the **Tanglewood** estate (just outside Lenox) has been the home of the summer Berkshire Music Festival, hosted now by the Boston Symphony Orchestra. Its Music Shed, designed by Finnish architect Eero Saarinen, seats up to 6,000. One of the nicest ways to enjoy the concerts in good weather is to come for a picnic a couple of hours early and listen to the music (much more cheaply) from the lawn. Saturday morning rehearsals are cheaper still. The Chamber Music Hall presents more concerts.

The Berkshire Theater Festival is at the Playhouse in **Stockbridge** (south of Tanglewood on Route 7). The town itself is well worth a visit. It was established in 1734 by only four white families who had the explicit goal of converting the local Mohican Indians. Reverend John Sergeant's **Mission House** (1739), Route 102, austere and even gloomy by modern standards but considered plush in that pious era, is now a museum of that pious era.

The **Old Corner House,** quite properly on Main Street, was the home of painter Norman Rockwell, acute observer of American Main Street life for the magazine covers of the *Saturday Evening* Post. In the collection exhibited near Stockbridge, you can trace the evolution of his work, from the details of small-town Americana in the De-pression years to the contemporary problems of racial integration and urban violence, along with portraits of his fellow Massachusetts men, the Kennedy brothers.

Further south, around Great Barrington, there is some first-class fishing and hiking country along the Housatonic Valley.

Newport (*Rhode Island*) (*From Boston, Interstate 93 and Route 24 south; from Cape Cod, Route 6 and Interstate 195*)

This playground of the legendary Astors and Vanderbilts, who accumulated fabulous fortunes from railroads and steamships in the 19th century, has remained a pleasant resort for those who like sailing, music—and gawking at the sumptuous relics of that playground. The summer music festival and yacht races have become world famous. Take the 3-mile **Cliff Walk** south from Newport Beach to visit these incredible mansions, inspired by—and often plundered from—the châteaux and *palazzi* of Europe, called "cottages" by their owners.

Imagine the dinners at the turn of the century, at which guests shared caviar and champagne with their pet poodles before going to Mrs. Astor's ballroom for the "400" (only room for 400 guests, but there were only 400 one could invite). Then look at the magnificent **Breakers,** Cornelius Vanderbilt II's 70-room cottage, designed by Richard Morris Hunt. To call this crypto-Renaissance palace "an incredible display of tasteless vulgarity"—as did a member of the Society of Architectural Historians—is to miss the point. The marble, bronze, alabaster and gilt of the interior, especially the Grand Salon and two-storey dining room, are the ornaments of fantasy, not the realities of anything so mundane as good taste. If you're unconvinced, go down the coast to William Vanderbilt's **Marble House,** with almost as much gold as marble in it. Conscientious art-historians argue whether Hunt's model was the White House in Washington or the Petit Trianon in Versailles.

The beautifully preserved **Touro Synagogue,** east of Washington Square, is one of Newport's historically most important buildings. Built in 1763, it was America's first synagogue, serving the Sephardic Jews from Lisbon and Amsterdam. Its austere beige façade contrasts with a richly handsome interior. The women's gallery is supported by 12 columns, Ionic below and Corinthian above, symbolizing the 12 tribes of Israel.

You can pick up a wealth of free material at the Chamber of Commerce Information Center.

MID-ATLANTIC REGION

Seven years after the end of the War of Independence, the northern and southern states finally agreed on a site for the nation's permanent capital—right between the two regions, on land ceded by Maryland and Virginia. Your visit to Washington and a swing through the surrounding states will give you an opportunity to compare the businesslike North with the more leisurely South. Is Philadelphia as earnest as its reputation or Virginia as stately as its old plantation-days image? And Washington? In a moment of irritation, President John F. Kennedy once exclaimed that the capital had all the charm of a northern city and the efficiency of a southern town.

WASHINGTON D.C.

You couldn't mistake this city for anything but the capital of a great republic. Everything about it smacks of government. Monuments and ministries abound. But the architecture leans more to the temples of ancient Greece and Rome than the palaces and cathedrals of the European monarchies, and the government buildings are set in a green and pleasant landscape. The 69 square miles of the city (an area conterminous with the District of Columbia) include 33 parks, relics of the old Maryland estates and plantations.

Over 3 million people live in Greater Metropolitan Washington and the suburbs in Virginia and Maryland; the city itself numbers well over 600,000 residents, more than half of them Black. The government centre of civil servants, congressmen, senators, diplomats and journalists leads a life largely separate from the concerns of the metropolis, which is beset like any other large American town with slums and crime. And so for foreign visitors, too, this underbelly remains mostly out of sight, as they stick to the downtown federal district and its residential neighbourhoods to the north-west.

When you see the attractive houses and diplomatic missions along and around Massachusetts Avenue and the university district of Georgetown, you may find it hard to believe that for a long time Washington was just a muddy mess, much of it marshland on the banks of the Potomac River. To lay out the new capital, George Washington called on the Paris-born engineer, Pierre Charles L'Enfant, the man who had remodelled Federal Hall in New York for the presidential inauguration. But the valiant Frenchman, a major with the U.S.

Army during the Revolutionary War, produced a radial plan inspired by Rome and Versailles for the central federal district that proved a little too ambitious for the young Republic's treasury. After a quarrel with the bureaucracy, who called him "L'Enfant terrible", he was fired and died in misery.

Apart from the White House—only half-finished when John Adams moved in in 1800—the place looked much like a ramshackle frontier town for most of the 19th century, in part because it was sacked and burned by the British in 1814. The Capitol took 70 years to complete and the streets weren't paved or properly lit till after the Civil War. It was only in the 20th century that Washington finally assumed the shape of L'Enfant's grand conception—perhaps it took that long to find the money—and the architect was reburied, with honours, at Arlington House.

Considering all there is to be seen, the area covering Washington's sights is mercifully compact. It's practically all in a rectangle extending from Union Station and the Library of Congress, on the east, to Watergate and the Lincoln Memorial near the Potomac River, on the west. Georgetown is just north-west of this rectangle and Arlington National Cemetery on the west bank of the Potomac.

(Nearly all the monuments and museums are free of charge.)

Getting Around. When you no longer feel like walking—Washington can be very hot and sticky in high summer—a very agreeable alternative is the system of open-sided Tourmobile shuttle trolleys. They follow a route past the main monuments, museums and government buildings, stopping at convenient points around the Capitol, the Mall and the White House. Guides provide cheerful commentaries as you ride. The great advantage is that you can get on and off as often as you like with one all-day ticket (bought on the trolley when you first board). The Tourmobile also undertakes excursions to Arlington and Mount Vernon.

Public transport in Washington includes an efficient municipal bus sevice together with an extensive underground Metrorail network. Taxis are plentiful, charging—not exorbitantly—by the zones into which they've divided the town (see the map in the cab) rather than by meter. Zone One covers most of the main sights. Keep your car for out-of-town excursions, because legal parking downtown is expensive and illegal parking disastrous. The police do not hesitate to tow vehicles away to one of 20 compounds without letting you know, even by telephone, which one.

The White House (*1600 Pennsylvania Avenue, N.W.*)

Unusually, the American president lets you visit his home. The White House is open Tuesday to Saturday, 10 a.m. to noon (business permitting). From June to August you collect a free, same-day ticket from the White House Visitors Center (1450 Pennsylvania Avenue, tel. 202 208-1631), which also has information and exhibits on the president's home. Plan to collect your tickets early—they may all be gone by 8.30 a.m. From September to May, just queue up at the East Gate on Executive Avenue. Read this beforehand—there is no guide inside.

Whatever detractors might say, the place is magic. The house really is incredibly white, Virginia sandstone, not marble, repainted the moment the gleam even threatens to fade. And the stately interior positively glows with the pride of American history.

It was designed in 1792 by Irish-born architect James Hoban in the English Palladian style popular with the landed gentry. In the competition for a $500 gold medal, Hoban beat an anonymous entry by Thomas Jefferson. Happy to reside there himself in 1801, Jefferson declared it "big enough for two em-

The Capitol Building

perors, one Pope and the grand Lama" and then promptly added a terrace pavilion on either side while Benjamin Latrobe was putting on the porticos. He was setting the pattern for nearly all his successors of remodelling or redecorating their temporary home—without the benefit of his architectural training.

The usual tourists' entrance is through the East Wing Lobby, decorated with portraits of the first ladies of past presidents. The cheerful **Garden Room** has the yellow-lacquered bamboo-style furniture of the early 19th-century English Regency period, when people liked things to look a little Chinese. Through the windows you can see the Jacqueline Kennedy Garden. Displayed in the East Foyer are gifts from foreign heads of state—

Toasting the White House
It wasn't always the president who redid the White House. In 1814, the dastardly British Admiral, George Cockburn, led an assault on Washington and the White House in retaliation for American pillage in Canada (see p. 24). While President James Madison had gone off to join the militia, wife Dolley stayed behind to take care of the valuables, getting out just before the British arrived and set fire to the place. A providential thunderstorm put out the fire but not before the White House turned decidedly black.

---

since Watergate very carefully inventoried.

Upstairs on the first floor, the **East Room,** familiar for presidential press conferences, is used for concerts, balls and receptions—weddings for the president's children, funeral services for presidents who die in office, notably Lincoln, Franklin Roosevelt and Kennedy. The White House's first First Lady, Abigail Adams, used it as a drying room for her laundry. The famous 1796 Gilbert Stuart portrait of George Washington was saved from the 1814 fire by good old Dolley Madison.

First ladies often hold tea parties in the elegant **Green Room** under a superb 1790 cut-glass chandelier offered by the English to President Herbert Hoover. Jefferson liked to take his dinner here, showing off to baffled Americans the latest gourmet ideas he'd imported from Europe, such as macaroni, waffles and ice-cream.

The oval **Blue Room** is decorated in French Empire style appropriate to the state dinners held here. Outside the windows is "Truman's Balcony" where the man from Missouri used to take the air.

The **Red Room** with its red satin walls has some impressive gilded and marble tables. Its opulence contrasts with the restrained décor of the **State Dining Room** at the western end of this first floor (underneath the presidential living quarters). Dominated by a portrait of Abraham Lincoln, it's done in fine 18th-century English style, walnut Queen Anne chairs against oak panelling with Corinthian pilasters.

The Mall and Potomac Park

The Mall—an expanse of greenery and water from the Capitol to the Lincoln Memorial, crossing the axis between the White House and the Tidal Basin at the Washington Monument—is undoubtedly one of the world's great urban vistas. The place is alive with people strolling around, relaxing on the grass, flying kites and spinning Frisbies, surrounded by monuments and museums. It's certainly a posthumous triumph for planner Pierre Charles L'Enfant, whose dream it had been to achieve this interaction of town and nature.

If the Statue of Liberty represents America to the world, then the **Washington Monument** symbolizes the nation for Americans themselves. This 555-foot white marble obelisk seems to state, with the noble simplicity of George Washington himself, the people's loftiest aspirations. Construction of the monument began in 1848 but dragged on for 36 years because of lack of funds and the interruption of the Civil War. Inside, an elevator will

take you to the top for a great **view** of the Virginia and Maryland countryside.

West of the obelisk, wander along the beautiful, tree-lined, 2,000-foot-long reflecting pool to the **Lincoln Memorial** (1922). This Greek-temple-like structure, a white rectangular box surrounded by 36 Doric columns, houses the 19-foot, seated statue of a pensive Abraham Lincoln by Daniel Chester French. If you care to make the vigil, there is a wonderful effect to be seen at daybreak when the majestic sculpture is first lit by the rising sun it faces, even more dramatic than its night-time illumination. On the left of the entrance is a plaque with Lincoln's speech after the Civil War Battle of Gettysburg, when he paid tribute to those who had died for a "nation conceived in liberty and dedicated to the proposition that all men are created equal".

Pause for a while at the Vietnam Veterans Memorial, nearby. This simple black monument to the Vietnam war dead carries the names of 58,000 soldiers killed or missing in action. The more conventional statuary group was added later at the request of many of those who served.

From here you can make a detour across Potomac Park and around the Tidal Basin to the domed

Watch 'em Work
It's very easy to see American government at work. When the Senate or House of Representatives is in session, a flag flies over their respective wings. In the mornings, you can visit Congressional committee public hearings. This is where the real legislative work is done. (Advance details are published every day in the Washington Post's *"In Congress" column.) You may be more interested in a floor debate, held after noon. Foreign visitors need only show their passports to get a pass to the Senate or House Visitors' Gallery, either from the Sergeant at Arms of the Senate or from the Doorkeeper of the House on the gallery floor. American citizens can get passes from their elected representatives. Senate debates tend to be more dignified, House debates more lively, because the latter's representatives are up for re-election every two years and must constantly impress visiting constituents. You'll rarely see all 100 Senators or more than half the 435 Representatives. Remember, Democrats sit to the Speaker's right, Republicans to his left, an arrangement that has no ideological significance.*

Jefferson Memorial (1943), inspired by the Pantheon in Rome. As you look at the bronze statue of this architect, philosopher, and most elegant of statesmen, think of the words of President Kennedy at a

Interior of the Library of Congress

dinner for Nobel Prize winners: "I think this is the most extraordinary collection of talent, of human knowledge, that has ever been gathered together at the White House—with the possible exception of when Thomas Jefferson dined alone".

The Mall takes you past one of the world's most impressive concentrations of museums and galleries (see pp. 96–98). At the end, south of the brooding statue of Civil War hero Ulysses S. Grant, stop off at the **Botanic Garden.** It's a joy to relax in spring among the azaleas. Year-round, orchid-lovers marvel at the 500 varieties.

Capitol Hill

The most powerful government in the Western world deserves a setting like the Capitol. This massive edifice imposes its will under a huge white dome that joins the Senate in the north wing to the House of Representatives in the south. The place exudes power.

William Thornton's original design in 1793 was a low-domed affair. When Benjamin Latrobe expanded the design after the British burning of 1814, the home-spun Congressmen complimented him only on the corncobs and tobacco leaves with which he rather whimsically decorated the Corinthian columns of their chamber. Charles Bulfinch came from Boston

to put on a bigger and better dome, but by 1850 Congress, sensing America was going places, wanted it even bigger. So Thomas Walter, with nothing less than St. Peter's in Rome for his model, hoisted an iron monster up on a grandiose columned "drum" and that, with Thomas Crawford's statue of Freedom topping it off in 1863, is the way it stands today.

You enter the Capitol from the east side, starting at the **Rotunda** (there are 45-minute guided tours). The vast ceiling is decorated by a fresco painted by Constantino Brumidi in 1865, *The Apotheosis of George Washington,* showing him glorified by the deities of Liberty, Victory and Fame and 13 ladies representing the 13 original states. Below is a 300-foot frieze devoted to American historical events from Columbus via Cornwallis's surrender at Yorktown to the flight of the Wright brothers' *Kitty Hawk* aircraft in 1903.

In **Statuary Hall** and the corridors leading off the Rotunda, you'll see what is widely regarded as one of the most delightfully horrendous sculpture collections in America. It's the result of an act of cultural democracy by which each of the 50 states was invited to exhibit two (now limited to one) of its most famous citizens, portrayed by the state's own sculptors.

Outside, the Capitol's grounds cover 131 acres of charming parkland designed by the 19th-century landscape architect, Frederick Law Olmsted, well known for his parks from Boston and New York via Chicago to California.

The **Library of Congress** (1st Street and Independence Avenue), packed with literally millions of books, maps, manuscripts, periodicals, photographs, recordings and rare instruments, is one of the great institutions of Capitol Hill. For the visitor, the permanent exhibition of documents includes the 1455 Gutenberg Bible, one of only three in the world to have survived in perfect condition. See also the poignant Civil War photographs of Matthew Brady, first of the great American photo-journalists, in the Prints and Photographs section.

Behind the Library of Congress, the **Folger Library** (201 E. Capitol Street) offers in its Tudor interior the largest collection of Shakespeareana outside Britain, including a nicely reproduced Elizabethan theatre. Next door, the awe-inspiring **Supreme Court,** built in 1935, is the last of Washington's government buildings in the Graeco-Roman style. For those who are interested in the workings of the American legal system, court hearings can be attended from October to June.

North and South of the Mall

The scene of Abraham Lincoln's assassination, **Ford's Theater** (511 10th Street, between E and F streets) has been preserved as a National Monument, meticulously restored to how it looked on the night of April 14, 1865. Since 1968, it has been operating again as a theatre, complete with presidential box. The basement is now a museum of Lincoln's life. It preserves the clothes he wore to the play, the Derringer pistol that killed him, and the diary of assassin John Wilkes Booth, Shakespearean actor and embittered supporter of the lost Southern cause. Across the street, at number 516, is **Petersen House,** where the dying president was taken—the streets of Washington being too badly paved for a safe trip back to the White House. You'll see the bleak little bedroom where the 6-foot 4-inch Lincoln had to be laid diagonally across the bed.

Officially named the J. Edgar Hoover Building (after the FBI's posthumously suspect director), the **Federal Bureau of Investigation** offers the most hair-raising tour in Washington (entrance E Street between 9th and 10th; reservations 324-3447). An introductory film explains the workings of the Bureau and documents its historic cases from the gang-busting days of the 1930s to the investigations of civil rights activities in the '60s and the threats to "national security" of the present day. Then you'll see the gangsters' guns and Hoover's Ten Most Wanted Men. The laboratory displays the FBI's latest gadgetry for uncovering criminals. For the tour's climax, you watch an agent shooting his .38 calibre revolver and a submachine-gun into a paper man-sized target—offered as a souvenir to someone's lucky child.

For a rather more enlightening experience, visit the **National Archives** (Constitution Avenue between 7th and 9th streets) where you can see the original documents of the Declaration of Independence, the Federal Constitution and the magnificent Bill of Rights, all of course handwritten on parchment. Some have faded badly but are now surrounded by light-filtering glass, with helium protection against decay.

South of the Mall, at 14th and C streets, is the fascinating **Bureau of Engraving and Printing,** where you can see the printing of U.S. paper money and postage stamps, anything from a one-cent stamp to a $500 million Treasury Note (you are not allowed to take photographs, and there are no free samples). Follow the block-long gallery-tour of the gentle art of greenback-growing from blank white paper sheets through inking and cutting to the delicious stacking of crisp dollar bills at the other end. A one-dollar bill takes 15 days to produce and will usually disintegrate after 18 months of normal use.

Arlington

Running north behind the Lincoln Parkway between the Rock Creek Parkway and the river is a delightful half-mile walk along the green river-bank. On weekends you can see polo, field hockey, even jousting on horseback, while less hectic types paddle by in canoes. On your way, you'll pass the **Kennedy Center for the Performing Arts,** less admired for its rather clumsy architecture than for its cultural activities in a capital that previously neglected the performing arts. The Center comprises two theatres, an opera house, a concert hall and the American Film Institute's excellent "cinémathèque". A little further north is the appropriately convoluted mass of the Watergate apartments where the 1972 dirty tricks were perpetrated, resulting in the downfall of Richard Nixon.

Beautifully situated on a hillside on the opposite bank of the Potomac is **Arlington House** (also known as the Custis-Lee Mansion). This sober Greek Revival mansion fronted by eight Doric columns was built by George Washington's adopted grandson, George Wash-ington P. Custis, in 1812. It was later the home of General Robert E. Lee until he left to lead the Confederate armies in 1861. Immediately in front of the house is the grave of the architect Pierre Charles L'Enfant, commanding the best view across the river of the capital he so lovingly planned. A granite slab is engraved with his original plan. It's a good vantage point from which to compare the plan with the result.

During the Civil War, Union troops confiscated Lee's house, and part of its surrounding plantation was used as a burial ground for the war dead. Out of this grew **Arlington National Cemetery,** in which any American soldier who has seen active duty can be buried.

Pride of place goes to the **Tomb of the Unknowns** (soldiers of the two world wars and the Korean War), guarded by a solitary infantryman ceremoniously changed every half hour in summer, every hour in winter. In its own small park, the **John F. Kennedy Grave** is a square of simple paving which is set around an eternal flame. Jacqueline Kennedy Onassis is buried in the same plot, and John's brother Robert is buried nearby.

The Marine Corps War Memorial, better known as the **Iwo Jima Statue,** is outside the north entrance to the cemetery. The huge bronze group shows five marines and a sailor hoisting the American flag (a real one raised daily by the Washington-based marines) on Mount Suribachi during the battle for the Japanese Pacific island base of Iwo Jima on February 23, 1945. It took three more weeks to capture the island, with the loss of over 5,000 men—Japanese losses were four times higher.

Georgetown

Immediately north-west of the downtown federal district, Georgetown is the home of Washington's élite in government, the diplomatic corps, university establishment and better-paid journalists. It's also the liveliest part of town, with bright, pleasant shops, art galleries, cafés and restaurants, centred on M Street and Wisconsin Avenue. It's the only part of Washington with a cheerful street life after dark—the perfect antidote to any overdose of museums and officialdom.

Right from the beginning, Georgetown was the smart end of town. It was laid out in 1751 and was already established as a major tobacco market when Washington was still in the planning. Georgetown exported tobacco along the Potomac and imported luxury goods such as silks, wines, tinware, tea and powder for the wigs of its high-stepping gentry. A couple of houses survive from that golden era

but most of its better residential architecture is elegant Georgian and Federal-style from the first half of the 19th century, with a little Victorian "heavy pastry" from after the Civil War. Its narrow, tree-shaded streets provide a welcome change from the broad avenues of governmental Washington.

The oldest house in town is the **Old Stone House** (3051 M Street), built in rough stone in 1766 with an entrance up on the first floor and bedrooms gabled in the roof. Worth noting among the Georgian houses is **Dumbarton House** (2715 Q Street), remodelled by Benjamin Latrobe in 1805. It's now headquarters for the venerable National Society of Colonial Dames of America and houses some fine furniture, silver and china from the late 18th century. **Dumbarton Oaks** (3101 R Street), an imposing mansion built in 1801, gained its place in history as the site of a 1944 conference at which the U.S., Britain, the Soviet Union and China drew up the blueprint for the United Nations. The 16 acres of grounds are a delightful mixture of formal terraces and reflecting pools with more informal English-style landscaping on a lower level. The gardens include (at 1702 32nd Street entrance) the elegant, mushroom-domed Museum of Pre-Columbian Art designed by Philip Johnson.

95

A charming surprise at the southern edge of Georgetown is the remnant of the **Chesapeake & Ohio Canal** (the "C & O"), restored as one of the finest recreational areas that Washington possesses. It's perfect for loafers, hikers, cyclists, canoeists and fishermen—and in winter, as in a Brueghel painting, skaters. Canal Square (1054 31st Street) is an old canalside warehouse converted into an attractive shopping centre.

Museums

National Gallery of Art (Constitution Avenue between 4th and 6th streets). The West Building, a classical, columned temple of art, is devoted to European and American painting and sculpture from the Middle Ages to the present day. Its great strength is in Italian art, but the French, Dutch, German, Flemish, Spanish, British and American schools are splendidly represented as well. I.M. Pei's design of the

Calder mobile, National Gallery of Art

East Building is a breathtaking combination of geometric forms—soaring triangles segmented into piercingly acute angles. The effect is even more exhilarating inside, where the museum's collection of contemporary art is on display.

The Smithsonian. Not one museum but a huge umbrella institution grouping 14 museums—13 in Washington and one in New York. The museums have a combined inventory of 75 million artistic and scientific items, only one per cent of which is ever on display.

National Air and Space Museum (Jefferson Drive and 6th Street). The whole adventure of flying, whether it be across a meadow in North Carolina with the Wright brothers in 1903 or just 66 years later from Cape Canaveral to the moon, is packed in 23 galleries.

National Museum of Natural History (10th Street and Constitution Avenue). Everything from an 80-foot-long *diplodocus* to the creepy, crawly Insect Zoo. The building also houses the Museum of Man, with a display of Eskimo and American Indian artefacts.

National Museum of American History (Madison Drive, 12th to 14th streets). Americana are presented here with a delightful mixture of dignity and humour.

Corcoran Gallery (17th and East Streets). A fine array of American Art, plus European Masters. Every two years there's an all-American roundup.

Hirshhorn Museum (Independence Avenue between 7th and 9th streets). Distinguished collection of modern art displayed in the drum-shaped building, highlighted by the sculpture garden featuring Rodin's *Burghers of Calais* and important

97

pieces by Moore, Picasso and David Smith. The painting collection does justice to Cubism, Social Realism, Op, Pop and Minimal.

Freer Gallery of Art (Jefferson at 12th). Oriental and American art.

Art and Industries (Jefferson at 9th) includes an important collection of Americana and other exhibits from the 1876 Philadelphia Centennial Exposition.

Arthur M. Sackler Gallery (1050 Independence Avenue SW). Buddhist sculpture, ancient Iranian metalwork, and about 1,000 works of art from China, Southeast Asia and the ancient Near East are housed in these beautiful subterranean galleries.

National Portrait Gallery (8th and F streets). All the presidents and great ladies are here, including Pocahontas, Eleanor Roosevelt and Gertrude Stein.

Museum of American Art (8th and G streets). Fine examples from colonial times via Winslow Homer, Cassatt and Whistler to O'Keefe and de Kooning.

Renwick Gallery (Pennsylvania Avenue and 17th Street). The best of American design, crafts and decorative arts.

The Phillips Collection (1600 21st Street) Duncan Phillips' fine home is a showcase for a small but select collection of mostly modern European and American paintings.

EXCURSIONS

Mount Vernon *(16 miles south on Mt Vernon Memorial Parkway, also by tourmobile in summer)*
Not just a dutiful pilgrimage to the home of George Washington, Father of the Nation, Mount Vernon offers a delightful journey back in time to the life of an 18th-century Virginia plantation, beautifully restored, the lawns perhaps a shade more tailored than in the old days. Make the 35-minute drive early in the morning to avoid the spring and summer crowds and sit, as George and Martha did, on the graceful square-columned veranda which overlooks the Potomac river valley and the Maryland hills beyond.

Great soldier and leader of men, George Washington was also an accomplished farmer. He owned some 8,000 acres of land, divided into 5 farms with 120 slaves to work them. At the border of the immaculate Bowling Green, you'll pass old trees planted by George himself. Inside the house, you can see Martha's account books, each item painstakingly recorded. The furniture is authentic 18th-century; George's bedroom has the original pieces, including the bed he died in in 1799 and the portmanteau trunk that accompanied him during the Revolutionary campaign.

Colonial Virginia *(South from Washington on Interstate 95 via Richmond to State Highway 5)*
Highway 5 takes you through some lovely James River plantation country to the Historic Triangle of Jamestown, where Virginia was founded, Williamsburg, its capital from 1699 to 1780, and Yorktown, where the Revolutionary War reached its triumphant climax in 1781. The towns are linked by the Colonial Parkway on which a Visitors Center dispenses tickets for Colonial Williamsburg.

Williamsburg is a complete "museum-town" where you can stroll around meticulously reconstructed 18th-century houses, shops and taverns—no cars, only horse-drawn carriages and oxcarts taking children for rides. Tour-guides and the artisans working at the cobbler's, gunsmith's, apothecary and printer's workshop are all dressed in colonial costume. The restoration was carried out with funds from John D. Rockefeller, Jr., in 1927. Drawing on 18th-century engravings found across the Atlantic in the Bodleian Library, Oxford, architectural historians were able to restore the 1705 **Capitol** building and **Governor's Palace** in exact detail. For the latter, they were helped by a precise plan of the interior drawn by Thomas Jefferson, who lived here for six months as Governor of Virginia. The major thoroughfare is **Duke of Gloucester Street** with some of the finest wooden weatherboard and red-brick Georgian houses. Revolutionary bigwigs met at Raleigh Tavern; you can eat authentic 18th-century food at the King's Arms, Chowning's and Christiana Campbell's taverns, all in fine restored state.

Jamestown, 6 miles south of Williamsburg, was the site settled by the first pioneers from London in May 1607 (13 years before the *Mayflower* reached Massachusetts). The only relic of colonial Jamestown is a crumbling church tower. The site was abandoned because of malarial mosquitoes (gone now). But **Jamestown Festival Park,** at the entrance to the causeway leading to Jamestown proper, has been built as a replica of the old three-sided fort, with a 17th-century pottery and an Indian ceremonial lodge. On the river are full-scale replicas of the tiny vessels, *Susan Constant, Discovery* and *Godspeed,* which brought John Smith and 103 settlers across the sea on their courageous voyage. You can even go aboard the *Susan Constant* to inspect living conditions.

Yorktown, 18 miles to the east, is where Lord Cornwallis surrendered his British troops in October 1781, effectively sealing Britain's loss of its American colonies.

Before visiting the battlefield, stop at the Yorktown Victory Center, just 2 miles out of town, where you can talk to costumed interpreters in farm and battlefield settings and see a display of revolutionary war artefacts. The most significant part of the fighting was actually a naval engagement in Chesapeake Bay between the British and the Americans' French allies. In town, you can visit **Moore House,** where the British negotiated their capitulation with the Americans and French.

BIG CITIES NEARBY

Baltimore and Philadelphia serve as interesting counterparts to the national capital. The birthplace of American nationhood, Philadelphia is a lively mixture of ethnic groups, while Baltimore, a major seaport

for Chesapeake Bay, has undergone exciting urban renewal, and is a great place for seafood.

Philadelphia *(Pennsylvania)*

It's one of the more charming aspects of America that a town which occupies such an important place in the history of the nation should also be a national joke. Philadelphia, after all, is the City of Brotherly Love that William Penn established as a model of religious freedom and colonial enterprise and where Benjamin Franklin and Thomas Jefferson championed the movement for independence. But it's a quiet, sedate town—to which comedian W.C. Fields preferred a graveyard, and where the master of horror, Edgar Allan Poe, wrote his famous poem "The Raven".

While the modern city has been enlivened by its thriving Italian and Jewish communities, it's the old Anglo-Saxon backbone that continues to set the dignified tone. According to Mark Twain, "In Boston, they ask 'How much does he know?' In New York, 'How much is he worth?' In Philadelphia, 'Who were his parents?'"

Today the town's past is still of vital importance to its citizens. And they proudly proclaim **Independence National Historical Park** at the heart of old Philadelphia, containing all the great buildings of early America's government, as the "most historic square mile in America". At the grand red-brick Georgian **Independence Hall** (5th and Chestnut) you can see where America's founding fathers signed the Declaration of Independence and later the United States Constitution. Next door, the states' representa-

Colonial houses in Williamsburg

tives met in **Congress Hall** and signed—without great enthusiasm—the Bill of Rights that forced the government to protect rather than interfere with individual freedoms. On the pleasant tree-shaded green of Independence Mall (Market and 5th streets) you can touch (but not ring) the famous **Liberty Bell** in its glass pavilion. This was the bell that came from England in 1751, cracked en route as if to symbolize the American fissure in Britain's empire, was repaired in time to ring out from the tower of Independence Hall on July 4, 1776, and cracked again in the 19th century. Now it's been laid to rest for visitors just to pat it with affection.

In case you still don't grasp the Philadelphians' view of their city's importance, take a look at the magnificently outrageous **City Hall** (Market and Broad streets). It took the Louvre in Paris as its architectural model and, locals like to point out, it's bigger than Washington's Capitol. On top stands William Penn.

The **Philadelphia Museum of Art** (26th and the Parkway) houses a very good collection of American works, plus some fine Impressionist and Post-Impressionist paintings. Perhaps the best known work here is Van Gogh's *Sunflowers*.

Edgar Allan Poe's House (530 N. 7th Street) is now a museum of Poe memorabilia. He lived here with his young wife.

The **Rodin Museum** (22nd and Parkway) has the biggest collection of the French sculptor's work outside Paris.

The **Franklin Institute** (20th and Parkway) is a marvellous science museum, especially for the youngsters, where you can see lightning being made—a permanent test for Ben's invention, the lightning rod.

Baltimore *(Maryland)*

Baltimore suffers even more than Philadelphia from what Baltimoreans consider unfair barbs. Edgar Allan Poe *died* here and was buried in Westminster Churchyard, but otherwise the town is somewhat lacking in historical monuments. However, it makes up for this with some of the boldest urban renewal in the country. **Charles Center** has turned the erstwhile blight of the downtown business district into a lively area of shops, theatres and cafés.

Equally successful and visually more attractive is the 95-acre **Inner Harbor** development transforming the once seedy waterfront of Baltimore Harbor into a stylish setting for hotels, theatres, ethnic and seafood restaurants, parks and promenades, bringing the place back to life. Art shows, concerts and sports

Bountiful Italian market, Philadelphia

activities keep the place hopping throughout the year. The restaurants around the harbour serve some fine fresh seafood from the bay—clams and oysters, soft-shell crab, crab cakes and a Baltimore speciality, hard-shell crabs.

At Constellation Dock you can tour the restored Navy frigate *Constellation*, which was originally launched here in 1797. Landlubbers who prefer old trains can see a superb collection at the **Baltimore & Ohio Railroad Museum** (Poppleton and Pratt streets).

Pride of the **Baltimore Museum of Art** (Charles and 31st streets) is the excellent Cone Collection of 19th- and 20th-century painting, very well endowed with works by Matisse and Picasso.

103

THE SOUTH

For the holiday-maker, the South is above all the place where the sun is. For Americans, it's also an almost mythical place perceived through its history—an ante-bellum serenity and paternalism, the blood and fire of civil war, bitter resentments of reconstruction, and a 20th-century struggle for parity with the North and a new pride and prosperity. Parity, but not conformity. The South has held on to an exotic quality that spices courtly mellow decadence with a hint of contained violence below the surface. To sort out myth and reality would require a prolonged stay of months or years, criss-crossing the Carolinas, Georgia, Florida, Alabama, Mississippi, Louisiana and Arkansas. But for an introduction, start with Florida for the exquisite hedonism of its subtropical sun, then to Charleston for an echo of the golden past, to Atlanta for a look at the new South, and over to New Orleans, a grand old river city with a unique Creole flavour.

There is nothing ambiguous about a visitor's intentions in Florida: pleasure, sheer pleasure. Take in the sun, sea and sand along the coast from Miami up to Palm Beach, but allow some time off to visit the dreamlands of Walt Disney around Orlando and the outer space adventures launched from Cape Canaveral or perhaps to drift by the alligators in the Everglades swamps. In Florida's subtropical climate with air and sea-water temperatures ranging from an average low of 23°C (74°F) in January to an average high of 31°C (88°F) in August, sunlovers should watch out. Sun-bathing here should begin with no more than 30 minutes the first day; the Florida sun can really scorch you even when the weather is overcast.

MIAMI BEACH *(Florida)*

Connected to mainland Miami by causeways across Biscayne Bay, this is where the pleasure begins: 7 miles of gleaming sandy beaches in front of high-rise hotels and condominium apartment buildings. A few years ago these beaches nearly disappeared because of the erosion caused by undisciplined construction along the seafront. At the end of the 1970s, the U.S. Army Corps of Engineers came to the rescue by dumping 13½ million cubic yards of white sand along the reclaimed 100-yard-wide strip of seashore. It's a good place to get away from it all, and is a popular place to retire to—most residents are over 60.

After a careful dose of sun your first day, you might like to check out the various beaches. If your hotel has commandeered its own piece of the shoreline—as is the case around 46th Street—you may be perfectly happy to stay there, but there are several good alternatives:

Haulover Beach, at the north end, is for the very active, with palm trees to shade their lazy companions. It's very good for surfing, Frisbee-spinning and fishing off the pier. There are barbecue grills to turn your catch into a picnic.

Bal Harbor is great for shell-collectors and jetsam-hunters with those strange battery-driven rods that may locate buried treasures— old Spanish coins or new Miami jewels, but most likely just beer cans. You can combine your beach stay with some shopping in the boutiques that quite happily proclaim themselves to be the most expensive in the world.

Surfside at 93rd Street and the **64th and 53rd Street beaches** are best for swimming, away from the crowds.

21st Street is a favourite with young people, who turn the fast-food stands into lively open-air clubs.

Away from the sands, Miami Beach offers architectural rewards for Art Deco buffs. In the area of **Washington Avenue,** on the blocks between 8th and 21st streets, you can stroll around hotels, apartment buildings, restaurants and shops that sprang up in the tourist boom

of the '20s and '30s, with a flourish of chrome and bakelite, gaily coloured ceramic tiles and mirrored glass, borrowing motifs from the Egyptians and Aztecs. After years of scorn by purists who found the buildings too "florid", it's now been declared by official art historians to be a "national preservation area".

Continuing the triumphant spirit from the '50s to the present day, **Collins Avenue** stretches for 100 blocks of more modern hotels, the flagship being the **Fontainebleau Hilton** (at 44th Street). Even if you're not staying there, plan to have a drink or meal (and a look around) in the unquestionable monument of American leisure. No expense has been spared at the serpentine pool, cabanas, waterfalls, grottoes, hidden bars, tennis courts, luxury shops and aquarium to make you feel anywhere but at home. After the extravagant décors of the '50s, it's gone beyond vulgarity— gilt and marble are "out"—to the higher realms of *de luxe* fantasy. Today everyone's a film star.

MIAMI *(Florida)*

The sun-sea-and-sand worshippers tend to avoid the city of Miami itself, but they're missing some major attractions. Like many Miami Beach residents, they've been frightened by the influx of immigrants from Cuba and Haiti and the stories of drugs, voodoo and violent crime. The stories are true—drugs are one of the four main sources of revenue in Florida, with tourism, citrus fruits and manufacturing—but with the reasonable care that you'd take in any large city these days, there's some fun to be had in this high-colour town.

Downtown is a conventionally bustling area of department stores, restaurants and nightclubs around Flagler Street and Biscayne Boulevard. But it's livelier south of downtown in the Cuban neighbourhood of **Little Havana,** centred on a 30-block section around "Calle Ocho" (8th Street) running east from 37th Avenue. More than a quarter of Miami's 2 million people are Cubans and here is where they hand-roll their cigars and dance the *salsa*. The street life makes New York City seem sedate.

Try the strong Cuban coffee, served espresso-style on the street in paper cups, or cocoa for dipping your *churro* (a long thin doughnut). At Ocho and 14th Avenue is the site of the open-air Domino Park where neighbourhood enthusiasts (male only, women can just watch) play with a concentration worthy of grand-master chess. A block further east is **La Ceiba,** the sacred kapok tree, where sorcery is very openly performed. (Miami cemetery guardians often have to clear up the dead chickens, goats' heads and voodoo dolls left by Haitian and Cuban voodoo-doctors.)

On Ocho and 12th Avenue, you can watch cigars being rolled, pressed, wrapped and cut with elegant dexterity.

The closest thing Miami has to a bohemian artists' quarter is a place called **Coconut Grove** (South Bay Shore Drive), which is a pleasant self-contained community of boutiques, galleries and parks, with quaint sailing boats bobbing in the harbour.

Across the Rickenbacker Causeway, **Key Biscayne** has some delightful beaches at Bill Baggs Cape Florida State Recreation Area. But the star of Miami's many wildlife attractions is **Seaquarium,** just off the cause-way on Virginia Key. There you'll find whales, dolphins, sharks and turtles at play and in repose. The dolphins will leap any height for a few fish and the spectator's delight. Seaquarium is one of the few places where you can see the rare manatee, or sea cow, a large seal-like mammal which used to live in great numbers in Florida's waterways. And in **Parrot Jungle** (57th Avenue and 112th Street) the birds perform more tricks than the dolphins—ride bicycles, roller-skate, do a bit of arithmetic. Some of them even fly. The flamingoes alone are well worth the visit.

But man remains the most fascinating trickster. Look at what industrialist James Deering did with his **Vizcaya** home (3251 S. Miami Avenue). Now also serving as the Dade County Museum, this 70-room Renaissance *palazzo* on Biscayne Bay contains in its opulent interior almost every artistic style known to Western man from the A.D. 200 altar to the 1915 gold plumbing fixtures. The formal gardens are bizarre and the huge barge in the harbour is made of stone, a piece of sculpture by A. Stirling Calder, less mobile than the works done later by his son Alexander.

If that doesn't impress you, how about the 12th-century Spanish cloisters intended for newspaper and copper tycoon William Randolph Hearst's home in California?

In 1925, **St. Bernard's Monastery** (16711 W. Dixie Highway, off Biscayne Boulevard) was brought over from Segovia stone by numbered stone in 11,000 crates. Unfortunately, they were packed with hay that the U.S. Department of Agriculture deemed a health hazard to animals (there'd been foot-and-mouth in Segovia), so the dismantled monastery stayed on the East Coast until it was bought and reassembled by some entrepreneur. It is now under the auspices of the Episcopal Diocese of South Florida. The choral recitals here offer one of the most deliciously anachronistic experiences on the North American continent.

AROUND FLORIDA

The Everglades *(Toll road south to Homestead then take State Route 27, follow signs to the National Park)*
This watery plain has given swamps a good name, replacing the image of a disease-ridden morass with that of a wonderland of natural beauty. A 50-mile band of brackish water from Lake Okeechobee flows lazily down through Florida and into the ocean. Called the "River of Grass", the slow-moving bog positively teems with wildlife. The **Everglades National Park** covering nearly 1½ million acres is under

the protection of U.S. Rangers, who are stationed at the various visitor centres throughout the park with advice about how best to enjoy— and not spoil—the wilderness.

From the park entrance south- west of Homestead (pick up a map at the Visitor Center), the road runs 38 miles to the coast. Several marked turnoffs along the way take you out to campsites and picnic grounds beside lakes or near "ham- mocks"—raised areas in the swamps. The first of these turnoffs leads you to **Royal Palm Visitor Center** on the edge of a fresh water slough. Look down into the clear waters of the pond to see shoals of fish, among them the Florida garfish much appreciated by the al- ligator. You might like to see one of the brief slide-shows introducing the Everglades at the Visitor Center before taking the Anhinga and Gumbo Limbo foot-trails leading from this area.

The Anhinga Trail's raised boardwalk circles over sawgrass marsh where you can see alligators, egrets, herons and the anhinga snake-bird. The Gumbo Limbo Trail is a circular half-mile track through jungle vegetation. Keep your eyes open for racoons, opos- sums, tree-snails and lizards, very big hereabouts.

At the end of the main road is **Flamingo,** a fishing village on a

Alligators
The Everglades alligators are coming back. Legislation against hunting or trapping the reptiles has helped to re- verse the population decline. There are well over 10,000 alligators today (and some 500 crocodiles), although once they numbered in the millions. To provide the raw material for de luxe handbags, belts and shoes, they were almost hunted out of existence.

Alligators prefer fresh water; crocodiles like sandy beaches and salt water. And if you get close enough, you'll notice that alligators have shorter, blunter snouts.

Never, never underestimate an alli- gator—even if it appears to be dozing. Small or large, it will thrash towards anything that moves, snap with 2,000 pounds of pressure and drag its prey under water before devouring it at leisure.

shallow bay dotted with islands. In the good old days, it produced illicit "moonshine" alcohol. Now it's a tourist centre with a motel, house- keeping cabins and campsite. At the Flamingo Marina, you can rent tackle, boats and canoes to fish for trout, redfish, snapper and snook (which has a taste reminiscent of pike). Find your own way up to Everglades City through a chain of lakes and rivers called "The Wilderness Waterway" or take a sightseeing boat from Flamingo.

The abundant wildlife on the coast and in the interior includes ibises, ospreys, white herons, bald eagles, snowy egrets, otters, roseate spoonbills, green turtles, manatees (the gentle "sea-cows" increasingly threatened by fast motorboats) and rare Florida panthers.

Coat yourself in insect repellent and follow the rangers' precautions about poisonous plants and snakes.

The Gold Coast

The 70-mile-long Gold Coast offers half a dozen vacation resorts favoured by Americans escaping the winter rigours of New York, New England and the Midwest. Hotels and condominiums gleam white across wide, palm-tree-lined boulevards that border on spotless beaches. Some of these resorts are in another world altogether.

Fort Lauderdale is crazy. Its peak moment of madness is the month-long Easter vacation when roughly a quarter of a million sun-starved northern students descend on the town like the merry Mongol hordes of yore. They come not to pillage and rape but to boogie on the beach and try some gentle mating in the moonlight. Early evening, the kids cruise their cars bumper to bumper up and down the A1A "Strip" along the seafront, climbing from one convertible to another in search of an extra giggle. Summer and winter, the town settles down as private boats and yachts (estimated to number 30,000 on and off the canals) drift along the network of **inland waterways** past elegant marina homes. The best way to view them—if you're not thinking of chartering a yacht—is to take one of the paddle-boat cruises from the Bahia Mar marina.

Boca Raton is lazy. It's the winter home of a highly regarded polo club, but you can also enjoy the superb beaches tucked behind the dunes. Or rent a rod and pretend to fish off the rocks around the inlet. If you must be active, go bird-watching or hiking around Deerfield Island Park, once the home of Chicago's own Al Capone.

And **Palm Beach** is another world, the place that put the "gold" in the Gold Coast. (The "palms" in Palm Beach are said to have grown from coconuts spilled in a Spanish shipwreck.) The town was created after oil and railway magnate Henry Flagler was persuaded at the end of the 19th century that Florida's warm winters made the state a viable proposition for his railway expansion. At the same

Cypress Gardens, Florida

time as the railway was being built down the Gold Coast, the secluded location of Palm Beach struck Flagler as just the kind of place for his kind of person. Now one of America's wealthiest communities, it stretches its splendid *palazzi* along Ocean Boulevard, not far from the proprietors' yachts in the harbour. You can catch glimpses of these opulent residences as you wind through the impeccable landscaping. Flagler's own home is on Coconut Row, a white marble palace named Whitehall, currently the **Henry Morrison Flagler Museum,** which traces the town's early history amid elegant old furnishings, with the master's private railway carriage also on show.

In this, Florida's ultimate consumer paradise, there is scarcely a luxury shop of the world that is not represented on its pride and joy: **Worth Avenue.** It's a street that ranks alongside Paris's Rue du Faubourg Saint-Honoré or London's Bond Street. Even if your budget doesn't allow you to go wild and buy all the elegant goodies you want, you can still press your nose against the windows.

You'll notice that the couturiers go a little crazy in the colours they choose here. It's the Florida sun that does it. You'll also see the most delightfully flamboyant golfing clothes ever offered to Western man and woman. What's more, there are people actually wearing them on this hallowed avenue. The Gucci store is worth the detour— nothing less than a Florentine *palazzo*, with fountains playing in the tree-shaded courtyard.

Kennedy Space Center

Situated a hundred-odd miles to the north on Merritt Island, this is the site of all manned-craft launchings. Unmanned flights are launched from Cape Canaveral, across the Banana River. An ideal trip here would include watching a launching. You can get the schedule and information about reservations for the special viewing by calling (407) 452-2121. Otherwise there's still plenty to see if you avoid the crowds by arriving very early at the Visitors Center on State Route 405 and catch one of the two-hour bus tours.

The Blue Tour takes you on a historical survey of space travel and includes visits to the Air Force Space Museum, former launching pads, and inside the old Mission Control building. The Red Tour concentrates on the facilities used by the current space-shuttle programme. The exhibits at the Visitors Center include films and simulated flights, the *Apollo-Soyuz* command module and a lunar roving vehicle.

Walt Disney World® Resort
(20 miles south-west of Orlando off Interstate 4 and State Highway 192)

With Walt Disney World, the grand old movie-maker's company has turned his fantasies into a mammoth holiday resort development, with its own hotels, campgrounds, golf courses, water theme parks, boating facilities, vacation villas and shops, surrounding the biggest theme park in the world. The area covers 27,400 acres—much of it reclaimed marshland.

The heart of the complex is the 100-acre theme park known as the Magic Kingdom. Just to the south is what might be called its brain, the EPCOT Center, a multimedia projection of the world's past and future filtered through a Disney-inspired imagination.

Adjoining EPCOT's south side, but with a separate entrance, the Disney-MGM Studios park celebrates America's love affair with the movies. To keep adults inside the Disney empire when the big three parks close, Pleasure Island offers some innocent night-life until the small hours.

Entering Disney's territory (from Highway 192 or I-4) you'll head for whichever of the three you have chosen. If you're driving, you'll pay to park in one of the enormous lots (note your area, row and space

> **Some Timely Tips**
>
> *Plan your visits to Walt Disney World so that you are at the entrance of your chosen park early in the morning—particularly if you're not staying in one of the Disney hotels. By early afternoon in peak season, the queues for the rides get extremely long, and if a park gets full, they close the gates. Besides, it gets too hot to tour the attractions in the afternoon sun—that's the time to be inside one of the air-conditioned halls. (From September 1 to mid-December and January 3 to mid-February, things are easier.)*

number) and walk or take the shuttle to the main gate. Hotel buses go straight to the gate.

Unless you have bought a package including entrance fees, you can choose between a one-day ticket, good for one park only, a four-day ticket (which allows you entrance to all three parks), a five-day ticket (all three parks plus Pleasure Island) or an annual ticket. The days don't have to be consecutive, and once you're inside, all rides and exhibits are free. At each park entrance, be sure to pick up a map and timetable.

The Magic Kingdom

Once past the ticket booths, choose between the ultra-modern monorail or the more leisurely ferryboat across the lake to the Magic King-

113

dom's entrance. Now you're in fairyland, with Cinderella's castle, and surrounded by Mickey Mouse and a host of Disney movie characters. Take your choice of the Kingdom's six different sections.

Main Street, USA, is the very symbol of the good old American Way of Life, from the entrance under the Railroad Station past gabled and turreted turn-of-the-century buildings to Town Square, where City Hall dispenses information about the rest of the Magic Kingdom and Walt Disney World in general.

Adventureland proposes exotic tropical flora and fauna. A gigantic (concrete) banyan tree supporting the Swiss Family Robinson Treehouse stands by the landing-stage for the Jungle Cruise, complete with trailing vines and (foam-rubber) wild animals.

Frontierland romanticizes the pioneer days—quick draw at the Shootin' Gallery, fast-food at Pecos Bill's Café or slow ride on the gaily coloured riverboat.

Liberty Square doesn't quite replace a visit to New England but makes a valiant effort to capture the atmosphere of the Republic's cradle at Liberty Tree Tavern.

Fantasyland takes you on a submarine voyage 20,000 Leagues Under the Sea or on a dizzying whirl in the Mad Hatter's gigantic teacup. Every childhood character seems to be here—Peter Pan, Snow White's Seven Dwarfs, not to mention Disney's own Mickey Mouse.

Tomorrowland is devoted to outer space and the accompanying technology. You can go on a Mission to Mars or pilot a Star-Jet. In the towering white-steel Space Mountain is a heart-stopping rollercoaster ride which simulates a race through space. More reassuring is the WED-Way People Mover, cars floating oh-so-smoothly on a cushion of electromagnetic force. You have free access to many of the technological attractions sponsored by the manufacturers—well worth the time.

EPCOT Center

Out of Walt Disney's last dream of an Experimental Prototype Community of Tomorrow has grown his company's most ambitious entertainment centre—partly built, constantly evolving—south of the Magic Kingdom. It attempts to present in exciting visual terms the past and future of our planet, together with a showcase of some of the world's nations, all within a few hundred acres around an artificial lake. Every night there is a spectacular firework display over the lake.

In **Future World** a monorail takes you around polygonal, spherical, dome-shaped or pyramidal

pavilions (each sponsored by a major American company) demonstrating the evolution of our civilization and the new technologies that will be tomorrow's tools. The centre-piece is **Spaceship Earth,** a 180-foot-high, white geosphere. Inside, you will coast along in an egg-shaped vehicle on a rail past 3D holograms of prehistoric man and lifelike robots of his descendants, through the ancient civilizations of Greece and Rome via the Renaissance to the present day, at the top of the sphere.

World Showcase presents nations of the world through their monuments, landmarks and cuisines. Enjoy French delicacies in a bistro at the foot of a model Eiffel Tower, or wander through an Italian market of fake onions, tomatoes and carrots before sitting down to a plate of real *fettucine* in a restaurant alongside a replica of Venice's Piazza San Marco.

Disney-MGM Studios

More like 1930s Hollywood, probably, than Hollywood ever was, the Art Deco streets of Disney's newest theme park lead to real and replica film sets. You'll see stunt shows, ride through movie history, meet the Muppets and learn some of the secrets of Walt Disney' animation techniques. On Star Tours you can experience "virtual reality" in a runaway spacecraft and in Catastrophe Canyon you'll get a close up of the special effects that gave disaster movies their name.

To see some of the highlights of all three parks, you would need at least three days, perhaps four. You'll walk miles and there's a lot of waiting in line when the parks are at their busiest. It's particularly tiring on a hot summer's day, although you can rent strollers (pushchairs) and wheelchairs. For more information, including on the wide range of Disney-run accommodation, contact Walt Disney World, PO Box 10100, Lake Buena Vista, FL 32830–0100, U.S.A.

Universal Studios Florida (Orlando)

Film and TV fans can live some of their favourites and see new productions in progress. Hundreds of millions of dollars have been spent to create thrilling special-effect rides and some real, some lookalike stars make their appearance. Make sure you arrive early in the day in order to find out about any special events which might be planned. You'll need to spend most of the day here: one- and two-day tickets are available. There's quite a lot of walking, though pushchairs and wheelchairs can be rented.

Mexico, EPCOT Center

CHARLESTON
(South Carolina)

Standing aloof at the point where the Ashley and Cooper Rivers flow together into the Atlantic, this town evokes that elegant, courtly atmosphere that people still associate with the "Old South". After South Carolina had led the Southern states' secession from the Union, Charleston was the town that fired the first shots in the Civil War. Ever since, it has maintained, with winning self-consciousness, a sense of dignified separateness.

The **harbourside**—along the Battery curving north up to East Bay Street—is a delightful palmetto-shaded area to stroll around the 18th- and 19th-century houses with beautiful gardens of dogwood, wisteria and azalea.

Running west from East Bay Street, follow Market Street, which takes you to the colourful **Market Square.** Here, open-air cafés, restaurants, art galleries and boutiques have been installed in renovated warehouses—very much in keeping with the nationwide movement for redeveloping derelict downtown neighbourhoods.

From the Municipal Marina at the junction of Calhoun Street and Lockwood Drive on the west, Ashley River side of the peninsula, you can take a boat trip out to historic **Fort Sumter.** This is the old military base that, during the Civil War, was wrested from the United States Army by South Carolina militia in April 1861, to the polite applause of the Charleston gentry assembled on the harbour. It was recaptured, after a two-year siege, in February 1865. The two hour boat cruise includes a visit to the Civil War museum and a tour of the remains of the fort.

Two excursions out of town will complete your glimpse of the old days of the cotton plantations. **Boone Hall,** situated 7 miles north on Highway 17, was used as the Tara plantation for the filming of *Gone with the Wind*—as Georgia, apparently, had nothing quite so appropriate. But the most spectacular grounds are the **Magnolia Gardens,** 14 miles north of Charleston on Highway 61. This lovely 400-acre nature reserve that was once a huge plantation combines exotic displays of flowers and shrubs with fine opportunities for activities including bird-watching, hiking, biking and canoeing.

ATLANTA *(Georgia)*

This historic capital of Georgia is also the bold and bouncing capital of the new South. The town's symbol, which you can see in two fine sculptures—one on Broad Street by the First National Bank, the other on Martin Luther King Drive—is the phoenix, the mythical bird that rose from the ashes. The town's modern prosperity has been motivated by its total destruction in 1864 during the Civil War. Two years later it was the federal headquarters for the South's Reconstruction and the dynamism has not yet abated.

Venue for the 1996 Olympic Games, the town also offers exhilarating contemporary architecture, elegant shops, smart restaurants and shiny discos—the backdrop for a people cannily combining Yankee sophistication with the savvy of those redneck good ol' boys who sometimes sound as if they just hit town, but hit it hard.

To get the ideal overview, start your tour with a trip to the 70th-floor revolving restaurant on top of the **Peachtree Plaza Hotel**—the elevators whiz up through glass tubes on the outside of the building. The **view** is spectacular, all the way to the Blue Ridge Mountains.

(No need to rent a car if you're on a brief visit, the buses of Atlanta's highly efficient MARTA public transport system give a comprehensive tour of the major sights, stopping off at the main hotels.)

Linked to the plaza, **Peachtree Center** is the unmistakeable heart of downtown, an airy shopping and business centre with attractive landscaping among the skyscrapers, drooping vines and tropical plants,

reflecting pools and splashing fountains. Even if you're not staying there, be sure to visit the Hyatt Regency Hotel, a pioneer in the updated atrium architecture: the skyscraper is built around a skylit courtyard with its own indoor-outdoor café-terrace inside the hotel.

The **Martin Luther King Memorial** (407 Auburn Avenue, NE) marks the tomb of the great civil rights leader assassinated in Memphis in 1968. Atlanta was his home, and the tomb, bearing the inscription "Free at last" stands beside the Ebenezer Baptist Church where he and his father preached the message of non-violence (his mother was murdered there in 1974). A research institute next door provides an information centre on King's life and works.

One of the newer testimonies to Atlanta's entrepreneurial energy is the **Omni International Complex** (100 Techwood Drive), a dazzling 34-acre megastructure, as Atlantans like to call it, containing a sports coliseum for ice-hockey, basketball, circuses and concerts and a convention centre with cinemas, shops, discothèques, a skating-rink and restaurants. Multicoloured laser beams light up the enormous interior at night while hundreds of "sun sculpture" prisms set in the skylight create a charming kaleidoscopic effect by day.

Sing with Care

A mistake that foreign visitors sometimes make in Atlanta is to whistle the tune of "Marching through Georgia". Atlantans don't dwell unduly on the past, but this ditty is still not appreciated here. It recalls the march of Northern troops who left Atlanta in September 1864, having carried out the orders of General William Tecumseh Sherman to burn it to the ground. Though he ruthlessly carried out the tactics of scorched earth throughout Georgia, Sherman was a soldier of much more compassion than Southerners understandably credit him with. Whether or not he actually made the remark often attributed to him: "War is hell", he did say to the protesting mayor of Atlanta: "War is cruel and you cannot refine it".

The **High Museum of Art** (Peachtree and 16th streets) is a stunning white structure containing a superb collection, including American decorative art, 19th- and 20th-century photography, African art and some fine modern paintings.

Atlanta is also the home-base of Coca-Cola, and the company's museum (310 North Avenue) gives a fascinating glimpse of the history and advertising of this bubbly symbol of Americana.

NEW ORLEANS *(Louisiana)*

Whatever is exotic, lurid, even sinful in the popular image of the South stems in large part from this port town at the mouth of the Mississippi River. In New Orleans, the jazz that grew up in its brothels and seamy saloons is still hot and the Creole cooking brought from the West Indies by the old French and Spanish settlers is as spicy as ever. You'll find them both in the French Quarter. And if the elegant decadence of the ante-bellum aristocracy is at best a whispered legend handed down to a few strutting diehards, take a look at their grand-daddies' splendid Greek Revival town-houses in the Garden District and you'll see what a proud world they lost when they had to give up their slaves. Mississippi gamblers no longer fleece wealthy widows on

riverboats coming all the way down from Natchez, but the sternwheeler steamboats are back in service again for cruises along Ol' Man River.

The closest they get to being exotic, lurid and sinful these days is at the great Mardi Gras carnival, so successful that the city fathers are now turning every imaginable occasion—St. Patrick's Day, Bastille Day, the arrival of spring or summer—into another festival, however hot and steamy it may get. New Orleans loves parades, but if they haven't found an excuse for one when you're visiting, you'll still find a public party going on somewhere, with all the trumpets and trombones blowing full blast.

French Quarter

Known locally as the Vieux Carré (Old Square), this is the historic heart of town, bounded by Canal Street and Rampart Street (originally a fortification), Esplanade Avenue and the Mississippi River. Great fires in 1788 and 1794 destroyed over 1,000 houses in the quarter, but the 19th-century reconstruction has maintained the old two- and three-storey houses with filigreed wrought-iron galleries providing the roof for shaded colonnades at street level. This, despite the encroachment of new hotels and saloons, remains the quarter's dominant architecture.

Start at **Jackson Square** where, around the statue of General Andrew Jackson, the place bustles all day long with clowns, magicians, balloon-vendors, and assorted eccentrics sporting strange costumes. Groups of children stage "tap-dancing" shows on street corners, embedding bottle tops in the soles and heels of their sneakers to provide the "tap". Flanking the cathedral are two relics of the colonial era—the **Cabildo,** originally a police station and later the City Hall, and the **Presbytère,** a priests' residence that became a courthouse. They are now part of the Louisiana State Museum. The Cabildo's exhibits tell the colourful history of trade on the Mississippi, while the Presbytère exhibits old Mardi Gras costumes and paraphernalia and tells the story of Louisiana's Blacks from slavery to the present day. St. Louis Cathedral is an 1851 restoration of the 18th-century church of the French Catholic diocese, more famous for the duels in its garden than for its architecture. Around the square are two rows of **Pontalba Buildings,** with elegant ironwork (cast rather than wrought) on the upper-storey galleries.

Walk down Dumaine Street past Madame John's Legacy, a nicely preserved French colonial cottage,

> ### Mardi Gras
> *Shrove Tuesday, the British call it, but people here like to translate the French—"Fat Tuesday" is the last hedonistic fling before an effort at Lenten austerity leading up to Easter. It's New Orleans' great moment of madness bringing hundreds of thousands of revellers—make sure you book your hotel room months in advance—to see the parade of papier-mâché floats down St. Charles Avenue, as well as many others throughout the city. King or Rex of the main parade is often a television or movie star. While the round of private masked balls starts on Twelfth Night (January 6), the pageants only begin 11 days before Mardi Gras. In costumes, anything goes—fat old men in baby's romper-suits, thin young ladies in fat old men's suits. The kinky may well wear a fabulous black leather cowboy suit on the front and absolutely nothing behind. Although Mardi Gras takes place in February or early March, the weather is delightfully balmy.*

to Royal Street, one of the most gracious in the quarter with some high-class antique shops. To the right, at 1132 Royal Street, is the **Gallier House,** named after its architect James Gallier, one of the few authentic old New Orleans houses open to the public. It has been lovingly restored to its original 1857 condition and if you walk out on the wrought-iron balcony

Jazz Town

Cotton is no longer king, but jazz has returned to its throne in New Orleans. The once disreputable music is now celebrated officially in the 14-acre Louis Armstrong Park on the edge of the French Quarter, complete with a 12-foot statue of "Satchmo", trumpet in one hand, handkerchief in the other. The local Tulane University's sociology department has special archives of recordings, photos and other documents devoted to the history of jazz.

It all began at the end of the 19th century when black marching bands wailed to the funerals and swung all the way home. At night, they played the bawdy-houses on Basin Street, and when the redlight district was closed in 1917, the action moved to Bourbon Street. The nightclubs and saloons there today are bouncing and shaking more loudly than ever—ragtime, blues, easy-going Dixieland or the heavier driving "Chicago" style, swing and boogie woogie, but none of the bop, cool and acid-electronic stuff that has come along since World War II.

The jazz joints dispensing beer and stronger stuff come and go, change their name and location from season to season, but one solid institution remains in place—Preservation Hall. Just old-time traditional jazz played straight by old black musicians.

NEW ORLEANS

you get a lovely view of the neighbourhood's old tranquillity before venturing out to attack the hurly-burly of **Bourbon Street's** saloons and nightclubs.

If you want to save Bourbon Street till night, cut down Governor Nicholls Street towards the waterfront. On the corner of Decatur is the old *Streetcar Named Desire* made famous by Tennessee Williams' play. (Desire is in fact a street a dozen or so blocks east of here—this streetcar doesn't run any more but you can still take the St.

Charles Avenue streetcar through the Garden District starting from Carondelet at Canal.)

Close to the waterfront is the ever-expanding **French Market,** pleasant boutiques and ice-cream parlours at this east end along with the traditional French (and Italian) fruit, vegetables and fish, and the lively 24-hour **Café du Monde** back near Jackson Square. It makes a good claim to the best coffee and *beignets* (doughnuts) in town, on a very Gallic terrace.

Try and save time to explore the **Riverwalk** marketplace, an interesting complex of shops and restaurants right on the river.

Mississippi paddle steamer

Garden District

South-west of the French Quarter, between Magazine Street and Louisiana, St. Charles and Jackson avenues, is the Garden District where the new American cotton and sugar aristocracy built their townhouses after the Louisiana Purchase, while the Creoles stayed on in the Vieux Carré. Surrounded by gardens of magnolias, oaks and palm trees, the mansions rival outlying plantation homes. There are some fine examples along **Prytania Street**.

The district's golden era ended with the double blow of the Civil War and the elimination of the Mississippi steamboat trade by the railways. The steamboats have now been restored to service for **river tours** starting from Toulouse Street Wharf or the Canal Street docks. Most of the cruises take you past Chalmette National Historical Park (also an easy 10-mile drive southeast on Route 46). Andrew Jackson's crushing victory here over the British in the Battle of New Orleans came after a peace treaty had been signed, but it was enough to give him the national renown that won him the White House 14 years later. For those who make the drive out here, the pretty **Beauregard Plantation House** serves as an information centre for the battlefield and cemetery.

THE MIDWEST

Americans who work hard bring a lot of energy and imagination to their leisure, too. Foreign visitors are often surprised at how attractive life can be in America's busiest cities and few are busier than those of the Midwest. The area, popularly known as the Heartland, is the industrial and agricultural core of the U.S. It covers Ohio, Indiana, Illinois, Michigan, Wisconsin, Minnesota, Iowa, Missouri, Kansas and Nebraska. From the Great Lakes across the prairies to the Great Plains, the Midwest is dominant in dairy and pig farming, corn and wheat, but it is also a flourishing industrial center specializing in steel and rubber and car manufacture.

Chicago, business headquarters for many of the big steel companies, is the transportation hub of the continent, main junction for the national railway system and today blessed—one might even say cursed—with the world's busiest airport. In the neighbouring state of Michigan, it's still an economic truth that if car-capital Detroit sneezes, America catches cold. These two cities have achieved their industrial and commercial pre-eminence with a rich and fascinating "ethnic" mix that makes them increasingly vibrant centres of cultural activity, too.

CHICAGO *(Illinois)*

Vigorous, tough, even brutal—these are the adjectives that many people associate with Chicago. But beautiful? Yes, there is a beauty to this vigorous, tough and sometimes brutal town that startles newcomers flying in over Lake Michigan or driving up from the south past the ugly steel towns of Gary and Hammond, Indiana. The skyline is simply one of the most spectacular in the world and something, for once, that does not make Chicago play second fiddle to New York.

For this is the city that taught the rest of the world how to build skyscrapers. It was a technique learned from necessity. In 1871, a fire swept through the largely wood-built city—scarcely 30 years old—leaving 100,000 homeless. Chicago had to rebuild in a hurry, new fireproof structures making maximum use of available ground space. The men who worked out how to construct a building around a metal skeleton so that it could "go as high as you like", but with elegance and style, became collectively known as the Chicago School. They included Louis Sullivan, Daniel Burnham and later Mies van der Rohe. Frank Lloyd Wright also worked in Chicago, but mostly on residential architecture. Their works and those of their pupils have made of Chicago a veritable lived-in and worked-in museum of modern architecture. In quality of design, architectural critics insist, the more famous Manhattan skyline is in no way superior to the urban panoramas along Chicago's lakefront and in the downtown area.

The other visual surprise in this resolutely commercial city is the 15-mile stretch of sandy beaches and green parkland along the lakefront. Unlike many other big cities on the Great Lakes, Chicago did not build factories or railways all along its lakeshore, but reserved most of the land for parks and residential neighbourhoods. As a result, it's possible to sunbathe, swim or go fishing just a couple of blocks from the major centres of town.

The population of Chicago is 3 million, big by any standards, but still a long way behind New York, giving them a "Second City" complex that sometimes makes them defensive, but also acts as a spur to achievement. It was inevitable that the town's proud architectural tradition would prompt it one day to build something higher than New York's Empire State Building or World Trade Center and, sure enough, the Sears Tower is now the world's tallest. The Chicago Symphony is one of the world's great orchestras and the Art Institute is a museum of international renown. But the people themselves, rather than aspire to the sophistication of Manhattanites, have a distinctively warm, robust and cheerfully sardonic attitude to life that makes them much more approachable in public places. That old image of gangland machine-gunnings is hard to live down, but you'll not find any monuments to Al Capone, and the Mafia is no more powerful here than in any other wealthy American city. There's an Anglo-Saxon business establishment, but the public tone is set much more by the Irish, Polish, German, Italian and Jewish segments of the population.

Getting Around. The Chicago Transit Authority (CTA) runs a very efficient bus system, taxis are not too expensive, but for once we recommend renting a car to move around the city, except in the congested downtown area, if you're staying more than a day. Orientation is not too difficult: the city centre is known as the Loop, after the elevated railway track that loops around the downtown business district immediately south of the Chicago River. The other neighbourhoods are defined in geographical relation to the Loop—North Side, South Side, West Side.

Michigan Avenue

Rather than start in the bustle of downtown, we suggest you first take stock of the city from its most elegant street, certainly busy, but more measured in its pace. With a well-developed knack for boosterism, Chicagoans call the tree-lined stretch from Oak Street to the river the **Magnificent Mile.** It contains the town's smartest high-fashion boutiques, jewellery shops, departments stores, art galleries and bookstores. Its image is such that when McDonald's fast-food chain (corporate HQ: Chicago) wanted to open a branch here, neighbouring merchants insisted that the décor be appropriate to the location. The result is a very dignified hamburger stand indeed.

But the dominant landmark is the gigantic black-steel 100-storey **John Hancock Center** with its

---

Stable Stable

It has been established that the Great Fire began in the stable of Patrick and Catherine O'Leary over on the West Side on the evening of October 8, 1871. Then Chicago bar legend takes over to insist—and it's not wise to question stories told in a Chicago bar—that it was all the fault of Mrs. O'Leary's cow kicking over a paraffin lamp. At any rate, history does record that the fire raged for 27 hours, wiping out over 17,000 buildings, and when a rainstorm put it out, not only was the Water Tower still standing, but—fact, no legend—so was Mrs. O'Leary's stable.

---

dramatic exterior—a diagonally strutted skeleton. This is a vertical street unto itself, soaring 1,107 feet into the air. The first five floors are taken up with shops, then there are half a dozen floors for parking, and above that the building has offices and apartments, with a supermarket and swimming pool for the residents. From the 94th floor observatory you have a view across to the Michigan shores of the lake, down over the Loop to the steel mills of Indiana, up the lakefront towards Wisconsin and out across the flat residential neighbourhoods of the West Side. Above or below, the effect of the Hancock is like Chicago itself, vigorous, tough, yet beautiful, too.

Down the street at Chicago Avenue is a strange white-limestone turret that is, in fact, the city's most cherished historic monument, the **Water Tower.** It was built in 1869 to house a pumping-station to take water from the lake, and was the only public building to survive the Great Chicago Fire. Today it is surrounded by a pleasant park.

One block west on Chicago Avenue, **Rush Street** is a lively entertainment area with outdoor cafés, nightclubs, restaurants and taverns that come alive after dark.

Going back to Magnificent Mile, Water Tower Place (845 N. Michigan) is—inside at least—a very attractive shopping centre with waterfalls playing alongside the escalators taking you up seven floors of shops and restaurants. Four blocks south, **Ontario Street** is "gallery row" for a thriving contemporary art scene.

Just before you reach the river, you should take note of one of the city's more bizarre skyscrapers, the cathedral-like **Tribune Tower** with its Gothic pinnacles and porch and 30 storeys in between them. It was built in 1925 for the *Chicago Tribune* newspaper, and was the successful entry in America's most famous architectural competition. Many of the world's leading architects—a total of 233 entries from 23 countries—submitted designs, with the Bauhaus master, Walter Gropius, and the great Finnish designer, Eero Saarinen, among the losers. Having persuaded the world by default that modern buildings should henceforth have modern designs, the tower became a unique and even lovable eccentricity.

There is an excellent ensemble view of the varied skyscrapers in the vicinity of the Chicago River from **Michigan Avenue Bridge**. The white terracotta, clocktowered building just north of the bridge is the **Wrigley** of chewing gum fame, which is particularly attractive

View of lakeside Chicago

when floodit at night. West along the river are the twin towers of **Marina City,** resembling two huge corncobs. The circular concrete towers, with apartments shaped like slices of pie on the upper floors, go right down to the river and have docking space for 500 boats for residents or for businessmen commuting to work by motorboat from the lake's north shore suburbs. In stark contrast behind is the pure black-steel-and-glass slab of Mies van der Rohe's **IBM Building.**

The Loop

With the "El" (elevated railway) rattling around its periphery of Wabash Avenue, Lake, Wells and Van Buren streets, the Loop unmistakably means business. LaSalle Street is the heart of the financial and banking district and has the same canyon-like quality as New York's Wall Street. The major downtown department stores are on State Street and Wabash Avenue. One of them, **Carson, Pirie & Scott,** is a mecca for architectural scholars attracted, like the earliest shoppers in 1899, by Louis Sullivan's incredibly intricate ironwork ornament over the Madison Street entrance, as well as by the then revolutionary, horizontally elongated windows.

But the most successful feature of Chicago's business district is the space devoted on its many open plazas to monumental modern sculpture and mosaics rather than statues of famous men. This **plaza art,** as it has become known, began with Picasso's great *Sculpture* (1967) in front of the Richard J. Daley Center (Washington and Dearborn streets), a complex of courthouse and local government buildings named after the late mayor. Like the elegant skyscraper courthouse, the 50-foot sculpture is made of CorTen steel that weathers to the colour of rust, but without the corrosion. To people who want to know whether the sculpture is to be understood as a woman or a horse, Picasso himself said they might just as well "try to understand the song of a bird". At any rate it draws to the plaza a constant flow of admirers and locals who just like to eat their sandwiches around it.

Other notable pieces of plaza art are Chagall's *Four Seasons,* a 70-foot mosaic on the First National Plaza (Monroe and Dearborn streets); a 53-foot, bright red *Flamingo* stabile by Calder (Adams and Dearborn streets)—this graces what is regarded as the most elegant set of U.S. Government buildings in the country, the **Federal Center,** designed by Mies van der Rohe; and, perhaps the most provocative, pop-artist Claes Oldenburg's filigreed *Batcolumn,* a 100-foot high

---

> **Beethoven on the Lawn**
> *Among the Windy City's many monuments, few are more respected than the world-famous Chicago Symphony Orchestra, where Hungarian George Solti was the latest of a long series of distinguished European resident conductors. Tickets for their autumn and winter concerts at Orchestra Hall (220 S. Michigan) are difficult to get, but if you know well in advance when you'll be in Chicago, you can write directly to Orchestra Hall for programme details and reservations. In summer, it's slightly easier to get tickets, when the orchestra plays at Ravinia Park in the northern suburb of Highland Park. There you can listen to their music and that of other major performers at this summer festival on the lawn with a traditional "Ravinia picnic" of chicken, strawberries and wine.*

tration. Actually the building consists of nine towers packed together, as its designers Skidmore, Owings & Merrill suggest, like squared cigarettes. They pop out of their packet at different heights. The structure's steel frame is sheathed in black aluminium with 16,000 bronze-tinted windows—that works out to one window for each of the workers employed there. Built for the Sears, Roebuck merchandising company as the ultimate status symbol, it has been criticized for packing all those people into a confined location without providing quick transport facilities for getting them out. Morning and evening rush hours are a bewildering sight. The impact of the building at ground level—some people lie on their backs on the plaza to take it all in—is enormous. Then there's the top, or at least the 103rd-floor **Skydeck** observatory. If you went up the Hancock in the daytime, try the Sears at night for a great view of the Hancock.

baseball-bat made of 1,608 pieces of welded steel (just outside the Loop at the Social Security Administration Building, 600 W. Madison Street).

On the edge of the Loop, but you really can't miss it, is, yes, the world's tallest building, the **Sears Tower** (Wacker Drive and Adams Street). Its 110 floors rise 1,454 feet and it's not likely that it will soon be topped, at least in the United States, because that's the limit set by the Federal Aviation Adminis-

Lake Shore Drive

A trip along the Outer Lake Shore Drive expressway is a delightful way to see the lakefront skyline unfold behind the parks. On the South Side you drive from Jackson Park past the sailboats moored in Chicago Harbor at Grant Park up around Oak Street Beach to Lincoln

131

Park on the North Side and the boats of Belmont Harbor.

(You can also make a boat tour of the lakefront on one of the cruises starting from Michigan Avenue Bridge on the Chicago River.)

Lincoln Park is worth a separate visit for the delight of the **zoo**. It has a terrific ape house, but better than all the usual tropical exotica (of which there's a good sample) is the charming idea of presenting farm animals—that's it, pigs, cows, goats, ducks and chickens—for city kids who never saw a chicken that wasn't fried or barbecued and know little else besides cats, dogs and pigeons. Similarly, the **Lincoln Park Conservatory** not only has

Fun and fantasy around Chicago

a beautiful orchid collection and amazing African and South American trees, but also the simple enchantment of hollyhocks and hyacinths and snapdragons and daisies in Grandmother's Garden.

Museums

The **Museum of Science and Industry** (South Lake Shore Drive and 57th Street) is the city's most popular museum because you don't just stand there and look, you get *into* the exhibits and do things. Go down a coal mine, walk through a 16-foot high model of the human heart, creep around a captured World War II German submarine, and press buttons and pull all kinds of levers with scarcely a "Don't Touch" in sight.

Museum Point (1300 S. Lake Shore Drive) combines three fascinating exhibitions. The **Shedd Aquarium,** largest in the world, has 7,500 species of fish, including a gorgeous Coral Reef collection of 350 Caribbean creatures. If you're lucky, you'll be there when scuba divers go down to feed the big fish. The **Field Museum of Natural History** also encourages visitors to "play" with some of the exhibits, though you may be intimidated at first by the giant rogue elephants fighting in the main hall. The **Adler Planetarium** offers attractive multi-

media sky shows. Apart from the well-presented but by now quite usual exhibits about space exploration, a highlight is the display of astronomical instruments dating back to the times when people still believed the earth was flat.

The **Museum of Surgical Sciences** (1524 N. Lake Shore Drive) is the place for those with a sense of the macabre. Inspect the

18th-century amputation devices, antique artificial limbs, but also a reassuring apothecary shop charmingly reconstituted from 1873.

The **Art Institute of Chicago** (Michigan Avenue and Adams Street), at first an art school, now ranks as one of the great American museums. In less than a century it has acquired a collection highlighted by a magnificent range of French Impressionist, Post-Impressionist and the major 20th-century movements.

Practically all of Chicago's ethnic groups have their own museum, often set in the neighbourhoods where they still live. Among them you'll find the Polish (984 N. Milwaukee Avenue), Swedish (5248 S. Michigan Avenue), Ukrainian (2247 W. Chicago Avenue), Jewish (618 S. Michigan Avenue), Lithuanian (4012 S. Archer Avenue) and Chinese (2238 S. Wentworth).

If you want to learn more about the riches of Chicago's architecture, the **ArchiCenter** (330 S. Dearborn) has a collection of historic models and photographs and organizes walking and bus tours of the city's landmarks. In Oak Park there are several tours of the many houses that the great Frank Lloyd Wright built, including his own home, in this western suburb, which has been declared a National Historic District.

DETROIT *(Michigan)*

Much older than Chicago, Detroit was established in 1701 by a French aristocrat, Antoine de la Mothe Cadillac, whose name is now attached to the aristocrat of General Motors' cars. To protect the burgeoning Canadian fur-trade, Cadillac set up Fort Ponchartrain d'Etroit—the fort on the straits, between Lake St. Clair and Lake Erie. Subsequently, as an important shipping centre on the Canadian border, its shipbuilding industry was accompanied in the 19th century by carriage-building. From that it was a natural step for Detroit to become the American capital of car manufacturing after Henry Ford built his first motor-driven vehicle in 1892 and revolutionized the American way of life in 1908 with his "Model T" which made cars available to everyman.

The car industry made the city the gauge of the country's economic health, but it was not always good for the town itself. Overindustrialization turned the city centre into a slum of derelict docks, warehouses and railway yards. In the 1950s and '60s, the middle classes fled to the suburbs. But dissatisfaction with the homogenized life out there has prompted civic leaders and most especially the Henry Ford family and fellow carmanufacturers to revive the downtown business district. The result is an exciting new interest in civic and cultural buildings around the core, quite rightly named Renaissance Center (known as RenCen to locals). It attracts thousands of people back to the new downtown shops, cafés and restaurants, and now apartment dwellings are going up along the waterfront to carry on the renewal.

The centrepiece of the **Renaissance Center** (Jefferson and Brush streets), in the dramatic group of five shining black-steel and tintedglass towers, is the 73-storey, cylindrical **Westin Hotel.** The vast lobby has an indoor "lake" surrounded by trees, and the lounges are reached by ramps and spiral staircases. There are bars and a revolving restaurant on the 73rd floor for you to view the city—and over the border to Canada. The interconnecting office buildings and hotel stand on a four-level podium that comprises 70 shops and four cinemas. The place is constantly abuzz with people.

Civic Center continues the new downtown bustle outdoors around **Hart Plaza** containing a striking Noguchi fountain. Jefferson Street takes you past the Ford Auditorium (corner of Woodward) where the fine Detroit Symphony Orchestra gives its winter concerts, along an esplanade enlivened in summer by street musicians, mimes and acrobats. You can take an old, reconditioned trolley car that rattles from the exhibition centre of Cobo Hall, past the outdoor cafés and boutiques on Washington Boulevard to **Grand Circus Park.**

The **Cultural Center** (around Woodward and Kirby avenues) brings the city's museums together. The **Detroit Institute of Arts** has some fine Old Masters, including Pieter Brueghel's **Wedding Dance,** but the most provocative works are the frescoes of Mexican Marxist painter Diego Rivera on work in Detroit automobile plants, as an epitome of industrial America.

The **International Institute** (111 E. Kirby) assembles under one roof the cultural artefacts, folklore, costumes and dolls of 50 different countries, many of them represented in the work force of the automobile plants.

To escape the city for a while, just take MacArthur Bridge at the end of Jefferson Avenue over to **Belle Isle,** a lovely island park in the Detroit River. You can play tennis or golf there and attend free open-air concerts by the Detroit Concert Band at the Remick Music Shell. For the children, there's a zoo reserved for baby animals and the **Dossin Great Lakes Museum** has a particularly fine exhibition of model ships.

THE ROCKIES

The Rockies are a series of mountain ranges extending all the way from Mexico to the Canadian Arctic, running along the great Continental Divide that forms the backbone of America. In Montana, Wyoming, Utah and Colorado, they bring the holiday-maker face to face with the inspiring natural beauties of America's back-country, its vast forests and torrents, delightful Alpine meadows in summer and superb ski-slopes in winter.

Formidable barrier to the 19th-century pioneers' westward trek beyond the Great Plains, the Rockies also proved to be sources of mineral wealth—gold, silver, copper and, today, uranium.

It was appropriate that the first natural region to receive the federally protected status of National Park (in 1872) should be Yellowstone, the mountain plateau 8,000 feet up in the Rockies. To the south, Denver is established as the major city to have grown out of the Rockies' old mining towns and provides the ideal starting point for exploring Colorado's mountain beauty. On the west of the Continental Divide the Mormons established their Salt Lake City, originally with the hope that the barrier of the Rockies would protect them from the intolerance of non-believers.

YELLOWSTONE NATIONAL PARK
(Wyoming)

Yellowstone is more than a vast landscape of mountains, valleys, rivers and forests—both living and petrified—it's a perpetual spectacle of exuberant geysers (including star performer Old Faithful) shooting hundreds of feet into the air, volcanic mudpots exploding, hot

springs bubbling out of the earth, and waterfalls so high they make Niagara look like an overflowing bathtub. All is set against a backdrop of colours that begin with the yellow of the canyon rock that gives the park its name.

Headquarters for the park are at **Mammoth Hot Springs** on the north side of Yellowstone. Visitors should, if possible, come through the north entrance at Gardiner (Montana Highway 89) or make their way up to Mammoth from the West Yellowstone entrance. The information centre provides important tips about camping sites as well as park regulations, trail maps and a museum of the region's flora, fauna and geological phenomena.

Old silver-mining town, Silverton

One of the great geological phenomena of the park is at Mammoth, the lovely silver travertine shelves of a **terrace mountain** being created daily before your eyes. Volcanically heated springs are thrusting up mineral-laden water from underground limestone beds and laying their deposits in terraced pools that form at least a couple of tons of new travertine each day.

Drive 21 miles south of Mammoth to the Norris junction on the 142-mile **Grand Loop** road that will take you around the major landmarks. A visitors centre at the junction organizes hikes (on boardwalks) across the steaming **Norris Geyser Basin.** You'll get good explanations of the workings of geysers and hot springs. With exceptional luck, you may even witness the world's biggest active geyser, the Steamboat. But unlike steady, reliable Old Faithful further down the road, its performance is almost as erratic as a volcano, varying in appearances from every few days to just once a year. When it does blow, it shoots water, steam, rocks and mud 300 to 400 feet into the air.

Further south, at Madison Junction, the Loop meets the road from the West Yellowstone entrance and curves down along the **Firehole River.** This well-named river is fed

Mammoth Hot Springs, Yellowstone

by hot springs and in places feels like a warm bath, compared with the plateau streams' chilly 39°F.

Old Faithful, the most famous sight in the park, is 16 miles south of Madison Junction. This is the geyser that you can rely on to blow every 65 minutes or so. Some geysers in the park are larger, but none is as dependable as Old Faithful, which erupts the most frequently of them all. Another Visitors Center nearby has excellent audio-visual exhibits to explain the phenomenon. This is also the region of three of the park's most active geyser basins, named simply Upper, Midway and Lower. Be on the lookout, too, for some intriguing, smelly mudpots. These vats of hot, soupy clay are activated by a steam vent or fumarole.

To escape the crowds that gather at Old Faithful, take the Loop east over to West Thumb (junction with the southern park-entrance road, the John D. Rockefeller Memorial Highway) on the shore of the beautiful **Yellowstone Lake.** Within strict limitations, you are allowed to fish for cut-throat trout, averaging 18 inches. Boats and tackle can be rented either at Grant Village on the lake's south-west tip or at Fishing Bridge on the north shore. Don't forget that you're competing for the fish with otters, osprey hawks and grizzly bears, as well as coyotes hanging around for what others drop.

From the lake's north shore, the Loop follows the Yellowstone River down to the **Grand Canyon** of the Yellowstone. Approaching from the south, you catch a first sight of the cascading waters of the 109-foot Upper Falls. Park a little further on near the short trail that

---

Leaving Well Alone

Human beings are only guests in the park and park guides will warn you not to interfere with the residents—the moose (elk), antelope, bighorn sheep, bear, bison and myriad fish and birds. Under no circumstances should you feed the bears. The ferocious grizzlies number about 250 in Yellowstone, the black bears about 600. A programme to remove the bears from the busiest tourist areas has reduced bear-related injuries, but they still seek out campgrounds for food. After being reduced in the 19th century by wanton slaughter from millions to just a few hundred on the whole continent, the bison are back up to 2,000 in this park. Yellowstone's ecological policy of strict non-interference with nature means, for instance, that no attempt is made to save the moose herds from starvation in the bitter winters. To do so would deprive predators—grizzlies, coyotes and eagles—of an important food source. Many moose survive the winter by standing in water warmed by hot springs, others fall into the springs and end up as a grizzly's hot supper.

---

will take you to **Inspiration Point** where you can survey the even more dramatic 308-foot **Lower Falls** and a panorama of the winding 24-mile-long canyon. It drops 1,200 to 4,000 feet to the banks of the Yellowstone River. The canyon walls are impregnated with arsenic sulfides that produce every shade

and variation of yellow, wonderfully enhanced by the brilliant greens of the surrounding lodge-pole-pine forests.

At the northern end of the canyon is **Tower Fall** (near the junction with the north-east park-entrance road from Cooke City). On a sunny day at noon you'll almost certainly see a double rainbow across the 132-foot-high falls. And if you

Bighorn sheep

think that the huge perched boulder is about to tumble down, "Discoverers" of the Tower Fall on August 27, 1870, placed bets that it would be gone by August 28.

East of Tower Junction, off the Lamar Valley Road, lies a **petrified forest.** These trees are still upright after millions of years, and include sycamores, magnolias, maples, oaks, redwoods, walnuts and willows, suggesting Yellowstone was once a lot warmer than today. The forest was covered by volcanic ash rich in silica with which groundwater impregnated the trees and plants, turning them to stone.

Yellowstone Logistics

Most of its 3,472 square-mile expanse is in Wyoming, but Yellowstone also spills over into Montana to the north and Idaho to the west. Only one of the park's entrances, Gardiner, remains open year-round; the others close between November and May. In winter, the park is snowbound and access is only with a rented snowmobile or in the park's own snowbus. Both Salt Lake City and Denver have local airline services to Yellowstone's airport, where you can rent a car. Though all of the major sights can be reached by car, plan on some good walking too.

Hotels, mostly comfortable but simple cabins, must be reserved well in advance, particularly in winter when only a few are open. Contact TW Services, Yellowstone National Park, WY 82190, tel. 307–344–7311 (for information: Superintendent, Yellowstone National Park, WY 82190, tel. 307–344–7381). Camping can be a scramble for the choice spots in high season, but it's worth the effort. It's best to visit Yellowstone outside the peak months of July and August, but even then the park is vast enough for you to be able to move off the beaten track.

DENVER (Colorado)

If you don't believe Denver was once the mining capital of Colorado, look at the 24-carat gold leaf dome on its Capitol Building, or at the local branch of the U.S. Mint that handles one quarter of the nation's gold supplies. The Wild West days have long gone, but locals still like to sport a stetson hat and checked shirt, for old times' sake. This is the mile-high town, but the air here is unfortunately as polluted as in many other major American cities and the architecture is relentlessly modern, apart from one colourfully preserved street from the old mining days. But what counts for the holiday-maker is what you see almost on the city's doorstep—the marvellous backdrop of the Rocky Mountains, Denver's backyard.

Take a look around town, get used to the altitude and then hit the road out to Colorado's mountains. There's no better place to start than the Visitors Bureau at 225 W. Colfax, well prepared to provide you with local and travel information.

Across the street, the **U.S. Mint** gives free weekday tours of its money-making plant. You can see gold bullion and the counting-room, full of the finished product.

Also on Colfax is the august **Capitol Building** (E. 14th and E. Colfax streets). Make sure to take the west staircase and stand on the 13th step—that's exactly one mile above sea level.

The best of the modern city is the dazzling **Denver Art Museum** (W. 14th Avenue and Bannock Street). When you see its seven-storey walls covered with one million glass tiles over a surface broken up higgledy-piggledy with slotted windows, you know what its Italian architect, Gio Ponti, meant when he said: "Architecture must create spectacles." The museum, by the way, contains a first-class collection of American Indian art—totem poles, costumes and rugs.

Old Denver is over on **Larimer Street,** which has conserved its Victorian buildings as art galleries, shops, leathersmiths', silversmiths' and cafés—some good Mexican restaurants, too. Larimer Square is done up with courtyards and arcades lit by gas lanterns. But the most authentic piece of old Denver is to be found in the grand lobby of the 1892 **Brown Palace Hotel**

(17th and Tremont Place), genteel forerunner of the skylit atrium style of today's glass tower hotels.

From September to May, the Denver Symphony Orchestra plays at **Boettcher Concert Hall** (14th and Curtis streets), an acoustically sophisticated auditorium-in-the-round with the audience encircling the performers. A unique opportunity to see the conductor's facial expressions. Classical and popular music concerts are held 16 miles south-west of town in the open-air arena of **Red Rocks,** set amidst towering red sandstone outcrops.

If you don't have time for an extended tour of the Rockies beyond Denver, you can still get a taste of one of the higher mountains by *driving* all the way to the top! Just west of Denver, **Mount Evans** is 14,260 feet high, with a paved road to its peak. (Drive 35 miles on Interstate Highway 70 to Idaho Springs and then south on Route 103 to Route 5.)

WEST CENTRAL COLORADO

An ambitious tour of the major resorts of West Central Colorado will take you on a beautiful 360-mile circuit through the Rockies, but you may prefer to aim for just one of the big three:

Aspen is the best known resort town in the state. At 7,937 feet it

143

provides wonderful winter sports opportunities, but it's also a delight in summer both for its music festival and for the hiking, camping, fishing and riding in the surrounding **White River National Forest.**

In the 1880s the town made its fortune out of seven silver mines, but the market collapsed in 1893 and the town was deserted until revived as a sports and cultural centre after World War II. Some of the old Victorian buildings have been preserved with considerable charm and taste, particularly the Opera House and the lovely Hotel Jerome.

The **Aspen Music Festival** in summer presents opera, classical music and jazz of the very highest order. International stars just like to hang out here. They take advantage of the easy-going atmosphere in the downtown mall of shops and outdoor cafés or excursions into the spectacular **Maroon Bells** mountains south-west of town. In winter, the skiing opportunities vary from the family slopes on Buttermilk and nearby Snowmass to the challenges on Aspen Highlands or the famous Ruthie's Run on Aspen Mountain.

Negotiating the Colorado River

Vail, north of the White River National Forest, is a very successful modern ski-resort with Swiss-style chalets. In summer it caters for tennis and golf enthusiasts—the only problem with the golf course is that the scenery is so spectacular it may distract you from your game. Surprisingly, there is also enough gentle landscape around to make bicycling a special pleasure. Anglers fish for some excellent trout in Gore Creek and Eagle River.

Glenwood Springs offers the ultimate luxury of a 405-foot-long swimming pool fed by a stream of natural warm water to a temperature of 85°–90°F. The waters were much prized by Indians as energizers before going on the hunt or warpath. They'll relax you before or after some exhilarating rafting down the **Colorado River.**

SALT LAKE CITY (Utah)

A unique phenomenon in American life, Salt Lake City is a community founded and sustained on theological doctrine—that of the Mormons, or, to give them their full name, the Church of Jesus Christ of Latter-day Saints. It also manages to be a highly agreeable town of friendly people, with bright shopping centres and outdoor cafés as well as impressive monuments to their historic spirit of adventure and courage.

All this is carved out of a desert of salt flats that stretch from the foot of the Wasatch Range of the Rockies around the Great Salt Lake clear across Utah to the mountains of Nevada. Their geographical isolation has motivated the people of Salt Lake City to keep up a busy cultural life of ballet, choral music and art exhibitions.

Temple Square is the all-important centre of Salt Lake City, a 10-acre compound surrounded by a 15-foot-high wall containing the nucleus of the Mormons' church buildings, including the Temple, Tabernacle and Visitors Center.

The solid granite Temple, 40 years in the building, is closed to non-believers but the celebrated **Tabernacle** is open to everyone. Its vast 250-foot-long and 150-foot-wide turtleback dome, originally made of wood shingles but now encased in aluminium, was constructed only with wooden dowels, no nails, since iron was too scarce in Utah in the 1860s. The dome stands on 44 sandstone pillars at its periphery and provides wonderful acoustics for the great Mormon Tabernacle Choir. The 375 singers hold free rehearsals on Thursday evenings. A monumental 10,814-pipe organ enhances the rather stark interior of the Tabernacle (you can attend free organ recitals every day at noon).

The **Church Office Building** (Temple Square East) contains a unique collection of genealogical records, possibly including a mention of your own ancestors.

Beehive House (67 E. South Temple), built in 1854 as Brigham Young's residence, is now a museum devoted to the great man.

Too Many Wives

The Mormons' founder, New Englander Joseph Smith, began and ended his religious career with divine revelations. The first, in the 1820s, was that the American Indians were the Lost Tribes of Israel to be redeemed from paganism by Smith and his followers. Twenty years later, with 15,000 converts in Nauvoo, Illinois, he was directed by revelation to follow the path of polygamy, since the prophet Isaiah had said in the Bible that "seven women shall take hold of one man". Smith in fact took 27 wives and others followed suit until a conflict with dissidents ended in his lynching. Brigham Young succeeded as the Mormons' Prophet, inheriting 5 of Smith's widows to add to a dozen of his own wives, and led his people on an arduous 1,000-mile trek across the prairies, Great Plains and the Rocky Mountains to a new promised land. "This is the place" were his much quoted words on surveying the dry expanses of Utah's salt flats. Polygamy remained the official practice until the United States made its disavowal the condition of Utah statehood in 1896.

The life of the early community is portrayed in the **Pioneer Museum** (300 N. Main Street). State Capitol, a copper-domed, Corinthian-style building of Utah granite and marble, affords a sensational view of the Wasatch Mountains.

The **ZCMI** (Zion Co-operative Mercantile Institution) at 15 S. Main was the country's first department store in 1868. Now its charming, ornate cast-iron façade with its slender Corinthian columns serves as the front of a bustling shopping mall with attractive boutiques, art galleries and gift shops. Similarly, **Trolley Square** (5th South and 7th East streets) has converted old trolley barns into restaurants, shops and a theatre. Monday night, the Mormons' Family Evening, is a popular time for locals to visit the ice-cream parlours and movie houses.

Just south of the square, **Liberty Park** makes a lovely picnic ground, with arbours, swimming pool, tennis courts and a boating lake. There are also summer concerts, an amusement park and an aviary.

The Salt Palace auditorium holds 28,000 people for concerts and sporting events. On the same grounds, the **Bicentennial Arts Center** combines theatre, ballet and the music of the Utah Symphony Orchestra with art exhibitions.

You should not leave without visiting the **Great Salt Lake** itself, even if you prefer not to float in its hot, sticky, 25 per cent saline water. The lake is surrounded by marshland and salt flats, and is indeed forbidding to all but the hardiest Mormons.

Much more refreshing is the lovely **Wasatch National Forest,** a haven of peace and a pleasure for hiking, camping, trout fishing or autumn hunting for deer, moose, antelope and elk. In winter this area is also popular for skiing and winter sports.

Visitors Center, Temple Square

THE SOUTH-WEST

The region *par excellence* of America's wide open spaces, the South-West stretches across most of the much touted "Sun Belt". It covers the vast ranchlands and oil country of Texas, the rugged highlands of New Mexico first settled by the Indians and Spanish conquistadors, and Arizona's deserts rising to pine-forested mountains. Their culmination is the nation's most awe-inspiring sight, a phenomenon that humbles the most blasé of world travellers—the Grand Canyon.

Perhaps it's the sheer majesty of these open spaces that sustains in the people of this region that particular brand of American individualism and independent spirit that have been a little tamed in the cities of the East and West coasts and the Midwest. It makes South-Westerners perhaps somewhat less accessible to the outsider at first, but if you take the trouble to win their confidence, you'll find the most cordial, cheerful and colourful company in the country.

Don't even consider visiting Texas, New Mexico and Arizona without a car. While buses and planes will take you from town to town, the distances around the

148

towns and between the sights are more than shoe leather or local bus services were meant to deal with. Spring and summer bring the great dry heat of the desert or the enervating humidity and high temperatures of towns like Houston. The region was settled by doughty pioneers and you must come to it with some of the same spirit.

Texas is an acquired taste. The endless cattle ranges, the inexorable pumping of the oil derricks and the sparkling prosperity of the skyscrapers in Dallas and Houston are insistently impressive. But in the end, the name Texas evokes not only a geographical location but a special people with a special attitude to life, and this is what is hard to get hold of. The pushy arrogance and braggadocio have become legendary, to a point where Texans who might by nature—just a few of them—be shy, retiring types feel obliged to live up to the popular image. Since the 1959 admission of Alaska (2½ times its size), Texas is no longer the largest state in the U.S., but the self-image as biggest and best has remained. Houston and Dallas will show you the dynamic modern form this Texan self-confidence has taken and San Antonio will show you the historic background from which it has come.

Part of the joy of New Mexico is the predominance of a completely different architecture from that of the rest of the U.S. Adobe (dried mud) houses with tranquil courtyards, arcaded plazas and fountains give a welcome illusion of coolness in the summer. You won't find them everywhere, but there are enough to make you forget for a while the rectangular blocks of skyscraper-land. Another special pleasure here is the desert landscape and the glowing pink and gold light which gives its aridity a jewel-like quality, an excellent ambiance for meditation. It's not surprising that the state attracted so many artists, flower-children and hippies in the 1960s. They've stayed on and grown into mellow forty-year-olds with a *mañana* view of life that fits in well with the local mores. Don't hurry around New Mexico, let it seep in slowly.

After the skyscrapers of New York City, the rugged desert and mountain landscapes of Arizona are the most likely component of the world's image of America. For history and Hollywood, this is as far as the Far West gets. The Hopi Indians settled here in what was Europe's Middle Ages and the Navaho followed. In the 19th century, the cattle and sheep ranchers fought for control of the plains and battled with Apache heroes Cochise and Geronimo. Copper, gold, silver, uranium and other ores made the state rich, and the year-round sun has since warmed the hearts of retired colonists from the cold Midwest. For the visitor, Arizona offers the matchless wonder of the Grand Canyon, the awe of the deserts and the mirage-like towers of Phoenix.

DALLAS *(Texas)*

Television, movies and the national tragedy of John F. Kennedy's assassination have made this one of the best-known cities in America. The skyline looming out of the plain says it all. A forest of towers sheathed in silver or bronze mirror-glass reflect the dawn as more golden, the noon's blue sky more blue, the rosy sunset blood-red.

From Dallas-Fort Worth Airport you may pass **Texas Stadium** on Route 183. It sets the stage. This gigantic, domed arena has a large hole in the roof. It's the home of the Dallas Cowboys American Football team, known locally as "God's Team". The hole in the roof, say the fans, is to let God watch the game. If you happen to be there in season, try to get a ticket. Even if you don't understand the game, the spectacle will not easily be forgotten.

Downtown, the most attractive skyscrapers are the glassy Allied Bank Tower and the gleaming slabs of the Hyatt Regency Hotel. They stand beside **Reunion Tower** (300 Reunion Boulevard, off the Stem-

mons Freeway). The Tower has a revolving cocktail lounge, restaurant and observation deck for a fine **view** of the Texas infinity.

The **John Fitzgerald Kennedy Memorial** (Main and Market) is a stark and eloquent monument to the shooting of the president on November 22, 1963, one of those dates when everyone remembers what he or she was doing when the news came. The 30-foot-high walls enclose a broken square which is approached along a gently sloping ramp, a space for meditation. The assassination is understandably

---

Bar Tips

If you want to make friends with Texans in a bar, don't order white wine or fancy cocktails. If you think you can manage it with a straight face and without spluttering, ask the bartender for a "long neck" (bottled beer) together with a shot of whisky. Don't say "Scotch", don't specify rye or Bourbon. Just drink the whisky, it'll be Bourbon, at one gulp. Smile politely at your neighbour. Ease your way gently into conversation, don't get bumptious or pushy. Don't talk dirty. Don't argue the merits of European and American football. Don't even try to explain the rules of soccer. Just ask how good the Dallas Cowboys are this year compared with the past. Don't talk about Houston in Dallas or about Dallas in Houston. They don't want to know.

Bathroom Cowboy

The cowboy look has come in and out of fashion a dozen times. Bankers wear pointed boots and stetson hats. The whole world wears blue jeans. But in any good Texas gentleman's outfitters, you can study and acquire the "real thing" (pronounced "thang"). Start with the hat. There are four basic cowboy hats: the Bullrider, straw for the summer, felt for the winter, with a slight crease in the high crown and the brim pulled down front and back. Normally it takes a season of rodeo bullriding to get the right shape, but you can work on it in the bathroom mirror. The R.C.A. takes its name from the Rodeo Cowboy Association and differs from the Bullrider by its side vents, wedge-shaped centre crease in the crown and narrower brim. The Rancher, as its name suggests, is for the boss and so made of beaver skin and is wide-brimmed. The Hi-Roller is for city-slickers, low crowned, curled brim, good for gambling, pulls well down over the eyes. Jeans, as people have known for a long time, should look worn-out from the beginning. But not just worn-out anywhere, only on the inside of the leg, from riding, and the back pocket, from your chewing-tobacco tin. Again, you can simulate all this in the bathroom, with a good floor-scrubbing brush. Belts should be of handtooled Texas cowhide with your full name (not just initials, that's sissy) on the inside. The buckle, loop and belt-tip should of course be sterling silver (not gold, that's considered vulgar ostentation) and should have a simple, elegant floral motif, no ranch or rodeo scenes. Similarly, your boots should not be ornamented, just good plain leather. Pointed toes are not indispensable but high heels are—not for making you taller, of course, but to hold the stirrup. Soak them in the bathtub, dry them in the oven, cover with mud, scrape with harsh knife, soak and dry again, kick them front and back against the wall. O.K., you're ready to ride.

---

something the people of Dallas would rather forget, but visitors just won't let them. And so the municipality has provided a map on a plaque near the Memorial showing, among other landmarks, the nearby **Texas Book Depository** (now used as a courthouse) from the sixth floor of which Lee Harvey Oswald is said to have fired the fatal shots. A **John Fitzgerald Kennedy Museum** (501 Elm Street) offers an audio-visual presentation of his life and assassination, called "The Incredible Hours".

West of the JFK Memorial is the little **Log Cabin** (Market and Elm), a replica of the one pioneer John Neely Bryan built in 1841 when he came to settle in this part of Texas, the site of the future city of Dallas. The tiny cabin, which was brought here, perhaps as a cheerful antidote to the assassination monument, served both as post office and courthouse.

This resolutely forward-looking town has preserved just one area in which it has assembled the remnants of its past—**Old City Park** (Gano and St. Paul streets). Here you can picnic on the grass among restored Victorian houses, old log cabins, an 1886 railway depot, a bandstand, 1900s shops and a Greek Revival mansion from 1855.

But otherwise, it's the people rather than the buildings that carry the past with them in this town. And you can see them at their best at **Farmer's Market** (1010 S. Pearl), a collection of ramshackle tin-roofed stalls where they sell Texas-sized fruit and vegetables, chew tobacco, spit or pick a mean guitar —good ol' boys to a man.

One of the more important local monuments is **Neiman Marcus** (Main and Ervay), a legendary department store. Nothing is too outrageous for them to sell—solid gold bathroom fittings, "His" and "Her" jet aircraft, pet lion cubs, a Monopoly game in which the board, the pieces, the money and property-cards are all made of chocolate (it doesn't specify whether the winner has to eat it all). The Christmas catalogue is a great collector's item.

The **Dallas Museum of Art** is a showcase of treasures you can't buy. But you can view the collection, particularly strong in 19th- and 20th-century art, housed in a starkly effective building designed by Edward Barnes.

In the midst of the formidable fanfare of downtown Dallas, you can retreat to a moment's tranquillity in the lovely triangle of Thanksgiving Square, a peaceful little oasis of immaculate lawns, trees, channels of water and a bridge leading to a spiral chapel inspired by the great mosque of al-Mutawakil at Samarra, Iraq.

HOUSTON *(Texas)*

Houston is oil and space. It's a hot, humid town that has burgeoned into one of the most prosperous business communities in America (though its Blacks and Mexicans are relegated to squalid slums for which Texan commercial ingenuity has not yet found a solution). To deal with the heat and humidity they have an underground network of air-conditioned concourses (fuelled by local oil) linking the downtown skyscrapers—and the highest air-conditioning bills in the nation.

Oil is proclaimed on its skyline by the striking black wedge-shaped towers of **Pennzoil Plaza**, designed by Philip Johnson, and the gabled, red granite Republic Bank Center. You can see how the black gold is drawn from the earth at the **Museum of Natural Science** (5800 Caroline Street at Hermann Park). The displays of drilling and refining technology include a fascinating model of an offshore oil rig.

The **Museum of Fine Arts** (1001 Bissonnet) has collections of Indian and pre-Columbian art, and the contemporary art section is a constant source of surprise as wealthy donors bring back new treasures. For local colour, the most exciting works on display are the studies of cowboy life by painter and sculptor Frederic Remington. His are the images that have made bucking broncos and gunfighters the icons of the Wild West.

The **Rothko Chapel** (3900 Yupon Street) is a lovely if somewhat austere non-denominational place of worship, housing the starkly contemplative, purple-and-black canvases of Mark Rothko. In the grounds is Barnet Newman's equally simple and moving rust-brown CorTen steel **Monument to Martin Luther King,** a shattered finger-like inverted obelisk balanced on a pyramid.

The chapel and neighbouring **Menil Collection** of art—strong on the surrealists and on primitive and oriental work—was given to Houston by philanthropists Jean and Dominique de Menil.

Twenty-five miles or so southeast of Houston on Interstate 45, the **Lyndon B. Johnson Space Center** is the controlling hub of the United States space programme, where astronauts train and NASA has its monitoring centre for manned space flights. The Visitor Orientation Center is a splendid museum of space equipment, rockets, lunar modules, space capsules and moon rock. It provides guided tours around the Mission Control Center by knowledgeable cadets, and you can also visit by yourself the Skylab Training Room, the living and working quarters of NASA's space laboratory.

SAN ANTONIO *(Texas)*

For the outsider, San Antonio is the most accessible of Texan towns, the historic centre of the state's Spanish-Mexican beginnings and delightfully inviting to the public today with its River Walk through the heart of downtown.

The **Alamo** (Alamo Plaza), built as the Spanish Mission San Antonio de Valero in 1718, is the hallowed fortress where 187 Americans fought and succumbed to 5,000 Mexican soldiers under General Santa Ana in 1836. They'd been sent to put down American resistance to Mexico's authoritarian rule of its Texas province. The Americans' heroic stand inspired the revolt which finally won Texas independence and subsequent admission to the U.S. as the Lone Star State. Today the Alamo is a museum of that momentous battle.

Among other memorabilia it displays the Bowie knife, the curved-bladed weapon fashioned by Colonel James Bowie, joint commander of the Alamo. It was the other commander, William Travis, who issued the order: "Victory or death." Best-known of the Alamo heroes was Davy Crockett, who'd devoted his life to self-promoting acts of courage in Tennessee before being defeated in a congressional election. He told his constituents "You can all go to hell, I'm going to Texas", and there he died.

You can see where the Spanish used to rule Texas at the **Spanish Governor's Palace,** a rather grim edifice dating back to 1749, still emblazoned with the Habsburg

Taos Pueblo

eagle of Spain's ruling family over the entrance. The house is furnished with authentic pieces from the Spanish and Mexican eras.

You can also see the Mexicans' old adobe houses and stone patios in **La Villita,** the residential neighbourhood south of the river along Villita Street. For Mexican shopping, go to the old market place, El Mercado (515 W. Commerce).

The river is San Antonio's pride and joy. The **Paseo del Rio,** or River Walk, takes you nearly 3 miles around a horseshoe curve through the town. Below the bustle of traffic, you can walk past banana plants and bougainvillea shading outdoor cafés and ice-cream parlours, nightclubs and craft shops. Water-taxis and river cruises are available at the Market Street

Bridge, or dine by candlelight on the pleasure barges. Beyond the river, the water garden of the Paseo del Alamo stretches to the Alamo.

The nicest museum in town is the **Hertzberg Circus Collection** (210 W. Market), part of the public library, where working models present a comprehensive history of the circus from its early days in England to the American heyday of the P. T. Barnum era. Clown costumes, Tom Thumb's dwarf carriage and a complete circus ring make a nostalgic exhibition.

For a panoramic **view** of San Antonio and the surrounding country go out to **HemisFair Park,** relic of the 1968 World's Fair, where there's an observatory on the 652-foot **Tower of the Americas.** The park is also the site of the **Institute of Texan Cultures,** devoted to the folklore of the 26 ethnic groups that together have created the state of Texas—Germans, Poles, Hungarians and Irish among others.

Mission Road running south of town takes you out to the missions which were the basis of Spanish colonization in the 18th century, with Catholic priests converting the Indians to Christianity while a garrison of soldiers subdued the recalcitrant and searched for gold. **Mission San José** (5 miles south on U.S. Highway 281) is the best preserved of these spiritual and military installations. Founded in 1720, this "Queen of the Missions" has a Spanish Baroque entrance, once lovely, now spoiled by gunmen who have used it for target practice, and souvenir-hunters who have chipped away pieces of the sculpture. Inside, you can visit the soldiers' spartan quarters, the granary and Indians' workshops.

SANTA FE *(New Mexico)*
Founded by the Spanish in 1610, Santa Fe is the oldest capital city in the United States. The atmosphere in the historic centre of town, for all the invasion of hotels and souvenir shops, still gives a hint of that more leisurely Spanish and Indian era. The rose-coloured adobe structures with their *vigas*, log-beams holding up the ceilings and roofs, managing miraculously to be both solid and graceful in form, offer their shady arcades as a delightful shelter from the heat of the day.

The **Plaza** is the focus of old Santa Fe. On its north side is the Palace of the Governors, the oldest public building in the U.S. (1610), now housing part of the **Museum of New Mexico** devoted to the history and prehistory of the state. In the arcade running along the façade of the palace Pueblo Indians sell handmade silver and turquoise jewellery (there is still turquoise of good quality coming in considerable quantities from the hills of New Mexico). Navajo and international folk art are displayed in annexes of the museum located along the old Santa Fe Trail.

Canyon Road, running along the south bank of the Santa Fe River, is the sleepy quarter where the painters, sculptors and craftsmen have their studios and galleries. Walk in and watch them work. The landscape artists tend to be the best, the ambient colour and light being such an inspiration.

The **Santa Fe Opera** is housed in a superb open-air setting, an amphitheatre carved out of the hillside (partially roofed in the unlikely event of rain) 7 miles north of town on the road to Taos.

TAOS *(New Mexico)*

In the early 20th century, Taos was an art colony much beloved by English novelist D.H. Lawrence. It continues to attract many artists and their groupies, who live an easy hand-to-mouth existence just off the town **Plaza.** The town's colourful street life blends society's bohemian element with Taos Indians, Spanish-American farmers and assorted sightseers. Back in the days of Spanish rule, Taos was the centre of the Pueblo Revolt (1680) which drove the Spaniards from New Mexico.

North of town, the **Taos Pueblo** is a centuries-old Indian village with 900 residents still inhabiting the sprawling five-storey apartment buildings—forerunner of modern America's condominiums. The jewellery, blankets and baskets sold here make good gifts.

At Ranchos de Taos, 4 miles south on Highway 68, the 1772 **San Francisco de Asis Mission** is the most attractive of the region's adobe churches. A sturdy, buttressed affair, it looks like a massive piece of sculpture.

PHOENIX *(Arizona)*

This may well be your starting point for the Grand Canyon. There are flights directly up to the Canyon or, if you like desert drives, rent your car here. One warning: drive within the 55 mph speed limit, the local highway patrol is very strict and the long straight roads encourage excess speeds. The most spectacular thing about Phoenix is its setting in the **Valley of the Sun,** the perfect backdrop to a Western movie, with the forbidding red Superstition Mountains to the east and towering Camelback Mountain north-east of town.

If you pass through Phoenix in summer, you may find that it's just too hot to get out of your air-conditioned car. However, there are a couple of museums well worth visiting. **Heard Museum** (22 E. Monte Vista) is one of the best Indian museums in the country. It traces the history of the Indians of the South-West from the first cave-dwellers and Pueblo Indians—with a superb collection of Kachina dolls—to modern times. It is fascinating to observe in the Indian art of our era the continuity in forms and themes from nature, virtually unchanged over the centuries.

The **Pueblo Grande Museum** (4619 E. Washington) is an on-site archaeological excavation of a Hohokam Indian settlement believed to date back some 2,000 years. The ruins, spread across a broad mound, mark out a civilization that disappeared with the Hohokam around the year 1400.

As preparation for the flora you'll see on your desert drive, why not visit the delightful **Desert Botanical Gardens,** 3 miles east of Pueblo Grande. They give a good idea of the marvellous variety of species in the world's cacti.

☑ THE GRAND CANYON

This is one place where you cannot rely on a writer or photographer to show you what it's like. No picture, no words ever matched the reality of the Grand Canyon's beauty. You have to see it for yourself. You'll see it and still won't believe it. There's a moment when nature combines magnitude with light, colour and texture to silence and

humble man into simple contemplation. That moment will come when you approach the **South Rim** of the 277-mile-long serpentine canyon. Look down to its mile-deep floor where the mighty Colorado River has eroded a passage and millions of years of earth up-heavals have gouged out a theatre for the performance of grand geological drama.

Plan your trip to the Grand Canyon like a military operation. There are camping facilities and hotels on the North Rim, but that's really for *habitués*. First-timers should concentrate on the South Rim. Make reservations well in advance (tel. 602 638-2401) whether you want to camp or lodge in the hotels and cabins of **Grand Canyon Village**. The Park Headquarters at Grand Canyon Village provides information about the bus tours of the main Rim Drive, bicycling around the rim, hiking or riding mules down to the canyon floor or rubber rafting along the Colorado River. Hiking and riding mules are for the hardy who are prepared to rise at dawn, face high temperatures at noon and generally rough it. Rafting is a spectacular way of seeing the canyon and perfectly safe in the hands of experienced guides, with good

The Grand Canyon

picnic and camping facilities en route.

The **Visitors Center** at Grand Canyon Village is a must for initial orientation. The rangers here and at key spots along the Rim Drive provide fascinating information on the geology, flowers, animal life and anthropological history—on Indians whose dwellings, built into the canyon cliffs, are still visible today on the North Rim.

There are some fine **nature trails** which the rangers will show you up on the rim through forests of juniper and piñon pine. Every now and again you emerge in a clearing on the edge of the canyon to peer down at the giant mounds or buttes rising like Egyptian pyramids or Aztec temples, and bearing such names as Zoroaster Temple or Cheops Pyramid. Some of the other fanciful rock formations bear such ominous names as Skeleton Point and the Phantom Ranch.

Free buses shuttle along the 8-mile **West Rim** (closed to private cars from May 1 to September 1) stopping off for superb views at Hopi Point, Mohave Point and Pina Point. Other buses pass frequently and will pick walkers up.

You should only attempt to hike if you are very fit and well prepared; although the distances are small, the terrain is rough and temperatures are extreme. Wear good

walking shoes, sunhat and protective clothing, and carry plenty of drinking water. The easiest route is the **Bright Angel Trail,** leaving from Bright Angel Lodge. Start at daybreak, as you can safely count on a good three hours going downhill, and six or seven hours coming back up. The trail zigzags down 1½ miles to a first resthouse (you'll find an emergency telephone installed there), another 1½ miles to the Jacob's Ladder Resthouse, still zigzagging and then straightening out to the beautiful **Indian Garden** at Garden Creek. You can stay overnight at this ranger station and campground providing you have a reservation, which should be made at least four months in advance.

Stalwart hikers will continue the next morning along Garden Creek around the self-explanatory **Devil's Corkscrew** down Pipe Creek to the River Resthouse beside the Colorado River. With an advanced reservation, hikers can also stay at the bunkhouse-style accommodation at Phantom Ranch. A more challenging hike is the steeper **Kaibab Trail** from the Yaki Point Road east of the village. The joy of the hikes is that they take you away from the madding crowd of the Rim Drive, though you can always walk a hundred yards away from them and enjoy the beauty of this phenomenon alone.

THE WEST COAST

The West Coast is America's most varied playground, catering to the crazy, the lazy and the easy-going. Only those in search of the hectic are discouraged: here, nobody rushes. While Las Vegas carries the madness inland to the desert, Seattle on the north Pacific coast introduces a note of sanity in its healthy green state of Washington.

But these are the appendages to the American mecca of all dreamers, European and American alike: California. A land blessed with sun and sea and oranges and ice-cream, California is quite simply the ultimate fantasy land. It is as far west as Western man can go without starting to go east. Stand on the beach at Malibu, stare out at the Pacific or back at the Santa Monica mountains and everything seems possible: balmy winters, shining summers, snow if you want it.

It's no accident that this is the chosen home of America's cinema. California offers every imaginable landscape—Swiss Alps, Sahara Desert, English meadows, African jungle, it's all just a few miles from the freeway. And what isn't already there—a Roman forum or Egyptian pyramid—can be built in a few days with the great wealth that California has amassed in a history of little more than a century.

Its prosperity is truly over-whelming, and constantly re-newed—beginning with the gold of the Sierras, spreading across the great Central Valley to the gigantic combines of agribusiness (mere agriculture was just a passing phase), and on to the coast for oil and the aerospace industry. Californians are perfectly prepared to work and work hard, but they can't wait to get back to the tennis court or swimming pool, go surfing in the Pacific or hiking in Yosemite.

In constant quest of the new, in clothes, music, ideas, toys and religions, the people cling to their joyously accepted role as America's latest pioneers. Hula-hoop, skateboard, wind-surfing, roller-disco—it all starts, flourishes and fizzles out in California, while the rest of the world takes note and, more often than not, follows suit. Tough-as-iron blue jeans began life in San Francisco to withstand the wear and tear of the 1849 Gold Rush and then became the universal unisex clothing of the last half of our century. Flimsy-as-gossamer bikinis made their first appearance on the beaches of Southern California to attract as much sun and attention as possible. With a few modifications and abbreviations, their principle of merry exhibitionism has survived.

Many Californians would like to divide their state into two new separate entities, North and South California—corresponding to two distinct frames of mind represented by San Francisco and Los Angeles. But in fact there's a little bit of both—San Francisco's sophistication and Los Angeles' sunny craziness—all over the place.

Our itinerary begins in San Francisco and its nearby wine valleys and works its way down the Pacific coast to Los Angeles and San Diego before taking off for the national parks of Yosemite, Sequoia and Death Valley National Monument. Whatever your own chosen itinerary, if time permits, you should also make an excursion to California's favourite out-of-state playground, Las Vegas.

You can get to almost all these places by train or bus, and air travel is relatively cheap compared with the rest of the country, and a great bargain compared with Europe. However, California is inevitably the land of the car and it will be difficult for you to enjoy the full scope of the vast and varied landscape without driving. San Francisco is a town for walking, with buses and cable cars to help you up and down the hills, but Los Angeles is resolutely a drivers' town. Yosemite and Sequoia are splendid places for hiking.

SAN FRANCISCO
(California)

San Franciscans are unashamedly in love with their town. All over the place you see the boast: "Everybody's Favorite City". The town's natural setting, nestling in the hills around the bay, make it uncommonly cosy, the zip in the air is invigorating and even the fog rolling off the ocean is romantic rather than chilling. The pervasive enthusiasm of the residents is difficult to resist. Just one tip: if you're thinking of showing your new-won familiarity with the city by calling it "Frisco", don't. It makes real San Franciscans shudder.

If you have a car, the best way to begin your visit is to take the **49 Mile Scenic Drive,** a comprehensive tour that gives you an overall picture before you start to explore in detail. Stop off at **Twin Peaks,** south of Golden Gate Park, for a panoramic view of the city and its bay.

Then put away the car and use the city's first-class public transport and a pair of good walking shoes. Start at the bridge. There are more than one, but *the* bridge is of course the **Golden Gate Bridge.** It is, in fact, not golden but a deep burnt sienna or reddish-brown, depending on the light; the masterpiece of engineer Joseph Strauss. At 4,200 feet, it's not the longest, but few would deny it's the most beautiful suspension bridge in the world. Completed in 1937, it took four years to build and takes four years to repaint—a job that begins again as soon as it's finished. Walking across the bridge is as exciting an adventure as climbing the Eiffel Tower or the Empire State Building. The bridge sways beneath your feet and the lamp-posts rattle as the wind blows through the cables.

(While you're here, spare a thought for **Oakland Bay Bridge** just visible in the distance. The silvery bridge swings across to Oakland via Yerba Buena island and at 8¼ miles is one of the world's longest. It's the bridge you'll take to Berkeley.)

South of the Golden Gate Bridge is the **Presidio**, site of the original garrison, built by the Spanish to protect their settlement in 1776. It is now the headquarters of the Sixth Army and remarkably green and pretty for a military establishment.

On your way down to the Yacht Harbor, you'll pass the **Palace of Fine Arts,** a weird rebuilt relic (the original was chicken wire and plaster) from the 1915 Panama-Pacific Exposition. The exterior, a hodge-podge of classical architecture and reinforced-concrete "Roman ruin", contrasts with the modern technological wizardry of the Exploratorium museum inside. What with

> ### The Cable Caper
> *One delightful way of coping with San Francisco's hills is aboard the fabled cable cars. It's clearly one of the most enjoyable rides imaginable. Especially standing on the outside step—dangerous but legal—hanging on for your life as the Powell Street car clangs up and down Nob Hill, with the sights passing by in slow but bumpy motion.*
>
> *The cable cars were first installed in 1873 and one of the originals can be seen in the museum, which is also the system's fascinating working centre at Washington and Mason streets. The handmade cars are constantly being refurbished and overhauled, so don't be surprised if one or another of the cable-lines is not in service.*
>
> *By the way, you're not allowed on with an ice-cream, because the bone-shaking ride would almost certainly land it on the lap of a fellow passenger.*

holography, lasers, solar-operated musical instruments, it's great for the kids on a rainy day.

From the western Yacht Harbor make your way along Marina Boulevard, past its fine waterfront houses, to **Fisherman's Wharf.** Stroll around, look at the boats and nibble shrimp or crab from the seafood stands along the wharf. It's also a major centre for the revival of street theatre and music that seems to have caught on the world over. Check out the delightful shopping

centres, **Ghirardelli Square,** a converted red-brick chocolate factory, and **The Cannery,** once a fruit processing plant. Both now include a variety of attractive shops and restaurants. Directly east of Fisherman's Wharf is the popular **Pier 39**, another large complex of shops, restaurants and entertainments. Visitors are rewarded with spectacular views of the bay, Alcatraz and the Golden Gate Bridge.

The Hills

There are 40 of them, and they're San Francisco's pride. A tour of Nob Hill (Powell or California Street cable car), Telegraph Hill (bus) and Russian Hill (cable car) will give you a good sense of the past and present splendours of San Francisco's wealthy.

The imposing Victorian houses of **Nob Hill,** where the "nobs" or nabobs lived, were wiped out in the 1906 earthquake—with one notable exception: the impressive brownstone house of James Flood, now the highly exclusive Pacific Union Club. You can't get in there, but you can loiter (with appropriate decorum) in the hill's two landmark hotels—the Fairmont and Mark Hopkins. Each has a panoramic bar and the stiff price you pay for a

Oakland Bay Bridge

167

drink in either of them is worth it for the view.

The best reason for climbing **Telegraph Hill** is to see the other hills from the top of Coit Tower. Built in 1934 to honour the city's fire department, its shape is meant to resemble the nozzle of a fire hose.

Russian Hill may be less opulent than the other two hills, but its gardens and immaculate little cottages make it the most appealing. The constant ups and downs of the city's streets reach a crazy climax on **Lombard Street,** between Hyde and Leavenworth. After you've negotiated the incredible serpentine plunge, weaving in and out of backyards and around seven sudden bends, you're not going to quibble about its claim to be the "crookedest street in the world".

Downtown

In spite of its name, **North Beach** can lay no claim to being a beach at all. It's the district north of the Broadway and Columbus intersection that is both centre of the Italian community and focus of the city's artistic and intellectual life. Part of it used to be known as the "Barbary Coast", an infamous den of iniquity where sailors came for the brothels, while their captains shanghaied drunken or otherwise unconscious civilians for their crews.

Since the 1950s when poet Lawrence Ferlinghetti gathered his fellow beatniks around his City Lights Bookshop, North Beach has been the place where California's new ideas, intellectual and other, are first tried out. The few relatively literate hippies of the '60s congregated here to escape the mindless nonsense of Haight-Ashbury. In the '70s it was the turn of the "mellows", the smiling younger brothers and sisters of the hippies, gliding around on quiet roller skates, eating frozen yoghurt and espousing low-risk ecological causes. Whatever trend emerges in the future, a couple of Grant Avenue coffee shops have survived to offer you ringside seats to watch it all begin.

Chinese newcomers are making inroads into the Oriental and Italian neighbourhood, clustered around Columbus, Stockton, Vallejo and Green streets. There are many small Oriental and Italian grocery stores, pastry shops, espresso bars and cafés and restaurants. But the seedy tradition of the Barbary Coast lives on in the dwindling number of "topless" joints on Broadway.

Chinatown has evolved from a ghetto imposed on the Chinese in the 19th century by the founders of the city into a proud, self-assertive community. Gone are the days of the Tong wars to establish control of the community's underworld and opium dens. The vicarious thrill that those adventures provided has been replaced by a general civic pride, though Chinatown's elders are showing some concern for the future: rising rents are driving out small family businesses and the upwardly mobile continue their exodus to the suburbs.

More than 82,000 Chinese live in San Francisco, making it the largest Chinese community outside Asia. The principal neighbourhood is bounded by Broadway, Bush, Kearny and Stockton, with eight blocks of Grant Avenue as its colourful centre.

An ornamental arch at the Bush Street end of Grant marks the entry to Chinatown. Flanking it are two hamburger houses of Chinese design. Beyond the arch, life is more resolutely Chinese.

On a smaller scale, but with the same cultural pride, is **Japan Town**,—J-Town to San Franciscans. Its Cultural and Trade Center at Geary between Laguna and Fillmore Streets includes schools of cookery and Japanese flower arrangement, a Japanese theatre and a hotel with Japanese amenities— sunken baths, mattresses on *tatami* mats, kimonoed maids and indoor rock gardens.

After which you may want to remind yourself of America' predominant culture, the Anglo-Saxon

variety. In the wedge formed by Market Street, the city's main thoroughfare, and Van Ness Street you will find a sprawling complex of municipal, state and federal buildings, known collectively as the **Civic Center.** It was initiated in an ambitious burst of city planning after the 1906 earthquake, and the early structures are in Renaissance style. Also part of the complex are the twin Veterans' Building (housing the San Francisco Museum of Modern Art) the Opera House, where the United Nations Charter was signed in 1945, and the Symphony Hall.

For a shopping detour, drive down Market Street (walking is best avoided to be on the safe side) and turn off at Powell. **Union Square** is the place to go for fashionable boutiques, speciality shops, flower stands and large department stores. Continue on to Montgomery Street, the heart of San Francisco's financial district; here, in the home of the Gold Rush heirs, take a look at the **Old Coin and Gold Exhibit** of the Bank of California (400 California Street). You're not likely to miss the **Transamerica Pyramid,** an 853-foot spike at the corner of Montgomery and Washington streets. It's one of those buildings which purists start off hating and then defend in the following generation.

Golden Gate Park

Away from the skyscrapers of downtown, take the number 5 Fulton bus to get to Golden Gate Park. Originally nothing but sand dunes, it was turned into its present lush parkland quite by chance—or so the story goes—when 19th-century urban planner John McLaren accidentally dropped the oats from his horse's nosebag and they sprouted. McLaren carried on from there and today San Franciscans have a delightful landscape of small lakes and hills, an arboretum, botanical gardens, playing fields, stables and a popular open-air chess hang-out. At the eastern end of the park there's a superb children's playground and beyond it, the Haight-Ashbury district of the 1960s "flower children". Although it is still a somewhat depressed area, a regular infusion of new shops and boutiques, along with steady "gentrification", promises continued improvement well into the future.

The park includes three major museums clustered around the Music Concourse. The **M.H. de Young Memorial Museum** has some fine American and British paintings and decorative arts, and is known as host to important travelling exhibitions. The **Asian Art Museum** next door contains the rich Avery Brundage collection and the **California Academy of**

Sciences houses a zoological museum, an aquarium and a planetarium. Afterwards, you can rest in the lovely **Japanese Tea Garden.**

Alcatraz

Of the cruises you can take on San Francisco Bay the most entertaining (from Pier 41, near Fisherman's Wharf) is to the abandoned prison of Alcatraz. The U.S. Rangers conduct informative and witty tours of the former home of A1 Capone and other convicts too hot for normal prisons. Alcatraz—the name comes from the Spanish Isla de los Alcotraces (Isle of Pelicans)—is a 12-acre rock with no arable soil. All the water for the shrubs and trees growing today had to be brought by the U.S. Army, for whom it was a "disciplinary barracks" until 1934. One and a half miles of ice-cold treacherous currents, sharks and raw sewage separate Alcatraz from the San Francisco shore. It was the ideal location for America's most notorious federal civil penitentiary, but enormously expensive in upkeep. In 1962, with each inmate costing $40,000 a year, they closed it down.

EXCURSIONS

The Bay Area

Immediately north of San Francisco are the two charming little

> *Getting Away from it All*
> Officially, nobody ever got away safely from Alcatraz. In all 39 tried, seven were killed in the attempt, and five have never been found but are assumed drowned.
>
> In 1962, at the very end of Alcatraz's grim history, John Paul Scott made it unharmed to San Francisco by greasing his body to resist the cold. Some students found him exhausted at Fort Point by the Golden Gate Bridge. Good-naturedly, not knowing he was an escaped prisoner, they called the police to help the poor fellow in his moment of distress.

harbour towns of **Sausalito** and **Tiburon,** which you can reach either by car across the Golden Gate Bridge or by ferry (from the Ferry Building for Sausalito or Pier 43 1/2 for Tiburon). Tiburon is the quieter of the two, although both towns have a colourful Mediterranean atmosphere, with a number of boutiques and pleasant bistros and cafés out on the boardwalk looking across the bay to San Francisco.

Sausalito and Tiburon are at the southern tip of the Californian phenomenon of Marin County, home of hot tubs, Jacuzzi whirlpool baths and other sensual delights of communal living. The perpetrators are not freaks, at least not any more, they've grown into lawyers and investment bankers.

The Wine Country

Wine-lovers will enjoy a drive through the vineyard of **Napa Valley** and across the Maacama Mountains to Sonoma. The valley is less than 50 miles from San Francisco and lies between the Mayacamas and the Howell Mountains, stretching from the town of Napa in the south to Calistoga to the north. Highway 29 is the main route through the valley. The Silverado Trail, which runs parallel to it, is the slower, quieter and more scenic route. Bus tours are available and you can even fly over the vineyard in a hot air balloon. The wineries, as they are known, provide tours and tastings in the cellars and organize picnics in the vineyards. Harvests begin around mid-August—the Californian weather being so much more predictably sunny than in Europe.

Some of the more interesting wineries are at Sterling, and at Mondavi, Martini, Beaulieu and Beringer in Napa, and at Souverain and Sebastiani in Sonoma. Homesick Frenchmen may want to visit the Domaine Chandon in Napa, owned by Moët et Chandon. The Hess Collection Winery near Napa exhibits artworks by Stella, Motherwell and some of the ultra-realists. A word of warning: the best restaurants of the region are closed on Tuesday.

California Vintage

California is proud of its wines and with good reason. Wine-growers have gradually refined and matured their techniques and have greatly improved their marketing strategies. In the old days, wineries churned out red and white wines and indiscriminately labelled them 'Burgundy' and 'Chablis'.

Now with a nationwide interest for good wine that is increasing every year, as well as international acclaim, California wine-growers are taking more care.

Generally, wines are distinguished by labels specifying the varieties of European grapes from which they were grown. The red wines include Cabernet Sauvignon from the French Médoc, Pinot Noir from Burgundy and Zinfandel, whose origin puzzles the experts (some believe it to be Italian, but you won't find it outside California).

The most important white wines are Chardonnay from Burgundy, Sauvignon Blanc from Bordeaux, Gewürztraminer and Riesling from Alsace, the German Mosel and Rhineland. The vintage displayed on the labels of these wines represents the authentic year of at least 95 per cent of the wine in the bottle.

Several French champagne houses are also now producing fine sparkling wines in California.

All these improvements have meant that there has been an inevitable increase in price, but Californian wines now hold their own with French, German and Italian ones.

PACIFIC COAST

Take Freeway 101 south from San Francisco and join Pacific Highway, Route 1, at Castroville, to get to **Monterey,** the old Spanish and Mexican capital of Alta (Upper) California. The bay was discovered in 1542 but was not settled until 1770 when Father Junipero Serra set up a mission here with the garrison protection of Gaspar de Portola's presidio. Monterey was a bleak, disease-ridden place and Portola recommended it be handed over to the Russians, who also coveted it, "as a punishment". But Father Serra accepted the hardships and led the taming of the Monterey wilderness. His statue keeps watch on Corporal Ewin Road.

The town is proud of its past and offers a sign-posted tour of the Old Town's historic buildings from the 19th-century Mexican administration and early American period. The architecture is a strange mixture of Spanish adobe and American colonial clapboard, two storeys with a balcony; an attractive enough hybrid to earn it the name of "Monterey style". At the Chamber of Commerce, on Alvarado Street, you can get a map showing the major houses.

Look for the **Larkin House** at Jefferson and Calle Principal, home of the first (and only) U.S. Consul in the 1840s, and the **Robert Louis Stevenson House,** 530 Houston Street, where the writer lived while he was working on *Treasure Island.* On Church Street you'll find the site of Father Serra's original baked-mud church; rebuilt in 1795, it is now the **Royal Presidio Chapel** or Cathedral of San Carlos de Borromeo. To the left of the altar is a colourful 18th-century Virgin Mary from Spanish Mexico.

Nearer the waterfront are the Pacific House, on Custom House Plaza, with a pleasant, flowery and tree-shaded arcaded courtyard, and the Custom House (1827), taken over as the first U.S. federal building on the Pacific coast.

More distinctively American is **California's First Theater** on Scott and Pacific streets, a pinewood shack built by one Jack Swan in 1847 as a saloon with a dubious boarding house upstairs. Customers were (and still are) attracted by Victorian melodramas, but the "boarding house" no longer operates.

Fisherman's Wharf, like San Francisco's, is a collection of shops and restaurants out on the dock, but offering a more intimate view of the

Big Sur, California

boats of the marina. The fish here are almost always fresh, but not abundant enough to keep Cannery Row going as more than a weather-beaten curiosity. The fisheries were the sardine capital of the western hemisphere from 1921 to 1946 but, by 1951, the sardines had disappeared. Today the timbered canneries made famous by novelist John Steinbeck as "a poem, a stink, a grating noise" are restaurants, boutiques and art galleries.

A big draw in the neighbourhood is the **Monterey Bay Aquarium,** featuring the denizens of the bay.

17-Mile Drive takes you down to **Carmel,** a delightful resort and artists' colony, which is ideal for a rest, a suntan and some serious shopping and gallery hopping. In spite of the golden light and the Spanish-style adobe houses, this immaculate tree-lined town with its leisurely, discreet atmosphere will remind you more of New England than of the California coast.

South-east of the town is situated the **Carmel Mission,** Basílica San Carlos Borromeo de Carmelo. Its restoration has been admirably carried out and its peacefulness is the perfect complement to the tranquility of the town. Father Serra is buried here.

The **coast road** from Carmel to Big Sur is only 30 miles long, but it takes more than an hour of careful driving. And every hairpin turn of the road opens up another spectacular vista of forest, hills and sea.

Big Sur and the Pfeiffer-Big Sur State Park offer marvellous opportunities for picnics, camping, hiking and fishing in the Big Sur River. This was the home of writer Henry Miller. Other artists lived here and you'll find it a great place to escape the crowd. Back on the coast, Orson Welles built a redwood honeymoon cottage for Rita Hayworth in the days when film stars did the romantic things expected of them. Now it has been expanded into a restaurant, worth a visit for its matchless view of the ocean, if nothing else.

The rugged shoreline road continues for 65 more miles to where William Randolph Hearst, the man Orson Welles immortalized in *Citizen Kane*, built his unbelievable dream castle at **San Simeon.** (Allow at least two hours for the guided tours. It's advisable to make a reservation, especially in the summer, by phoning 1–800–444–PARK. Hearst himself referred to the 123 acres of castle, guesthouse *palazzi*, terraces, gardens, Roman baths, private zoo and tennis courts as "the Ranch". Building began in 1919 and was still not completed when Hearst died in 1951.

The 275,000-acre estate lies 1,600 feet up in the hills. After parking your car in the lot, you take a tour bus which drives past zebras, barbary sheep and goats grazing on the slopes, remnants of Hearst's private zoo.

San Francisco architect Julia Morgan built "the Ranch" to Hearst's specifications as a "functional showcase" for his art collection. The incredible mixture of that collection registers as you pass the 100-foot swimming pool with its Greek colonnade and a copy of Donatello's Florentine statue of David standing on two authentic 17th-century Baroque Venetian fountains that Hearst had joined together. A Roman sarcophagus and 3,500-year-old Egyptian goddess are both genuine, but the "Ranch House" façade, its equestrian friezes on the balcony and Gothic canopies are made of reinforced concrete. Over the gigantic main entrance, in quiet simplicity, is a (genuine) 13th-century Madonna and Child.

Inside, the hodge-podge runs riot. A vestibule with a 60 B.C. Pompeian mosaic floor leads to a salon with 15th-century Flemish tapestries over Italian choir stalls behind sofas that have 1930s slip-covers borrowing motifs from the tapestries. The dining room has a magnificent cedarwood coffer ceiling from a Bologna monastery and is decorated with the flags from the Sienna *palio* pageant.

LOS ANGELES *(California)*

Los Angeles is the quintessential 20th-century creation. Only modern technology could have turned this desert into one of the most flourishing metropolises on earth. Engineering genius brought water hundreds of miles across mountains and deserts to feed the city and its industry and nurture its lush gardens. The fabled freeway system arrived in time to link the people scattered across its vast area and create the burgeoning monster that never ceases to astonish.

People who don't know it complain that Los Angeles is nothing but a bunch of suburbs looking for a city. The cliché is not so much untrue as irrelevant. When you visit the various neighbourhoods and townships that make up greater Los Angeles—Hollywood, Westwood, Santa Monica, Malibu, and dozens more—you find that nobody's looking for a city, they know where they are. Up in the hills, down at the beach, in the valley, around the university campus, they're all integral parts of Los Angeles. It is not a city in the traditional sense of a downtown urban core interacting with surrounding neighbourhoods, outskirts and suburbs. LA is more a state of mind. And a huge state of mind at that, covering 460 square miles, bounded by sea and sand to the west, mountains to the north and east and desert to the south, all topped off by an almost permanent canopy of sun. With all these possibilities, it's not surprising that leisure and pleasure are worshipped here.

"The Beach"

The beach (Angelenos always refer to it in the singular) stretches some 40 miles from Malibu through Santa Monica, Venice, Marina del Rey, Hermosa and Redondo to Palos Verdes before the sands hit the pollution of Los Angeles Harbor and the Long Beach shipyards. There's no better way to get the special feel of Los Angeles than to go straight down there. In L.A., beaches are not just resorts for holidays and weekend cottages, they are year-round residential areas.

Malibu is the favoured beach home of the more relaxed members of the film community. Rather than barricade themselves behind electric fences guarded by Doberman pinschers as they do in Bel Air and Beverly Hills, film stars and hot young directors can be seen jogging along the sands or shopping for yoghurt and diet drinks in the supermarket. Malibu Lagoon's Surfrider Beach attracts champion surfers from all over the world. Sunning and swimming are a little more peaceful down at Las Tunas and Topanga. Malibu Pier is a good place to fish. The one hazard disturbing Malibu's sunny peace is the occasional "cat's paw" tide or mountain landslide that washes the handsome beach houses into the Pacific.

Santa Monica is built on more solid ground, and its beaches are more of a family affair. But it's neighbouring **Venice** that attracts all the attention. The beach and

178

beach-park here are a non-stop open-air amateur circus of freaks, acrobats, weight-lifters, clowns and jugglers entertaining themselves quite as much as the passing crowd. In 1892, millionaire Albert Kinney had wanted to set down on the Pacific coast a replica of Italy's Venice, complete with canals, gondolas, a *palazzo* or two, hotels and amusement arcades. Then somebody discovered oil and the idea was abandoned. Four canals remain with a Lighthouse Bridge that traverses the Lagoon area feeding the canals. The neighbourhood has revived as a diverse community of serious artists, upscale galleries and the ever-present bohemian types.

Movieland

London buries its heroes in Westminster Abbey, Paris puts great Frenchmen to rest in the Pantheon, and Los Angeles offers the hand, foot and hoof prints of its stars in the cement courtyard of **Mann's Chinese Theater** (at 6925 Hollywood Boulevard). Start your pilgrimage here. Sid Grauman had the idea in 1927 of getting the immortals' prints when they attended gala premières at his great exotic cinema. Most stars followed the example of Mary Pickford, the Marx Brothers and Rita Hayworth: they got down on their knees and made a hand print. But it was natural for

Fred Astaire to leave a foot print, and cowboy Tom Mix preferred leaving the hoof print of his horse. If you go to see a film in L.A.—and it would seem silly not to, like not eating in Paris—go to one of the old preposterous movie palaces like the Chinese or the Egyptian across the street. The outrageous pagoda and Theban temple décors may be better than the film.

Walk along **Hollywood Boulevard**—one of the parts of L.A. where walking is customary—and you'll see over 2,500 actors' names on bronze stars embedded in the pavement. The street itself is less scintillating—rundown shops and pizza parlours—but the second-hand bookstores are excellent. You'll pass Frederic's of Hollywood with its lingerie museum and the beautifully restored Roosevelt Hotel. Between La Brea and Western Avenue, the boulevard has the fine, tacky splendour of the 1920s and '30s, with its low, flat stucco buildings and a droopy palm tree or two; even pre-war Packards and Buicks parked on the street.

A few blocks north of the boulevard is **Hollywood Bowl,** the splendid open-air auditorium where the Los Angeles Philharmonic Orchestra holds concerts against a background of the gigantic illuminated letters of H-O-L-L-Y-W-O-O-D, planted up in the hills.

South of Hollywood Boulevard lies L.A.'s most famous street, **Sunset Boulevard.** The Hollywood section is known simply as "The Strip". It's where people cruise up and down in convertibles, and where sleazy nightclubs and cheap motels vie with upmarket boutiques and elegant restaurants.

One of the most enjoyable Hollywood trips is a **tour of the film and television studios.** Two major TV networks (CBS and NBC) welcome you onto the sets for a look behind the scenes of some of America's most popular shows. A limited number of tickets to live shows are available on request. Universal Studios (Lankershim Boulevard, north of the Hollywood Freeway) offers an elaborate tour in open trolleys with guides who have all the show-biz flair of Hollywood itself. Participating in the special effects trickery, you'll be attacked by spaceships and the shark from *Jaws,* you'll meet up with a 3-storey-tall King Kong and generally be subjected to all the earthquakes, flash floods and fires you ever saw in a disaster film. You'll visit sound-stages and back-lots and learn the screen techniques used to create film's great illusions. You'll see how Moses parted the waters of the Red Sea in *The Ten Commandments* and ride through a "town" that includes a New England fishing village, a Bavarian square, French bistros and an Italian pizzeria, all in the space of four blocks.

Beverly Hills is exclusive and assertively separate from Los Angeles. The streets are lined with Rolls Royces and Mercedes and the architecture of the mansions is an astounding mixture of Spanish, Gothic, Bauhaus and Renaissance.

The town is phenomenally clean and litter is almost a capital crime. It's policed with formidable efficiency and, except for in the great shopping streets such as Rodeo Drive, walking is viewed with suspicion, especially at night. If you do want to take a walk here, it's a good idea to put on tennis or jogging clothes; the police will assume you're a sportsman. Only burglars, it seems, walk around Beverly Hills in "normal" clothes.

Downtown

Downtown Los Angeles is steadily becoming a more attractive and culturally active community. Some downtown institutions that have surfaced in recent years are the Museum of Contemporary Art and the Los Angeles Music Center, where the Academy awards are presented. The colourful Mexican life of the city is best enjoyed at **Grand Central Market,** north of Pershing Square. (The other great food market is Farmer's Market, west of Beverly Hills at Fairfax and Third.)

If you're going west again from downtown, avoid the freeway and take another great thoroughfare, **Wilshire Boulevard,** shining with the prosperity of its department stores and big hotels, but also a living museum of the ornate art deco architecture that characterized Los Angeles' rise to greatness in the 1920s and 1930s; among other examples, look for the **Franklin Life** insurance building at Van Ness and the **5209 Wilshire.**

Disneyland

Anaheim (27 miles south-east of downtown L.A. on the Santa Ana Freeway) is the home of Disneyland. Since 1955, Walt Disney and his successors have been dispensing the good clean pleasures of a make-believe world inspired by the uplifting fantasies of his films. Applying the techniques of the cinema and advanced electronics technology, Disney takes you around this smiling Technicoloured theme-park on a day-long outing that is simply stupefying in scope and impact. You can buy a 1-, 2- or 3-day Passport that covers the whole Disneyland complex, good for unlimited use of the attractions.

Pick up a booklet with maps at City Hall and head down **Main**

Street, which sets the tone with its sunny evocation of small-town U.S.A. at the turn of the century. You may notice that all the houses and shops are three-quarter size. In this effort to escape from the realities of the outside world, everything is a little smaller than life-size, and larger than life. Don't linger in the shops: head for **Fantasyland**, with Sleeping Beauty Castle, Pinoc- chio's Ride and a boat cruise through the charming, disarming "It's a Small World". **Adventure- land** is a boat ride through simu- lated jungle foliage on a river that passes successively through Asia, Africa and the South Pacific, com- plete with plastic tigers and alliga- tors. A miniature railroad takes you through **Frontierland,** the pioneer country of the Old West where a

loudspeaker warns you to "watch out for Indians and wild animals". Just the faintest unease is aroused by a settler's cabin on fire with a wax-model pioneer lying outside, killed by an Indian's arrow. But at the end of each ride are reassuring ice-cream and soft-drinks stands. One of the most exciting themes is **Tomorrowland,** constantly needing renovation to keep pace with progress. The rides include a submarine, the head-spinning Space Mountain, Star Tours, and the most up-to-date experiments in public transport.

Museums

Museum lovers have much to be excited about in L.A. The **L.A. County Museum of Art** (5905 Wilshire Boulevard) was designed by William Pereira and is one of the largest museums of its kind in the country. The extensive permanent collections include Impressionist paintings, contemporary art, Indian and Islamic art, American art and the Armand Hammer collection of Roman glass. In addition, the Pavilion for Japanese Art and the sculpture garden also contain some outstanding works, and there are regular changing exhibitions of contemporary art.

The **Norton Simon Museum** at Pasadena (Orange Grove and Colorado, off the Ventura Freeway)

contains a collection of European paintings, drawings and sculpture from the early Renaissance to the 20th century, along with Indian bronzes and Asian stone carvings.

The **J. Paul Getty Museum** (17985 W. Pacific Coast Highway, Malibu—call ahead 458–2003 for reserved parking in the museum garage) combines elements of the Norton Simon collection and of Hearst Castle. The legendary collections are housed in a replica of the Villa dei Papiri (excavated from volcanic mud left by Mount Vesuvius in A.D. 79), complete with mosaics, geometric gardens and Corinthian colonnades.

The **Armand Hammer Museum of Art** (10899 Wilshire Boulevard), the legacy of yet another billionaire, contains the world's largest collection of Daumier's works, in addition to much other Western European art.

SAN DIEGO *(California)*

This is the place where California's history began, as Juan Rodríguez Cabrillo, a Portuguese captain, first set foot on Californian soil in 1542. Sixty years later, its bay was explored by the Spanish but it wasn't until 1769 that Father Serra built his first mission.

The best way to appreciate San Diego's beauty is from the sea. Take a **cruise** along the bay—they

183

start from Harbor Drive at the end of Broadway—past the man-made Harbor and Shelter islands around the tip of the peninsula to Point Loma out on the Pacific.

Back on dry land, you can visit one of the 19th-century ships which are moored on the Embarcadero as part of the Maritime Museum Fleet, the most picturesque being the iron-hulled square rigger, *Star of India,* built in 1863. Or drop into Seaport Village, a lively complex of shops, restaurants and galleries.

San Diego's discoverer is celebrated by the **Cabrillo National Monument** on the Point Loma promontory (follow the signs south-west on Rosecrans Street). Cabrillo's statue, donated by the Portuguese government, faces the spot at which he landed.

Old Town (bounded by Juan, Twiggs, Congress and Wallace streets) is a six-block area of restored adobe buildings from the city's Mexican era, plus the brick houses of early American settlers. You'll enjoy a rest under the palms and eucalyptus trees of Plaza Vieja, originally the centre and bullring of the old pueblo. More restoration is under way in the Gaslamp Quarter, a mostly Victorian neighbourhood.

The modern town is fortunately blessed with enlightened urban planning, the popular Horton Plaza shopping centre—and the superb **Balboa Park.** Set right in the centre of town, the park offers a wealth of sports facilities and many of the city's cultural attractions. There's even an Elizabethan playhouse, site of the summer Shakespeare festival, running the gamut from space and science to fine arts.

But the star of the park is the **San Diego Zoo,** justly acclaimed as one of the world's finest. Certainly it's one of the most humane, giving the animals as large, free and natural a living space as possible in the confines of a man-made park. Australian species are particularly well represented. You can fly over the zoo in the Skyfari aerial tramway or take a guided tour by bus.

Another great park is at **Mission Bay,** offering first class aquatic facilities. Paddle around tiny islands and lagoons in canoes, or sail in catamarans and full-size sloops. It is also the home of **Sea World,** where you can see the famous 3-ton killer whale, not to mention sea lions, otters and a walrus performing in the "Pirates of Pinnipeds".

NATIONAL PARKS

The best times of the year for Yosemite and Sequoia are spring and autumn, but there isn't a bad time of year. Winter offers some good cross-country and even downhill skiing in Yosemite and lovely snowscapes in Sequoia, but you should check ahead to find out which roads are closed. Summer in both parks is high season and relatively crowded, but the peace of the high country is always within reach. Death Valley is best from late autumn to early spring. In the height of summer temperatures can rise to 100°F or more.

Yosemite *(California)*

"Base camp"—which might be a plush hotel room, modest lodge accommodation or simply a tent—is at the heart of Yosemite Valley along the Merced River. From the valley meadow, you can hike, bike (rentals at Yosemite Lodge or Curry Village), ride a horse or mule, or take the shuttle-bus to all the great sights. Soaring granite cliffs enclose the valleys—Half Dome at the north-east end (8,842 feet above sea level), Glacier Point, Sentinel and Cathedral Spires down the south wall, El Capitan, Three Brothers and Washington Column up the north wall.

You can grade the hikes according to your capacity and endurance, but try at least one hike, in sturdy shoes, for the sheer exhilaration of making it to the end. In the Merced River Canyon, **Vernal Falls** is within the scope of any normally healthy person. You follow a well-marked path that begins at Happy Isles Nature Center, where knowl-

edgeable U.S. Rangers will answer your questions.

If you're up to it, push on along the Mist Trail, past Emerald Pool to **Nevada Falls** and you'll begin to lose the crowd. Here you're on the John Muir Trail, named after the Scottish naturalist who explored the Sierra Nevada and made their conservation against the encroachments of civilization his life's work. The trail goes on past Merced Lake and heads for the lovely **Tuolumne Meadows** in the high country. The final destination is Mount Whitney over 200 miles away; Muir did it, but perhaps it's a little more than you'd prefer.

Less exhausting is a drive or shuttle-bus ride past Badger Pass to **Glacier Point,** 7,214 feet above sea level. Both the altitude and the view over the whole valley and the High Sierras beyond are, yes, breathtaking. You can see Yosemite Creek drop half a mile from the opposite wall in two spectacular plunges (Upper and Lower **Yosemite Falls**) and you'll get an outstanding view of the majestic **Half Dome.** From here you may be willing to leave the bus and hike and picnic on your way back along the Panorama Trail via the Nevada and Vernal falls—8 miles downhill in all.

Another beautiful hike is out to **Mirror Lake,** especially in spring or early summer when the waters

are perfectly still in the early morning or at sunset, capturing the marvellous colours from the trees and Mount Watkins behind.

Sequoia/Kings Canyon
(California)

A haven of peace and contemplation among the giant sequoias, many of them approaching 3,000 years old, the forest offers a gorgeous array of dogwoods, sugar pines and white firs, and a rich flora of orange leopard lily, white corn lily, lupine, chinquapin and bracken fern. This is no place for a hurried look; walk slowly, sit quietly and listen, fall asleep under a tree. Watch for the birds—woodpecker, raven, spotted owl, but also W.C. Field's favourite, the mountain chickadee, and the Steller's Jay.

Start at the Giant Forest Village with its motel and the Park Rangers' Visitor Center at Lodgepole. You can get a map and infor-

Death Valley National Monument

mation about the best walks in the forest and hikes in the back country. It's also a good idea to watch the informative documentary film about the sequoias.

 The best introduction to the forest is the **Congress Trail.** It's an easy two-mile walk, well worth lingering over for a couple of hours to absorb the beauty of the largest living creations. The trail begins at the **General Sherman Tree,** biggest of all, 275 feet high, 103 feet around

its base and still growing. Reaching up for their light well above the rest of the forest, the branches start 130 feet above the ground. As you move among the great sequoias—the President, the Senate Group, the House Group and the General Lee—you can understand John Muir waxing lyrical about "the first tree in the forest to feel the touch of rosy beams of morning and the last to bid the sun goodnight".

Another beautiful walk, by no means an exhausting hike, is out to **Crescent Meadow,** passing more of the stately giants along the way.

If you want to get away and explore the back country, carry on along the High Sierra Trail running 11 miles from Crescent Meadow to **Bearpaw Meadow.** This is not too formidable a hike. A nearby lake and streams offer good fishing for trout. You will have a fair chance of spotting some of the park's wildlife—bobcats, coyotes, golden eagles, black bear, spotted skunk, and cougar.

Death Valley National Monument *(California)*

A convenient way to see Death Valley is to combine it with an excursion to Las Vegas. Come in from the east, either on highway 95 and via Death Valley Junction on 190, or further north via Beatty, on 58.

This desert is perhaps the greatest surprise of all the wonders of California. It's not one but a dozen landscapes, not a monotonous expanse of sand dunes but an endless variety of terrains, rock formations, colours and plants. Go there in winter and you may see a flood of spring flowers blooming in the wake of the sparse rains. But above

all, there's the light, uncannily clear, distorting distances, pink at dawn, white at mid-morning, piercing silver at noon and then shimmering into gold as the afternoon progresses.

Don't be put off by the name, Death Valley. It was bequeathed by gold-rush hopefuls who crossed from Arizona and Nevada and suffered bitter hardships here. There are now some excellent facilities at Furnace Creek. However, if you are crossing the desert in summer, do not drive off the main road and, if you break down, wait in your car for the next police patrol to arrive.

Get up at dawn—really, you won't regret it—and drive out south-east along highway 190 to **Zabriskie Point.** As the sun rises and the light hits Tucki Mountain and the tips of the Panamints to the west before plunging into the valley's primeval salt lake-bed below, you're likely to be set wondering about the world's creation. By mid-morning (if you visit in winter) the temperature will still be in the cool 50s on your exposed ridge, but walk down the hill to the lake-bed and you'll feel the heat rising to meet you, reaching the 80s by the time you get to the bottom.

Continue over to **Dante's View** (altitude 5,745 feet), looking down at Badwater, 282 feet below sea level. It is the lowest point in the

United States. Make up your own mind whether this is paradise, purgatory or hell. On the other side of the valley you can see Wildrose, Bennett and Telescope peaks.

Retrace the road towards Furnace Creek and turn off left, travelling along the Death Valley floor. Follow the crumbling lake-bed known as the Devil's Golf Course as far as Badwater and walk out across that expanse of baked salt. The degree of desolation is almost exhilarating. Look closer at the salt and you'll discover it's set into bizarre funnel shapes, swirls and other intricate patterns. Drive back north again and cut off at the arrow pointing to **Artist's Drive.** Here you can explore a canyon of multi-coloured rocks and shrubs that culminates in Artist's Palette. The rocks have oxidized into bright mauve, vermillion, ochre, lime-green, turquoise and purple.

LAS VEGAS (Nevada)

If European and American dreamers go to California, where do Californian dreamers go? Well, they take Interstate Highway 15 from Los Angeles north-east across the Mojave Desert and over the Nevada state line to Las Vegas. While once the resort may have been considered Sodom and Gomorrah with air-conditioning and neon lights, today it seeks to project a whole-some image as an internationally known city hosting massive conventions and major sporting events, and welcoming millions of tourists. The city has a resident population of 800,000—in large part living in fancy retirement complexes—that enjoys a wealth of cultural and sports amenities offered by the area's health clubs, art centres and numerous churches. The squeaky-clean aura notwithstanding, Las Vegas remains one of those myth-laden towns that everybody should see once before they die. No amount of familiarity with films showing the marvels of this gambler's paradise can quite prepare you for the shock of the real thing.

At **Casino Center** downtown, which has banks and professional buildings cheek to jowl with casinos, the neon lights are so over-poweringly bright that midnight can look like noon back in the Mojave. Focus for the action is up-and-coming **Fremont,** better known as "Glitter Gulch". Every lit-up window shows dozens of people frenetically tugging the levers of the "one-armed bandit" slot machines. One sign declares: "For every U.S. coin you got, we got the slot."

The famous **Strip** (officially Las Vegas Boulevard), between Sahara and Tropicana Avenues, is four solid miles of hotels and casinos, each with a nightclub advertising

189

America's top comedians and singers and a score of girlie-shows, on ice, in water, even on an ordinary stage. There's plenty by way of family entertainment, including several theme parks; **Wet'n Wild** is a vast water-theme park right on *The Strip*. Some of the major hotels also provide family entertainment, and food and accommodation are both extremely cheap (subsidized by gambling profits!).

Even if you're not staying there, visit the most extravagant hotels on The Strip. These are the true monuments of Las Vegas, palaces of the Orient, Ancient Rome, Persia and many other fabled places. The most flamboyant are **Caesar's Palace,** complete with its fountains and colonnades, the **Tropicana** and its Island Paradise, and the **Mirage** with its expansive gardens boasting waterfalls, palm trees and erupting volcano.

But the décor is overwhelmed by the gambling—hundreds of slot machines spill out from the casinos into the lobbies, plus roulette tables, baccarat, blackjack and bingo. Poker is usually played in a roped-off area at amazingly sedate tables dealt to by house-dealers too busy keeping the game going to crack a joke. The most enjoyable tables to watch are the dice or craps games, where the players get excited, whoop, yell and groan as their for-

tunes go up and down. You'll notice there are no clocks or windows in the casinos—the management doesn't like you to think about what time of day it is; action is available non-stop.

Even if you don't gamble, the spectacle in the casino is fascinating and the floor shows are first-rate. The best way to handle Las Vegas and survive is to arrive at sunset—for that view of the first neon lights in the desert—stay up all night, sleep late, have a good breakfast and leave immediately.

SEATTLE *(Washington)*

Bright and energetic, Seattle is blessed with one of those natural locations that render public relations superfluous. Its bay on Puget Sound is surrounded by the green, green country of Washington with the snow-capped Olympic and Cascade mountains looming in the background and, at 14,410-foot, Mount Rainier towering over them all. The climate is fresh and moist enough to earn the town's sobriquet of the "Emerald City". In spring and summer, the place positively sparkles.

Seattle's fortunes are very much tied to those of the Boeing aircraft manufacturers, though the lumber industry, which got the town started in the 1850s, is still thriving. The town's deepwater Pacific harbour

has made it a natural gateway for trade with the Orient and the town benefits from a lively Chinatown, as well as a Japanese community. It was also the springboard for the Alaska and Klondike gold rushes of the 1880s and 1890s.

Pioneer Square (First Avenue and Yeslerway) is the only vestige of the good days. Its Victorian red-brick has been spared the urban developers' wrecking ball, and the pleasant tree-shaded little square is surrounded by some good restaurants (both expensive and moderate) quality boutiques and excellent jazz clubs. Look out for the ornate pergola, in fact a bus shelter.

You can explore Seattle's lower depths on an **Underground Tour** (from 610 First Avenue; call 682-4646 for reservations). It leads you through the subterranean city that was burned out in 1889 and buried under today's sidewalks, streets and buildings, which were simply

191

erected on top. You'll see old shops and façades and eerie galleries, illuminated by the guide's amusing stories of the town's beginnings.

Like any self-respecting port, Seattle is liveliest along the **waterfront.** Seafood restaurants, fish stalls and chandlers share the area along Elliott Bay with parks and the **Seattle Aquarium** (Pier 59). Stop by to feast your eyes on octopus, sharks, eels, seals and salmon, or watch a film on the watery depths in the Omnidome theatre. Afterwards, when it's time to get out on the water yourself, harbour tours (Pier 56) and a variety of ferry rides (Pier 52) will fit the bill.

Also on the waterfront, **Pike Place Market** (Pike Street and First Avenue) presents a delightful mixture of stalls with farmers, fishmongers and butchers selling their own produce.

The **International District,** bounded by Fourth and Eighth avenues and Main and Lane streets, includes Chinatown and the Japanese neighbourhood. You'll find dozens of jade and jewellery shops here, as well as great restaurants, a Buddhist temple and the **Wing Luke Memorial Museum** (414 Eighth Street), which traces the history of Chinese immigration to the West Coast during the mining and railway construction days of the 19th century.

The great symbol of Seattle is the 607-foot **Space Needle** standing on a tripod, a proud relic of the 1962 World's Fair that gave Seattle a much-needed boost after its 1950s slump. There is a revolving restaurant and an observatory at the top from which you have a splendid **view** across the city to the Olympic mountains and the Cascade Range dominated by Mount Rainier.

Immediately below the Needle is the **Seattle Center,** which also grew out of the World's Fair. It groups the Opera House, Playhouse, Coliseum and two first-rate museums, and is well worth a visit.

The **Pacific Science Center** is a spectacular structure designed by Minoru Yamasaki to house exhibits on space exploration, laser technology, the rich Indian culture of America's north-west, but above all the oceanography of Puget Sound. The **Art Museum Pavilion** (a branch of the Seattle Art Museum in Volunteer Park, known for its excellent Asian collection) features contemporary American and regional artists, as well as major travelling exhibitions.

If the silhouette of Mount Rainier has proved too inviting to resist, why not take an excursion out to the **Mount Rainier National Park,** two hours south of town, and enjoy some exhilarating hiking on its rugged slopes.

BRIEFINGS

Alaska, largest state of the U.S.A., encompasses a vast area full of infinite variety—a popular misconception is that it is all one frozen wasteland.

The **south-eastern Panhandle,** from Ketchikan via Juneau up to Haines and Skagway, has a moderate climate, plentiful rain, a green and fertile land, with considerable forests. The **Gulf Coast,** north and west of Haines around the Gulf of Alaska, is the most densely populated, centring on Anchorage, the state's only real metropolis.

The **Western region,** including the Alaskan Peninsula and the Aleutian and Pribilof islands, is foggy, wet and windy, great for sea- and bird-life. The **Interior** south of the Brooks Range from the Canadian Yukon border towards the Bering Sea has a dry climate, a land of extremes, hot in summer, bitterly cold in winter. And the **Arctic,** extending from Kotzebue above the Seward Peninsula in the west around Barrow to the North Slope at Prudhoe Bay offers the bleak polar landscape of permanently frozen soil.

A good way to see Alaska is by boat. Cruise ships leave from Seattle and (in summer) Vancouver, San Francisco and Los Angeles.

Hawaii. This 50th state of the U.S.A. is an archipelago of seven inhabited islands, a collection of islets, reefs, sandbars and rocks strung out over 1,500 miles in the North Pacific.

The state's capital, Honolulu, is a modern, high-rise city on the island of **Oahu.** The long white beaches and blue ocean are perfect for swimming and sunbathing, and surfers swear by the waves to be found on Oahu's north shore. When the sun has gone down, Waikiki offers the most vigorous nightlife.

The island of **Hawaii,** with Hilo its main city, is known locally as the Big Island because of its size and to distinguish it from the state name. There is plenty of sun and sand on the island's west coast, but the main feature remains its volcanoes, particularly the still-active Kilauea Crater.

Maui has superb beaches and plenty of sports facilities, as well as the old royal capital of Lahaina. A visit to the 10,000-foot, dormant volcano, Haleakala, is a must.

Further north, **Molokai** and **Lanai,** are ideal for those who want a quiet holiday—splendid opportunities for hiking, mule-trekking or rugged jeep-trips, while the rivers and waterfalls of **Kauai,** the Garden Island, are a delight for fishing enthusiasts.

The Berlitz HAWAII travel guide provides a comprehensive survey of all there is to see and do on the islands.

WHAT TO DO

Sports

Few countries are more sports-conscious than America. The competitive spirit runs high in every activity. With no new geographical frontiers to conquer, the urge remains to swim and run faster, jump further, climb higher and hit the ball harder than last week. The facilities are first-rate.

The Atlantic coasts of New England, New York and New Jersey, the Carolinas and Florida and the Pacific coast of California provide every imaginable **water sport**—swimming, diving, boating—and they're inventing new ones every season. For surfing, snorkelling, scuba-diving, wind-surfing and water-skiing, there are shops at the seaside resorts where you can rent the necessary equipment. Inland towns like Chicago or Detroit provide the same kind of facilities on their lakes and rivers.

(Many hotels have their own swimming pools, perfect to cool off and relax in after a long hot drive.)

Comparisons are invidious, but long-time reputations hold that southern California is best for surfing and the Florida Keys is best for scuba-diving. For surfing, the best

Hawaiian waters are ideal for surfing

waves are to be found at Malibu on Point Duma and Surfrider, at Santa Monica State Beach north of the pier and at La Jolla on Windansea and Boomer.

For sailing, Long Island Sound (New York and Connecticut), Cape Cod (Massachusetts), Newport (Rhode Island), the Chesapeake Bay (Maryland and Virginia) and Fort Lauderdale (Florida) are among the best on the East Coast, while Pacific sailors swear by San Diego (California) and Seattle (Washington).

Canoeing, a leisurely sport in the Florida Everglades, becomes an exhilarating test of endurance on the Colorado River in Arizona and Utah or in Yellowstone Park.

Deep-sea **fishing** provides high adventure in the Caribbean waters off Florida, but it's equally satisfying up around Cape Cod, along the Outer Banks of North Carolina or off the northern California coast.

For freshwater fishing check with local information centres for licensing regulations. **Hunting** in the Rockies for moose, elk and gamebirds is carefully regulated but by no means forbidden.

Hiking has become a major sport in these health-conscious times. There are marvellous opportunities in the national parks of the West or the hills of New England. The famous Appalachian Trail runs all

195

the way from Maine down to Georgia. It's the best way to get away from the crowd. Wear good walking shoes or boots, not just tennis shoes, for the longer hikes, and warm clothes for the sudden cool of the evening in the mountains. The rangers who run the national parks can help you with maps for the more interesting nature trails.

If you want to try **mountain climbing,** it's best to go with an experienced guide, especially over unfamiliar terrain. You can usually rent equipment in the national parks.

Jogging is still a popular pastime, healthiest of all barefoot along a sandy beach. The sports stores will try to sell you a lot of jogging "equipment"—haute-couture track-suits, Swiss timers, sweat bands, pedometers. But all you really need is a good pair of shoes and a towel. The town parks often have marked trails with exercise stations en route. In Boston, for instance, the parks, which locals call their "emerald necklace" strung along both banks of the Charles River, are perfect places for jogging. If you want to get around a little faster, rent a **bicycle** or—if you don't mind grazed knees and elbows—**roller-skates.**

Tennis, **golf** and **squash** are also popular. Tennis has become such an obsession that many towns provide floodlit courts for night-time games. Frequently the hotels have at least one tennis court in their grounds and can sometimes help you gain access to the local golf clubs. It helps to take your home golf-club membership card, but there are also many municipal golf courses open to the public.

Horse riding is good in New England and California. In the national parks, it's one of the more satisfying ways to get off the tourists' beaten track. In Yellowstone, Yosemite and Grand Canyon, **mule riding** is a more sedate alternative—and often a wiser one over the rugged terrain.

If you're taking a winter holiday, **skiing,** both cross-country and downhill, is spectacular in Colorado, Utah and California, but there are also first-class family resorts in New England. You may find the après-ski a little slow, but the slopes are fine and the people more disciplined at the ski lifts than in Europe.

Spectator Sports

Don't let ignorance of the basic rules of **American football** or **baseball** discourage you from watching these wonderfully colourful pastimes. Consider them rituals of anthropological interest. They

Perfect ski conditions in Colorado

provide fascinating insights into the mysteries of American society. An hour of the raucous humour of a baseball crowd at the New York Yankees or the Boston Red Sox, the militant religious fervour of the football fans at the Dallas Cowboys or the stoical fatalism at the Chicago Bears will teach you more about the local community than any sociological monograph. Hot-dogs taste better at baseball. And if you feel the need for some exercise of your own, you can always take advantage of baseball's "seventh inning stretch"—midway through the seventh of the nine innings, there is a pause while the spectators stand up and stretch.

Other sports that are better known outside America, such as **basketball** and **ice-hockey,** are played out in a particularly electric atmosphere, charged up by a lot of gambling on the "points-spread" (points difference between the two teams) in the one and by the violent body contact in the other. This is the stuff of Roman circuses. In comparison, the American version of **soccer** is rather tame.

Just what 20th-century America can do to the once sedate game of **tennis** is best witnessed at the U.S. Open Championships at New York's Flushing Meadow in September. The only thing drowning out the roar of the jumbo jets flying over from La Guardia Airport is the clamour of the spectators. And yet the tension somehow brings the best out of the players.

An unusual sport played in Newport, Rhode Island, and in Florida is **jai alai** (pronounced "high lie"), a local version of the high-speed Basque game, pelota. It's played in a three-walled court, trapping and hurling the ball with a scooped reed-basket known as a cesta. Night games are played at the Biscayne Fronton in Miami.

Horse racing attracts some colourful characters to Aqueduct and Belmont in New York and to Santa Anita in Los Angeles. But the great moment of the racing year is in Louisville for the Kentucky Derby (pronounced Der-bee) in May. If you are in the country at the time, but can't get to Louisville, you can still attend one of the countless Kentucky Derby parties held around the country, often in neighbourhood bars. Several hours are spent in drinking mint juleps (Bourbon whisky with crushed ice, sugar and fresh mint), while the race itself lasts just two minutes.

Shopping

The most important advice we can give you on shopping in the U.S. is not to start on your first day or you may find you'll have to go home early. For Americans, the business of seducing the consumer has become a fine art. Advertising, promotional stunts, discounts and perpetual "sales" have been developed to a point where the only time it is safe to go out merely window-shopping is after closing time.

Best Buys on the East Coast…

The best bargain in **New York** is window-shopping. Some of Manhattan's store windows are the most imaginatively dressed in the world, an ongoing street-museum of creative salesmanship. Of course, there is also junk, piled high, but at least it doesn't cost you anything.

Europeans will find the New York discount practice, widely advertised in the Sunday papers, particularly advantageous for cameras, radios and electronic calculators from Japan. In the realm of gadgets, Hammacher Schlemmer (456 E. 57th Street) reigns supreme with such extravagant oddities as electronic weighing machines that talk to you in the bathroom. The ultimate store to visit for toys is F.A.O. Schwarz (fifth Avenue and 58th Street; GM building). In a world of diminishing quality and synthetic fabrics, American men's all-cotton shirts are an excellent buy.

Manhattan's large department stores make up an exciting world of their own. The most imaginative

merchandiser is Bloomingdale's (Lexington and 59th Street).

Boston's importance in the nation's history makes it an ideal place to find the best of old Americana, but it becomes increasingly difficult to get the authentic stuff at less than historic prices. In antique shops in Charles Street on Beacon Hill or around Harvard Square in Cambridge, you'll happen on some original, sturdy colonial furniture, but more often some very good reproductions. Look out, as well, for beautifully painted, wooden decoy-ducks possibly used by Pilgrim pot-shotters. Patchwork quilts are another speciality of the colonial days, as well as decorative lacy-patterned glassware and handmade pewter (the latter at Faneuil Hall's Heritage Shop). Although whaling days are over, you can still find delicately carved scrimshaw ornaments made from whale bone and walrus tusks (particularly in curio shops in Back Bay or around Cape Cod and, above all, on Nantucket Island). Fragrant green candles made from bayberries are a speciality of Cape Cod.

Washington being such a terrific museum town, the museums also provide the best place to buy unusual and attractive gifts. The Air and Space Museum shop has some great model aircraft and spaceships for children and their fathers. The

199

Museum of Natural History is your best bet for jewellery of semi-precious stones and beautifully mounted pieces of rare minerals. The main Smithsonian Bookstore, located in the Museum of American History, offers a splendidly comprehensive selection of the country's arts, history and technology. Near the Mall entrance, take time to browse through the museum shop, which sells replicas of the more popular exhibits of old Americana. The National Geographic Society (17th and M streets) is also well worth visiting for its wonderful maps and picture-books of places near and far. For posters of the great masters, art calendars and art books, try the shops at the National Gallery of Art, both East and West, and the Hirshhorn.

Study the newspapers, especially the Sunday editions which are usually filled with advertising about the sales or "specials" currently promoted in the big stores. The major cities have discount stores, particularly good for records, cameras, electronic equipment and sporting goods. The press also gives details of local flea markets, generally held only at weekends.

...And Everywhere Else

Clothes. All the big cities import the fashionable clothes of French and Italian couturiers—the trick is to find them cheaper here than back home. But we also recommend that you take a look at California sportswear for women and at the American designers in men's clothing

High fashion and local crafts

201

who seem to have the knack of combining style *and* comfort, particularly in casual attire—great shirts and well-made moccasins. Apart from cowboy clothing, styles are international.

For children. Baby equipment, such as push chairs, back packs, and travel cots, is much cheaper in the U.S. than in Europe. Children's clothing also costs a lot less, and there are great bargains in the sales.

Jewellery. If you're looking for diamonds, concentrate on Diamond Row in New York. You'll find lovely turquoise in New Mexico, silver in Texas.

Compact Discs. The range of classical, jazz and popular recordings is probably the best in the world and the frequent discounts make them a good bargain. Prices are far lower than in Europe.

Gadgets and tools. Americans will do anything to make life easier in the kitchen, the bathroom or the toolshed, and there is a wide range of gadgets to choose from. Make sure, if it's electric, that it will adapt to your home voltage and plug system.

Cosmetics and toiletries. Whereas Europeans still produce a larger range of quality perfumes and eau-de-Cologne, the Americans have a bigger selection of lotions and creams, and good quality make-up is generally cheaper than in Europe. Try these out at the *beginning* of your trip so that you'll know which ones to stock up on at the end. There are some great-tasting toothpastes in a huge range of flavours. And the giant cans of shaving foam last almost forever.

Stationery. For some reason, Americans make the best notebooks, and they're always coming up with bright new ideas for filing-systems, address books, folders, labels and sticking tape. Good gifts for school kids—and their parents.

Craftwork and curios. As a rule, the artwork you'll find in shopping centres and in souvenir shops is junk, mass-produced in

---

One Man's Poison

A fine American institution for bargains in second-hand goods is the garage sale. Families moving away or just periodically emptying out their attics and cellars offer old clothes, furniture, books, records and ornaments displayed in the driveway of their garage. Track them down from their hand-written advertisements posted on walls, lampposts or supermarket notice boards or by just driving slowly around residential neighbourhoods on summer Saturdays—you're bound to find half a dozen. They're great places to discover the kind of old Americana—even ash-trays, car licence-plates and tobacco tins—that Americans consider junk and Europeans consider antiques.

Taiwan, Hong Kong and South Korea (though this stuff is apparently acquiring value as Low Kitsch, the more ludicrous, the better). Your best chance of finding authentic craftwork and high quality replicas is in the gift shops of art museums. These are usually run by people who care about the aesthetic reputation of their institution and some care goes into the selection of articles for sale. Try the Museum of Modern Art and the Metropolitan in New York, the museums of the Smithsonian in Washington, and the Art Institute of Chicago. As well as the usual posters and reproductions of paintings and sculpture, these and other museum shops sell fine jewellery of semi-precious stones set in good silver and gold, and handwoven rugs and clothes.

Entertainment

Nightlife in America is strictly a phenomenon of the big cities. In New York, Boston, Philadelphia, Washington, Chicago, San Francisco and Los Angeles, the **opera, ballet** and **symphony concerts** are major events of the social calendar. You have to plan well ahead to get tickets for these, but it's worth the effort. Your travel agency will probably be happy to help you contact the relevant city visitors information centres and arrange advance bookings.

The best **theatre** is still in New York, but other major towns have good repertory groups and experimental drama, particularly where there's a large university.

Discotheques continue in force, though with more varied music (even golden oldies) than the monotonous 1970s stuff. **Nightclubs** range from the spectacular extravaganzas of Las Vegas with top-flight singers and comedians, via the seedy strip-joints (both male *and* female) of San Francisco to quiet supper-clubs with a dance band, or just a piano bar in the smarter hotels. Jazz is king in New Orleans. New comedians try out on Sunset Strip in Los Angeles or in Greenwich Village, New York. And satirical cabaret knocks everything it can lay its hands on in Chicago. In Miami's Little Havana, they dance in the streets. In Texas, some of the nightclubs offer electronic bucking broncos and mud-wrestling. But the fashions change as fast as the light bulbs.

If you're a **cinema** buff and like to be ahead of your crowd, many of the big American movies that open in Europe in the autumn or at Christmas are released in the U.S. during the summer. These days, the major films rapidly become cult movies, and the queues of eager fans form twice around the block. Waiting to see a film, often for the

203

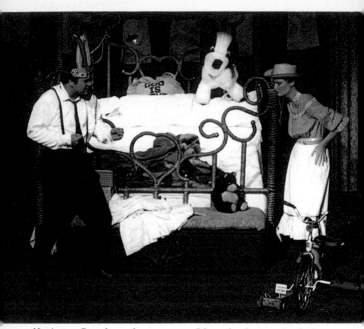

Not just on Broadway, theatre groups thrive throughout the U.S.

fourth or fifth time, has become a ritual complete with musical entertainment and picnics in the street. Focal points for this delightful madness are Westwood in Los Angeles and Third Avenue, New York.

Another great cultural phenomenon is the all-night **television,** a good way of curing your jet lag.

Often the best part of the programmes is the used-car commercial. But it's also a chance to catch up on the classics—the Marx brothers cavorting in *Duck Soup* or Woody Allen's *Manhattan*.

Night Time in New York

If you could do proper justice to night-time New York, you'd never have the energy to see it by day.

Theatre is still Broadway, on side-streets between West 44th and 50th

Opera is almost equally richly endowed with the huge classical resources of the Met and the modern repertoire of the New York City Opera, both at the Lincoln Center. The New York Philharmonic is the flagship for the 30 or so classical music concerts you can choose from on any one evening—with the added summer joy of free Philharmonic and Metropolitan Opera performances in the city's parks. Going to the cinema is a highly respected pursuit in Manhattan, both for first-run fare around Times Square and up on Third Avenue above 57th Street and for old Hollywood classics and subtitled foreign films in the smaller art-houses. The Film Society of Lincoln Center features programmes of retrospectives and hosts the autumn New York Film Festival.

streets for the big show and big ticket-prices. Off-Broadway and "Off-Off-Broadway" shows are smaller and cheaper. Dance undeniably has its world capital in New York. The excellent resident companies—the New York City Ballet, Robert Joffrey, Merce Cunningham, Alvin Ailey, Paul Taylor, Dance Theater of Harlem and the American Ballet Theater—also attract the competition of the very best foreign companies on tour.

On the nightclub scene, which only really livens up after midnight, disco rolls on with its own fathomable momentum, with modish New Yorkers predicting its imminent death since the day it was born. But jazz is making a strong comeback, especially in the clubs in Greenwich Village and SoHo, the West 50s and on the Upper East Side. For a quieter night, go dancing at the supper-clubs in the classic hotels around Rockefeller Center.

Unless you have your heart set on seeing the season's smash hit musical, you can usually pick up theatre tickets at the box office a day or two in advance (Friday and Saturday nights excepted). Look for discount vouchers at the Visitors Bureau (2 Columbus Circle) or, if you don't mind queues, head for TKTS (47th Street and Broadway or 2 World Trade Center) for half-price seats on the day of the performance.

But, if you like to play it safe, buy a copy of the *New Yorker* magazine before you leave home and order your tickets by mail.

Night Time in Washington

Under the direction of the cellist-turned-conductor Mstislav Rostropovitch, the National Symphony has become a world-class orchestra. The visiting ballet and opera performances make grand galas—and people at the Kennedy Center love dressing up. The Eisenhower Theater (political balance in choosing names was necessary though the old soldier wasn't much of a theatre-buff) stages pre- and post-Broadway productions.

For tickets, we suggest you pick up an out-of-town copy of the *Washington Post* before you even get to Washington—best of all, the Friday edition with the "Weekend" section—to plan and book ahead for plays, operas or concerts. Otherwise your hotel can sometimes help, or else try your luck with returned tickets at the box office an hour before curtain time.

Night Time in Boston

Those invidious categories of "highbrow" and "lowbrow"—nobody likes being called either—are both catered for among music-lovers by the highly respected Boston Symphony Orchestra and the jolly Boston Pops. Both perform at Symphony Hall on Huntington Avenue. The Pops moves outdoors in summer to give free concerts at the Hatch Memorial Shell on the Charles River Esplanade just west of Beacon Hill. For a magical experience, try to catch a chamber music concert in the courtyard of the Isabella Stewart Gardner Museum. The Boston Ballet and the Opera Company both perform at the Wang Center (270 Tremont Street). Theatre productions bound for New York try out "on the road" at Boston's Shubert, Colonial or Wilbut theatres. Critics being notoriously unreliable and investors too impressionable, you may be lucky enough to see a good play unfairly panned here that never makes it to Broadway because the backers get cold feet.

Night Time in San Francisco

In this instance, San Francisco is much more fun than Los Angeles.

Most people in L.A. seem to prefer to have their fun in private at home. But San Franciscans go out a lot and the coffee-house and street life is booming and bouncing with vitality every night.

Bars in San Francisco are a whole way of life—downtown Irish bars on Geary, Italian coffee houses and every other ethnic variety in North Beach, and a host of late-night waterfront "joints" along Embarcadero to Fisherman's Wharf. There is no obvious distinction to be made between "tourist traps" and local hang-outs, perhaps because San Franciscans are the most enthusiastic tourists in their own town, so you'll be mixing with the locals wherever you go. Some bar-cafés around North Beach specialize in good amateur opera singing—you'll hear it as you walk by the open doors. If it sounds too much like Pavarotti or Callas, it probably is—played on the jukebox between "sets". The San Francisco Opera is exceptionally good, but you'll be lucky to find a seat.

Broadway is also the main thoroughfare for jazz **nightclubs** and "topless", "bottomless" and other forms of strip-joint. The South of Market District, or SoMa, is home of a dynamic new night-life scene; you'll be able to dance the night away in clubs which stay open until the sun comes up.

EATING OUT

The nation's Latin motto *E Pluribus Unum* (One From Many) could well apply to American eating habits. It's a country of cuisines as diversified as its ethnic groups and at the same time a great uniformity in the everyday meals. Texas draws on its Mexican beginnings for spicy chilli and barbecued dishes and Florida takes inspiration both from Cuban rice dishes and Jewish delicatessen. Yet in both states and all the way to Maine in the north-east corner or to the state of Washington in the north-west, you'll find the same straightforward vegetable soups, plain green salads, steak and potatoes, fruit pies and ice-cream. The great mobility of Americans has spread the original unadorned, often rather bland cooking of the Anglo-Saxons right across the country. This basic unity of taste has, for instance, guaranteed the phenomenal success of the fast-food franchises.

You'll find many areas have distinctive cuisines, notably New York on the East Coast, New England, Miami and New Orleans in the South. For the all-important wines to accompany a fine meal, the vineyards of California naturally merit particular mention in the West Coast section. But first a few basic facts worth noting.

207

Eating Habits

For Europeans, American eating habits may need some introduction. As soon as you sit down for breakfast, you're likely to see the waitress advancing on you armed with a pot of coffee. Serving coffee is a hospitable way of saying "good morning" and it takes firm, clear action to stop this automatic gesture if you don't want coffee immediately. The coffee is weak by European standards, but your cup will be refilled several times.

If you're having fried eggs, don't forget to specify "sunny side up" (cooked from below only) or "over, easy" (turned and cooked lightly on top). Toast may be white, whole wheat or rye, and English muffins (something like a crumpet) are usually available, too.

At lunch and dinner, salad is served before the main dish, which used to upset habitues of French cuisine; now, in these slimmer times of diets and health-foods, the salad makes a good appetizer. Salad dressings are often surprising concoctions not familiar to every European palate. If you want a simple dressing you can always order oil, vinegar and a little mustard and mix your own vinaigrette.

You may find that you are offered a cocktail before, during and after the meal; cocktails are not necessarily considered as aperitifs.

Alternatively, you can order wine immediately.

One aspect of dining out that might surprise non-Americans is the formality often demanded by the "smarter" restaurants in the evenings. That means ties and jackets for men and and no jeans or sneakers for either men or women. This is enforced to maintain a certain "respectability" in the clientele. If you arrive without a tie or jacket, the establishment will occasionally lend you something from their own stock—most often horrendously ugly and even emblazoned with the restaurant's name in case you were thinking of walking off with it. Dresses are *not* provided for women, but female customers have been known to take their jeans off and use their blouse as a minidress—and be allowed in!

What to Eat

Sandwiches. Usually served on white, rye, pumpernickel or whole-wheat bread, a roll or a bagel (doughnut-shaped rolls) or perhaps on *pitta*, Arab flat bread. Classic fillings include chicken, tuna and egg salads; lox (smoked salmon) and cream cheese, a delicious Jewish speciality served on a bagel; corned beef or pastrami (a kind of cured beef), also Jewish specialities. Club sandwiches consist of three slices of toast in layers filled with turkey, lettuce, tomato, bacon and sometimes cheese. Hoagies, heroes, submarines and grinders all refer to the same thing: a fat, mouth-stretching sandwich of French bread, stuffed with meatballs, sausages or ham- cheese-salami-onions-lettuce-peppers-tomatoes and olive oil.

Soups. These days many Americans will lunch on soup rather than a hamburger, and more and more small restaurants include soups on the menu. Vichyssoise (don't let the name mislead you, it's an American dish) is a chilled concoction of leeks, potatoes and onions; chilli con carne, often served as a soup, is in fact a substantial and spicy stew of kidney beans, ground beef, onions and tomatoes.

Salads. The usual kind, served with dinner, consists of iceberg lettuce and a few slices of tomato and cucumber, but many American-style restaurants nowadays feature a self-service salad bar with an attractive assortment of greens and garnishes. Your choice of dressings may include "tomatoey" French, Thousand Islands (mayonnaise, ketchup, hard-boiled egg), Russian (mayonnaise and chilli sauce), Italian (oil, vinegar, garlic and herbs) or Roquefort.

The "chef's salad", which may contain ham, cheese and chicken, is a meal in itself; raw spinach salad with mushrooms ranks as a great American original; Caesar salad has romaine lettuce and a raw egg in the dressing; coleslaw (cabbage salad) often appears with sandwiches. Cold pasta salads often served with crisp raw vegetables or seafood are also extremely popular.

Meat. Beef still takes first place—though in health-conscious America the trend is away from red meat. It comes in enormous portions and is almost invariably tender. In steakhouses, you often pay a flat rate for a steak, a baked potato with sour cream or French fries (chips), a self-service salad bar, and in some cases a glass or two of wine, beer or *sangría*.

"Spare ribs" are pork ribs, marinated in a spicy sauce, baked or broiled and eaten with your fingers.

Fish and Seafood. Americans don't like fish as much as Europeans or the Japanese. But the fish itself is often of excellent quality, both the ocean fish of the East and West coasts and the Gulf of Mexico and the freshwater fish of the mountain rivers and lakes. Look out in particular for red snapper, blue fish, sea bass, salmon and trout.

Shellfish are perhaps best of all, particularly the clams, crab, shrimp, scallops, lobster, abalone and oysters, the latter more often cooked than they are in Europe. You can overcome the local tendency to deep fry everything by politely stating a preference for sautéeing or broiling. Lobster is best boiled rather than grilled.

Vegetables. Beans, peas, broccoli and cauliflower tend to be impeccable in appearance and colour but bland in taste. The great American vegetable is the Idaho potato, baked and served with sour cream, butter and chives. Corn on the cob is fine, off the cob it's watery. Succotash is corn mixed with lima beans.

Cheese. Swiss-, Dutch- and British-style cheeses are manufactured in Wisconsin, New York and Vermont; the sharper ones approach their European equivalents. The French cheeses, imported or locally imitated, tend to be too pasteurized to approximate their taste on the

other side of the Atlantic, but the creamier versions are spiced with herbs and garlic. It's rare to find a cheese-board served except in French restaurants, though cheese-and-wine bars are spreading.

Desserts. Ice-cream is undeniably where America excels. Amazing flavours are invented every week—spearmint, peanut butter, apple pie, cinnamon—and their vanilla is terrific. Put it on the fruit pies, *à la mode*, and you're heading for blissful calorific catastrophe. Apple Brown Betty is a kind of apple crumble. Brownies are a good, rich chocolate cake usually served in small squares. In early summer when the strawberries are at their peak, strawberry short-cake—scone-like biscuit on the bottom with dollops of whipped

cream on top—can be sublime. Enjoy things, you're on holiday.

Regional Cuisines and Resources
New York restaurants can be very good but their chefs tend to move around as often as baseball managers. The best ones are lured away by better offers from a competitor or do well enough to open up their own places—until they discover they're better cooks than businessmen and move on again to someone else's kitchen. The best selection of restaurants is in the theatre district, the East Side or Upper West Side or down in the Village. But rather than be told where to go *this* year, just consider the variety of cuisines.

The town benefits enormously from its cosmopolitan tradition. Italian restaurants are legion. With the French, you have to choose carefully between the few authentic —and very expensive—establishments and those run by tax-dodgers with French accents. The Chinese are much more reliably competent and more varied in their regional cuisines, especially down in Chinatown itself. And then there's the whole gamut of "ethnic" restaurants—Greek, Spanish, Japanese, Jewish, Mexican, Brazilian and Indian. Increasingly, they're taking their exotica out on to the streets, vending Arab *falafel* sandwiches, spicy Indian *samosas* or Turkish *shish-kebab* in hot competition with the local pretzels and hot-dogs.

New York's own contribution to world gastronomy begins with the hot-dog, which you can have either with sauerkraut or fried onions but not, authentically, without mustard—if only for the aesthetics of the yellow stripe down the middle of the sausage. The deli sandwich is a special Broadway institution, naming permutations of turkey, corned beef, pastrami, bacon, lettuce, tomato or whatever after some film star, pop singer or sports champion who may or may not once have ordered it. The New York strip steak is a good, thick cut of tenderloin, best eaten rare. Long Island Blue Point oysters are too good to spoil with the cocktail sauce that inevitably accompanies them. Manhattan clam chowder has tomato in it (as opposed to the creamy New England type). Although cheesecake may have come from Central Europe, it didn't taste heavenly until it reached Brooklyn and the delis on Broadway.

New York wines are mostly inferior to California's, but Napa Valley has nothing to match the Manhattan, a cocktail of four parts Bourbon whisky, one part vermouth and a dash of bitters. Here's lookin' at you, kid.

New Orleans prides itself on the most distinctive cooking in America. It certainly is very evocative of the city's own personality—or is it that the city derives its personality from the cuisine, rich, Latin and spicy? The Creole tradition combines a French love of intricate sauces, the Spanish penchant for mixing fish, meat and vegetables with rice, and a taste developed in the West Indies and Africa for liberal seasoning with hot peppers. Plus plain old Southern cooking.

The classic dish is jambalaya, a paella-like dish of rice and chicken, crab or shrimp with bits of sausage or ham, pepper and tomato. The poor man's version is the simple bean 'n rice, red kidney beans and rice flavoured with pork, deliciously filling. Gumbo, a West African word for okra (the green vegetable known to British India as "lady's fingers"), is the basic ingredient and generic name for thick soups of chicken or seafood, a meal in itself. Crayfish, pronounced and often spelled in Louisiana "crawfish", best served, for a change, straight boiled, is a favourite springtime shellfish to which whole festivals are devoted in April. The oysters here are plentiful and relatively cheap, encouraging New Orleans chefs to prepare them in a number of marvellous ways: fried or in gumbo; as oysters Rockefeller—rich as its name, baked with spinach and breadcrumbs; or oysters Bienville, cooked in white wine with shrimp, mushrooms and shallots; or an oysters brochette, skewered and wrapped in bacon.

The local version of the all-American submarine sandwich is the "po-boy" (long) and muffuletta (round), French bread stuffed with cold meats, oysters or other seafood, cheese and salads, often pepped up to local taste.

New Orleans claims to have invented the cocktail, or at least the word. It is, they say, a distortion of the French for egg-cup, *coquetier,* in which a Creole bartender by the name of Antoine Peychaud served his brandy and bitters in the 19th century. The dictionary, a little more soberly, suggests that cocktail was originally "a horse of racing qualities, but not a thoroughbred", a fair description of two New Orleans specialities: the Sazarac is rye whisky or bourbon and bitters served in a glass coated with anisette; the Ramos Gin Fizz adds sugar, lemon, lime, orange-flower water, egg-white, crushed ice and soda water to your poor, defenceless gin. If you're still conscious, try a *café brûlot,* coffee flavoured with cinnamon, cloves, orange peel and *flambé.*

In **Boston,** start your day with some of the "home-baked" muffins offered at breakfast time. Blueberry, cranberry, apple and date-nut are among the more interesting varieties. Or start with pancakes swimming in maple syrup.

New Englanders are proud of their culinary specialities, not the least of which is Boston baked beans. Simmered in molasses with a chunk of salt pork, this hearty dish is said to have been a decisive factor in the British abandoning their American colonies.

If that's true, the French were probably delighted to become America's first allies for a chance to sample the lobster caught off the coasts of Maine and Massachusetts, simply boiled or grilled with melted butter. The oysters, too, are good, as are the haddock, sea bass, flounder and scrod (local white fish, usually young cod). Cod turns up in fried fishcakes, a traditional Friday night supper. But clams are king hereabouts. Clam chowder is a uniquely New England soup (beware the heretical "Manhattan" version with tomatoes) of clams with potato, onions, milk and a few other seasonings that each cook keeps secret. A great summer ritual at the beach is the clambake. Over a wood fire, heat some rocks covered with seaweed. Then add potatoes, clams, lobsters and corn to steam under a second layer of saltwatery seaweed. When the potatoes are done, the feasting begins, accompanied by lashings of cold beer.

For dessert, as in the rest of America, fruit pies are legion but the cranberry is a New England innovation. Boston cream pie is actually sponge cake filled with custard and glazed with chocolate icing. For real authenticity, try Indian pudding made of cornmeal, molasses and milk.

Ethnic Food

Nearly every large city has its Little Italy, Chinatown or neighbourhood Jewish delicatessens and Mexican restaurants. **Italian** food follows traditional lines, except that a favourite spaghetti dish tends to be with meat balls rather than *bolognese*. On the West Coast you'll find a superb Italian version of bouillabaisse, a thick fish soup known as *cioppino,* more fish than soup, with every available shellfish spiced up or down, according to taste.

Chinese food does not have to be a full blown meal. At a dimsum parlour or tea shop you can select a smorgasbord of shrimp balls, steamed dumplings, deep-fried sweet potatoes and chopped mushrooms in wedges of rice-pastry, accompanied by pots of sauce.

Restaurants offer many variations of Chinese regional cooking—Peking, Szechuan, Shanghai, Hunan, as well as the familiar Cantonese. It's worth calling up a day in advance to order a whole Peking duck, glazed with honey and roasted slowly with spring onions. This gentle delicacy finds a sharp contrast in the spicy smoked duck you might try in a Szechuan or Hunan restaurant. But don't overlook seafood. The steamed sea bass prepared with chopped green onions, black beans, garlic, ginger and sesame oil or the Szechuan shrimp, are served piping hot in both senses of the word.

In recent years, **Thai**, **Vietnamese** and **Japanese** restaurants have proliferated, adding new accents to the Asian food scene.

Mexican eating houses offer an array of snack-like food—crispy *tacos* and *tostadas* and moist *tortillas* (cornmeal pancakes) stuffed with shredded beef or chicken, grated cheese, avocado and lettuce. But the best dishes are more substantial and sophisticated—*camarones con salsa verde* (shrimp in green sauce), *carne de puerco en adobo* (pork in chilli sauce) or *mole poblano* (chicken with almonds, sesame seeds, peanuts, chilli, raisins and savoury chocolate sauce).

For the uninitiated, **Jewish** food features Eastern European borscht, cabbage soups (red or green) with sour cream, gefilte fish and minced fish balls. Blintzes, a crisper version of the Russian blini, are folded over minced meat as an appetizer or sweet cream cheese as a dessert. Corned beef and spicy, smoked, Rumanian-style pastrami make delicious sandwiches; they're served on rye bread with potato salad and pickled cucumbers.

Drinks

The cold drinks are almost invariably served iced.If you want a good serving of cola or lemonade in the coffee shops and fast-food places, specify "little ice". Beer is of course also served icc cold. You'll find a wide variety of foreign beers as well as the home-grown variety.

New York State has some decent wines; those from California are better, especially the red ones. You can order domestic wine by the bottle or, in many places, in carafes as the "house wine". French and Italian wines, at quite reasonable prices, also appear on menus.

Since Americans discovered wine, hard liquor has gone somewhat out of fashion. But not the cocktail hour! Dry martinis (gin and a few drops of dry vermouth) are very potent. Bourbon, a mellow whisky distilled in Kentucky, is made of corn (maize), malt and rye; drink it straight, on the rocks or with soda. Many bars have a late-afternoon "happy hour" when they'll give you two drinks for the price of one or serve free snacks. Liquor (alcohol) licensing laws are explained on p. 228.

BERLITZ-INFO

CONTENTS

A ACCOMMODATION

Hotels and motels. It's always wise to book your accommodation in advance. You can also make reservations directly through the nation-wide toll-free booking services operated by the large hotel and motel chains (listed in the Yellow Pages of the telephone directory).

American hotels and motels usually charge by the room, not by number of occupants. Rates indicated normally do not include the state and city sales taxes or daily occupancy tax. Although hotel rates are not subject to control, they are comparable within similar categories of establishment. The larger hotel chains divide into luxury, moderate and budget class. Most rooms have air conditioning, private bathroom and television. When booking your room, you normally have the choice of twin (two beds) or double (room for two with one bed). Many motels furnish all their rooms with two double beds—very convenient for family travel. Most resort hotels offer special rates to guests who take their meals on the premises: A.P. (American Plan) includes three meals a day and M.A.P. (Modified American Plan), breakfast and lunch or dinner.

Motor hotels or motels are one of America's great bargains. Many belong to national or international chains, so you can make all the bookings for your trip at the same time.

Country Inns are usually luxurious and well restored. They are particularly popular in New England, but also exist in other areas.

Tourist homes (guest houses) and **Bed-and-Breakfast** establishments (usually fancier than European versions) are found in smaller towns and holiday centres. Local tourist authorities usually have lists.

Ranches. The *Country Vacation Guide* is an excellent source of information about accommodation on ranches. There are luxury ranches, enormous complexes with all facilities from swimming pools and tennis courts to barbecues, and the simpler—but nevertheless comfortable—dude ranches, where you can take part in everyday ranch and cowboy life. For further information, contact a travel agency. Cheaper accommodation can be found on farms and family ranches.

Youth hostels offer inexpensive accommodation, usually outside towns. They are open to members of national youth hostel organizations abroad. For further details, contact your national youth hostel association or write to American Youth Hostels, Inc.:
733 15th St., NW, Suite 840, Washington, DC 20005.

There are a number of centrally located residences run by the **YMCA** and **YWCA.** Rates are quite reasonable. You do not have to belong to the association to stay at the "Y", but demand is high so you should book at least two months ahead.

Students and young people can also find inexpensive accommodation at university campuses and through local student associations.

Camping. Camping in America generally involves some kind of recreational vehicle—campers, motor homes or caravans (trailers). So if you are camping the American way, follow the indispensable Rand McNally *Campground & Trailer Park Guide* or the voluminous Woodall's *Campground Directory*, both issued annually, which grade campsites according to facilities. Sites are divided into two categories: public campgrounds (found in the national parks, state parks and state forests) and private sites. Accommodation in the most popular parks must be booked directly with the individual lodge, anywhere from eight weeks to a year in advance, depending on the season. If you are sleeping rough, you must obtain a permit from the park.

AIRPORT INFORMATION FOR MAIN GATEWAY CITIES

New York. *John F. Kennedy International* (JFK), 16 miles south-east of midtown Manhattan. Hotel limousine (shared-car) and mini-bus service at frequent intervals throughout the day. Express bus (Carey Transportation) to Grand Central Airlines Terminal and the Air TransCenter at Port Authority Bus Terminal (West 42nd Street) every 30 min.; a separate shuttle service operates from the Grand Central stop to major midtown hotels. The journey from JFK takes from 60 to 70 minutes (longer at peak hours). JFK Express (bus and underground/subway) every 20 min. during the day; travel time 50–60 min. Helicopter to East 34th Street every 30–40 min. during the day; travel time 20 min.

Transfer by coach from JFK to *LaGuardia* (25–40 min.), by limousine to *Newark International* (45–75 min.). Regular inter-airport helicopter service (10–15 min. depending on airport).

Miami. *Miami International* (MIA), 7 miles west of downtown Miami. Super Shuttle mini-bus service available; travel time 25 min. Municipal buses run regularly from the airport bus station (on the first level of concourse E, opposite U.S. customs) to Miami and Miami Beach.

Transfer by coach to *Fort Lauderdale Airport* (60 min.).

Los Angeles. *Los Angeles International* (LAX), 16 miles south of central business district. Airport bus service to downtown Los Angeles, Hollywood, Beverly Hills, Westwood, etc., every 10–20 min. during the day. Numerous connections to surrounding areas.

Transfer to *Van Nuys Airport* every 30 min.

Chicago. *O'Hare International* (ORD), 18 miles north-west. Airport bus service to hotels every 20 min. during the day; travel time 30 min. Subway (rapid transit train) service every 15–30 min. during the day, every 60 min. at night.

Boston. *Logan International* (BOS), 2 miles east of business district. Airport bus service to major hotels every 30 min. during the day; travel time 20–30 min. Shuttle bus (Massport) to subway (Blue Line) service every 15 min. during the day; travel time 15 min. Shared-cab service to surrounding towns. Free airport bus to Water Shuttle—runs every 15 minutes during daylight across inner harbour to downtown Boston.

C CLIMATE AND CLOTHING

The U.S. climate varies considerably from frozen north to southern sun-belt, so take your destination into account as you pack your suitcase. In summer it's warm pretty well everywhere—except northern New England, Oregon and Washington. In winter, heavy outer wear is essential, unless you're restricting your visit to the southernmost states. For New York and Chicago, rubber overshoes, or galoshes, are a good idea; some swear by "long johns"—long underwear. Even in Florida and California, temperatures can plummet to freezing point in December, January and February. Yet cold spells never last long and can be followed by a heat wave; be prepared for every eventuality. North and south, air conditioning takes the edge off summer heat and humidity, so have a jacket or light wrap handy for the chilly indoors.

With the high crime rate prevailing in cities nowadays, unobtrusive attire is the rule—no flashy clothing or jewellery. Tourists would be wise to follow suit.

Monthly average maximum and minimum daytime temperatures in degrees Fahrenheit:

		J	F	M	A	M	J	J	A	S	O	N	D
Chicago	max.	32	35	45	59	70	81	84	83	76	65	48	35
	min.	17	20	29	40	50	60	65	64	56	46	33	22
L.A.	max.	67	68	69	71	73	77	83	84	83	78	73	68
	min.	47	49	50	53	56	60	64	64	63	59	52	48
Miami	max.	76	77	80	83	85	88	89	90	88	85	80	77
	min.	59	59	63	67	71	74	76	76	75	71	65	60

| New York | max. | 39 | 40 | 48 | 61 | 71 | 81 | 85 | 83 | 77 | 67 | 54 | 41 |
| | min. | 26 | 27 | 34 | 44 | 53 | 63 | 68 | 66 | 60 | 51 | 41 | 30 |

And in degrees Celsius:

Chicago	max.	0	2	7	15	21	27	29	28	24	18	9	2
	min.	−8	−7	−2	5	10	16	18	18	13	8	1	−6
LA	max.	19	20	21	22	23	25	28	29	28	26	23	20
	min.	8	10	10	12	13	16	18	18	17	15	11	9
Miami	max.	24	25	27	28	29	31	32	32	31	29	27	25
	min.	15	15	17	19	22	23	24	24	23	22	18	16
New York	max.	4	5	9	16	22	27	29	28	25	19	12	5
	min.	−3	−3	1	7	12	17	20	19	16	11	5	−1

COMMUNICATIONS

Post offices. The U.S. postal service deals only with mail. Post office hours are from 8.30 or 9 a.m. to 5 or 5.30 p.m. Monday to Friday, and from 8 or 9 a.m. to 12 noon or 1 p.m. on Saturday. Some branches have longer hours. Smaller branches close one afternoon a week, often Wednesday; all are closed on Sunday. Stamps can also be purchased from vending machines in drugstores, air, rail and bus terminals and other public places, but you will pay a surcharge.

Poste restante (general delivery). You can have mail marked "General Delivery" sent to you care of the main post office of any town. The letters will be held for no more than a month. American Express offices also keep post for 30 days; envelopes should be marked "Client's Mail". Take your driving licence or passport with you for identification.

Telegrams and faxes. American telegraph companies are privately run. They offer domestic and overseas services, as well as domestic telex facilities, and are listed in the Yellow Pages. You can telephone the telegraph office, dictate the message and have the charge added to your hotel bill, or dictate it from a coin-operated phone and pay on the spot. A letter telegram (night letter) costs about half the rate of a normal telegram., but takes at least twice as long to arrive. Most hotels are equipped to handle faxes—at a price. However, most shopping malls have an office services store which can send faxes much more cheaply.

Telephone. The telephone is part of the American private enterprise system. Public telephones can be found just about everywhere. Directions for use are on the instrument. Telephone rates are listed and explained in the front of the general directory or White Pages. Also included is a map showing area code numbers, information on personal (person-to-person) calls, reverse-charge (collect) calls, conference, station-to-station and credit-card calls. For local directory enquiries (Information) call 411. Evening (after 5 p.m.), night (after 11 p.m.) and weekend rates are lower.

Long-distance and many international calls may be dialled direct, even from a pay phone if you follow the posted directions and have plenty of coins on you. Certain credit cards are also accepted. For long-distance calls where a 3-digit code is required, you must dial 1 before the area code. Dial "O" for operator assistance. If you don't know the subscriber's number, dial 1 before the area code plus 555-1212 (free of charge from a pay phone) and give the operator the name and address of the person you want to call. Long-distance calls cost more from a pay phone than from a private one.

All numbers with an 800 prefix are toll-free (no charge). Always dial 1 before the 800. For information on toll-free numbers dial 1-800-555-1212.

CRIME AND THEFT

Petty theft and non-violent crime have become almost commonplace in many American cities and towns, and crimes of violence occur ever more frequently. But there's no need to panic. Follow a few common-sense rules and relax and enjoy yourself.

- Store valuables and any reserves of cash, traveller's cheques, etc., in your hotel safe. Carry only what you actually need from day to day. Make sure your handbag is securely fastened and keep your wallet in an inside rather than hip pocket. Never leave belongings unattended—at an airport, in a store, on the beach, or open to view in a car. It may be wise to cultivate a modest appearance: leave the glittering rings and fine gold chains at home.

- If you are in unfamiliar territory, enquire if there are any neighbourhoods which are unsafe—and keep away from them. After dark, go where the crowds are, avoiding side streets and poorly lit areas.

- If you are driving, keep car doors locked and windows up, lest some malefactor leap in when you're stopped at a traffic light. By the same token, never drive around with the windows wide open and your handbag or valuables on the seat: an invitation to some snatch-and-grab artists.

- As in most countries, be on the alert for pickpockets and bag-snatchers in any crowded atmosphere, from a packed bus to a circus tent.

CUSTOMS AND ENTRY REGULATIONS

To enter the United States, most foreign visitors need a valid passport and a visitor's visa, which can be obtained at any U.S. embassy or consulate. In general, British visitors with a valid ten-year passport and a return ticket purchased from one of the major airlines do not need a U.S. visa for stays of less than 90 days. Canadians need only present proof of nationality. Everyone must fill out customs declaration forms before arrival (usually distributed by your airline near the end of the flight).

Red and green customs channels are in operation at major international airports like New York's JFK, Chicago, Miami and Houston, where, on the whole, customs formalities have become less time-consuming than in the past.

The following chart shows certain duty-free items you, as a non-resident, may take into the U.S. (if you are over 21 where alcohol is concerned) and, when returning home, into your own country:

Into:	Cigarettes		Cigars		Tobacco	Spirits		Wine
U.S.A.	200	and	50	or	1,350 g.	1 l.	or	1 l.
Australia	200	or	250 g. or		250 g.	1 l.	or	1 l.
Canada	200	and	50	and	900 g.	1.1 l.	or	1.1 l.
Eire	200	or	50	or	250 g.	1 l.	and	2 l.
N. Zealand	200	or	50	or	250 g.	1 l.	and	4.5 l.
S. Africa	400	and	50	and	250 g.	1 l.	and	2 l.
U.K.	200	or	50	or	250 g.	1 l.	and	2 l.

A non-resident may claim, free of duty and taxes, articles up to $100 in value for use as gifts for other persons. The exemption is valid only if the gifts accompany you, if you stay 72 hours or more and have not claimed this exemption within the preceeding 6 months. Up to 100 cigars may be included within this gift exemption.

Plants and foodstuffs also are subject to strict control; visitors from abroad may not import fruits, vegetables or meat. The same goes for chocolates that contain liqueur.

Arriving and departing passengers are required to report any money or cheques, etc., exceeding a total of $10,000.

E   ELECTRIC CURRENT

110-volt 60-cycle A.C. is standard throughout the U.S. Plugs are the flat, two- and three-pronged variety. Visitors from abroad will need a transformer (240–110 V) and an adaptor plug for their electric razors.

EMBASSIES

Australia.   1601 Massachusetts Ave., NW, Washington, DC 20036; tel. (202) 797–3000

Canada.   501 Pennsylvania Avenue, NW, Washington, DC 20001; tel. (202) 682–1740

Eire.   2234 Massachusetts Ave., NW, Washington, DC 20008; tel. (202) 462–3939

New Zealand.   37 Observatory Circle, NW, Washington, DC 20008; tel. (202) 328–4800

South Africa.   3051 Massachusetts Ave., NW, Washington, DC 20008; tel. (202) 232–4400

United Kingdom. 3100 Massachusetts Ave., NW, Washington, DC 20008; tel. (202) 462–1340

EMERGENCIES

Many cities and towns have a special 911 number for emergencies— fire, police, ambulance and paramedics. Otherwise, dial "0" and the operator will connect you with the service you need.

G   GETTING AROUND THE UNITED STATES

By Car

Rental. Cars can generally be hired at airports and in most towns. Charges vary, so be sure to shop around for the best deal. Most car-rental companies offer a flat rate that includes unlimited mileage. If you are planning to drive more than 70 miles a day, this is probably the solution for you. There are also companies specializing in older (3 or 4 years), worn but mechanically sound cars. They are much cheaper and good for local touring. You may also want to look into rent-here, leave-there deals. A major credit card is essential to avoid paying an enormous deposit; some companies even refuse to accept cash as a deposit.

For tourists from non-English-speaking countries, a translation of your driving licence is highly recommended, together with the national licence itself, or failing this, an International Driving Permit. Collision damage insurance can substantially increase car rental costs. Check your own car insurance, holiday insurance or credit card cover to make sure you are not already covered for collision damage.

Auto driveaway. If you'd like to cross the country cheaply, look into an auto-driveaway deal. Several companies engage people to drive someone else's car from one part of the country to a specified destination. A refundable security deposit and an International Driving Permit are required, and the driver must be at least 21 years old. You pay petrol expenses yourself, and you have to take a reasonably direct route established in advance. Consult the Yellow Pages of the telephone directory under "Automobile Transporters & Driveaway Companies".

American Automobile Association. The AAA offers information on travelling in the U.S., as well as short-term insurance for visitors. Contact AAA World Travel:
1000 AAA Drive, Heathrow, Florida 32746-5603

AAA helps members, as well as foreign visitors affiliated with recognized automobile associations, in case of breakdown or other problems.

On the road. Drive on the right. In many states it is legal to overtake on both sides on major highways. Intersections are generally marked with stop or yield signs to indicate who has priority. Speed limits, almost always posted, are rather strictly enforced. An excellent interstate highway system crosses the U.S. Odd numbers designate highways running north-south, while even-numbered interstates run east-west. Interstate 80, for example, links New York with San Francisco, Interstate 5 goes from Vancouver to San Diego.

Highway terminology in the U.S. is confusing and not particularly consistent. But in general, turnpikes and thruways are high-speed, dual carriageways (divided highways) that collect tolls; parkways, which do not allow lorries (trucks), may or may not charge; freeways and expressways are usually free. Most road maps indicate which highways collect tolls. It's wise to have a stock of change on hand for the tolls— the "exact change" lanes (you drop the coins in a basket) move faster.

Speed limits are clearly signposted. Generally the limit on highways is 55 mph, but it goes up to 65 mph on rural stretches of interstate highways in many states. If you keep within the flow of traffic, you'll have no problem, but go any faster, and a patrol car will pull you over.

Expressway driving follows certain rules of the road. Rather than accelerate up the slip road (ramp) to join the traffic at its own speed, you hesitate at the top of the ramp and wait for an opening.

If you have a breakdown on an expressway, pull over onto the right-hand shoulder, tie a handkerchief to the doorhandle or radio aerial, raise the bonnet (hood) and wait in the car for assistance. At night, use the blinker.

Petrol (gas) and services. Stations are numerous and easy to locate. Many stations might be closed in the evenings and on weekends. At night, petrol stations require exact change or a credit card.

By Bus

Greyhound-Trailways U.S.A provides transport to and from cities all over the United States. Passengers can make as many stopovers en route as they wish, provided the destination is reached before the ticket expires. Sometimes travel by bus costs about the same—or even more—than flying. So don't automatically assume the bus is cheaper. Flat-rate rover passes for specified periods of unlimited travel are available. These tickets must be purchased outside the U.S.

Areas not served by Greyhound-Trailways are usually covered by regional and local bus companies.

By Train

500 major cities and towns are linked daily by Amtrak, America's National Railroad Passenger Corporation. Amtrak is currently advertising a variety of bargain fares, including excursion and family fares; the *U.S.A. Railpass*, the equivalent of the Eurailpass, can only be purchased abroad but many package tours are available in the U.S. Trains are a far less efficient means of transport than in Europe—buses are usually a better option for long-distance travel.

By Air

Air travel is by far the quickest and most convenient way of getting round the U.S. and less expensive than in Europe. Shuttle services operate on some heavily travelled routes.

The *Visit U.S.A.* fares on offer may not represent a saving for those only making one or two stops, though the rover tickets on offer outside the country usually do.

Fares change constantly, so it would be wise to consult an airline or travel agency for the latest information about discounts and special deals.

Local Transport

Municipal buses operate in most cities and towns. Some big cities have underground-railway (subway) systems. Maps of the network are usually posted at every station and in every train, and can be obtained at the ticket booth in any station. To take the subway, you need a token (purchased at the booth) which you insert in the turnstile.

Taxis are lined up at airports, railway stations and bus terminals, or you can hail a cab in the street or telephone for one. A tip of at least 15% is expected. On arrival in the U.S., if you take a taxi from the airport into town, make sure you have several small banknotes with you, as cab drivers will not give change for large denominations.

GETTING TO THE UNITED STATES

Because of the complexity and variability of the many fares, you should ask the advice of an informed travel agent well before your departure.

Scheduled flights. New York is the principal gateway to the U.S. from the British Isles, but major transatlantic carriers offer direct flights from Heathrow to some 20 other U.S. destinations. Direct flights are also available from Gatwick, Glasgow, Dublin and Shannon. Flying time from London to New York is 7 hours, to Los Angeles, 11 hours. Apart from the standard first-class and economy fares, main types of fares available are:

Super APEX: book 21 days prior to departure for stays of 7 days to 6 months; no stopovers.

Special Economy: book any time; offers plenty of flexibility.

Standby: bookable only on the day of travel, minimum 2 hours prior to departure.

From Sydney and Auckland, scheduled flights leave daily for Los Angeles, with connecting flights to other U.S. destinations.

Charter flights. Some are organized by scheduled airlines, others by special holiday companies. ABC (Advance Booking Charter) flights must be reserved at least 21 days in advance for a minimum stay of 7 days.

Package holidays. A wide variety are available, ranging from fully organized to flexible. Some packages include hire of a camper or camping equipment.

Baggage. You are allowed to check in, free, two suitcases of normal size on scheduled transatlantic flights. In addition, one piece of hand baggage of a size which fits easily under the aircraft seat may be carried on board. Check size and weight restrictions with your travel agent or air carrier when booking your ticket.

It is advisable to insure all luggage for the duration of your trip. Any travel agent can make the necessary arrangements.

H HEALTH AND MEDICAL CARE

Free medical service is not available in the U.S., and a visit to the doctor can be expensive, hospitalization an economic disaster. Holiday medical insurance is therefore a wise precaution. You can arrange for coverage through one of the big international companies or your travel agent.

Foreign visitors may wish to ask their embassy or consulate for a list of doctors. In an emergency, local telephone operators are an excellent source of advice (dial "0").

Visitors from abroad will find that certain medicines sold over the counter at home can only be purchased with a prescription (and vice versa).

HITCH-HIKING

Except on expressways and parkways it is legal to hitch-hike—but not really advisable. The practice does not have the best reputation—one hears too many stories of assault, robbery and worse. As a result, Americans, usually a warm-hearted lot, are wary of picking up anybody, and you may find yourself waiting hours for a ride.

L LIQUOR (ALCOHOL) REGULATIONS

Liquor laws vary a good deal from state to state and sometimes within a state. Utah is strictest, Nevada the most liberal. In certain areas you may buy alcoholic beverages in a supermarket or drugstore, in others you must go to a licensed liquor (or "package") store, even for beer. And the sale of alcohol on Sundays and holidays is frequently restricted or prohibited.

Ordering a drink in a bar or restaurant is encouraged, restricted or illegal depending on where you are. In some areas it may be necessary to join a "club"—usually a formality for nominal fee—to get a martini. Small restaurants that don't have the expensive permit to sell alcohol will generally let customers bring their own beer or wine ("brown bag" it)—but only in certain states. Only weak (3.2) beer is served in "dry" counties.

The minimum age for purchasing or drinking alcoholic beverages in a public place ranges from 18 to 21, according to the state. You may be asked for some identification ("I.D.") when buying alcohol, whether or not you look under age, and you can be refused if you have no I.D.

LOST PROPERTY

Air, rail and bus terminals and many stores have "lost-and-found" departments, and restaurants also put aside lost articles. If your lost property is valuable, contact the police. If you lose your passport, get in touch with your embassy or nearest consulate immediately.

M MAPS

Tourist information authorities distribute free maps and brochures. City and state maps can be purchased in bookstores and stationery stores and at many petrol stations.

The maps in this book were provided by Falk-Verlag, Hamburg, who also publish a complete road atlas to the U.S.

MONEY MATTERS

Currency. The dollar is divided into 100 cents.
Coins: 1 (penny), 5 (nickel), 10 (dime), 25 (quarter), 50 (half dollar) and $1.
Banknotes: $1, $2 (rare), $5, $10, $20, $50 and $100. Larger denominations ($500 and $1,000) are not in general circulation. All denominations are the same size and same green colour, so be sure to check each banknote before paying.

For currency restrictions, see CUSTOMS AND ENTRY REGULATIONS.

Currency exchange. Normal banking hours are from 9 a.m. to 3 p.m., Monday to Friday.

Only major banks in larger cities or at international airports will change foreign money or foreign-currency traveller's cheques, so it's important to carry cash or traveller's cheques in dollars. However, make sure you always have a supply of $1–$10 banknotes on hand for taxis, tipping and small purchases.

Credit cards. Credit cards play an even greater role here than in Europe. In the U.S., they are a way of life, and most Americans have several. The major credit cards are accepted as cash almost everywhere. When paying for goods or services, including hotel and restaurant bills, you will be asked: "Cash or charge?", meaning you have the choice of paying either in cash or in "plastic money".

Traveller's cheques. Visitors from abroad will find traveller's cheques drawn on American banks far easier to deal with, and they are widely accepted in stores, restaurants and hotels. Only cash small amounts at a time, and keep the balance of your cheques in the hotel safe if possible.

N NATIONAL PARKS

Government protected reserves are found all over the U.S. and take in everything from stretches of coastland and wayside campgrounds to wildlife reserves and wilderness areas. The 37 sites designated "National Park" or "National Monument" are areas of outstanding historical, geological and scenic importance. Almost all can be reached by car or bus and some have direct connections to major cities by rail or air. Each state also has numerous "State Parks", of lesser consequence but with pleasant scenic and recreational resources.

High season is mid-July to mid-August, when the most popular parks are likely to be crowded and advance reservations for campsites recommended. Parks often provide guided tours and usually lay on organized summer and winter activities.

Entrance fees vary. The reasonably priced *Golden Eagle Passport* (available at parks) entitles all the occupants of a private car to unlimited access to national parks. Seniors are entitled to reduced rates.

A few of the greatest parks have been dealt with in detail in this guide. Here are a few more that you may like to visit.

Shenandoah National Park (Virginia). Nearest wilderness park to the nation's capital, this park consists of a 105-mile stretch of wooded Blue Ridge Mountain.

Petrified Forest National Park (Arizona). In the most colourful area of the Painted Desert, six forests of fallen logs, 200 million years old, have been turned into jasper and agate.

Mesa Verde National Park (Colorado). Indians abandoned this prehistoric "green tabletop" 800 years ago, leaving behind stone cities built into the cliffside.

Bryce Canyon National Park (Utah). A fantasy land of pink cliffs, dramatic rock formations and breathtaking scenery.

For further information see your travel agent or write to the National Park Service, Washington, DC. For state parks, write to the state tourist department.

P PHOTOGRAPHY AND VIDEO

All popular brands of film and photographic equipment are available. Try to buy in discount stores where prices are much lower. Colour-print film usually takes 2 to 5 days to be developed, black-and-white film and slides up to a week.

Video tape is available for all machines, but pre-recorded U.S. tapes will not play on European systems (nor vice versa). They can be converted, but this is very expensive.

POLICE

City police are concerned with local crime and traffic violations, while Highway Patrol officers (also called State Troopers) ensure road safety, and are on the lookout for people speeding or driving under the influence of alcohol or drugs.

The American police officer is usually fair and friendly. Do not hesitate to approach any policeman and ask for assistance or information; helping you is part of their job. In case of emergency, find a phone, dial "911" or "0" and ask the operator to contact the police.

PRICES

The U.S. has a larger range of prices for any one item than you will find anywhere else, as well as a greater choice. The best prices are usually offered by huge discount houses, located just off highways and in suburban areas. Independent service stations are cheaper than those run by the large oil companies. Most prices do not include a state sales tax (normally 4 to 8%) and a city or resort tax.

To give you an idea of what to expect, here's a list of average prices in U.S. dollars. However, due to inflation as well as seasonal and regional variations, these figures must be regarded as approximate.

Camping. Entry fee $6–14 per vehicle, reservation fee $2.50–4, trail camps (hikers) $7 per night, developed campsites $14–16 per night, primitive sites $7 per night, caravan (trailer) and camper hookups from $16 to $24 per night.

Car rental. *Small* (e.g. Toyota Tercel) $42 per day, $250 per week. *Medium* (e.g. Ford Fairmont) $47 per day, $270 per week. *Large* (e.g. Ford LTD) $52 per day, $290 per week. Note: car rental is cheaper in Florida.

Cigarettes (20). $1.85 and up.

Entertainment. Cinema $6–7, theatre $25–60, nightclub/discotheque $10–50 for cover charge, $3–5 for drinks, jazz club $14–30.

Hairdressers. *Man's* haircut from $20. *Woman's* cut from $20, shampoo and set from $18.50, shampoo and colour rinse from $20.

Hotels (double room). Expensive $150 and up, moderate $75–150, budget or motel $45–75.

Meals and drinks. Breakfast $3–14, lunch $7–15, dinner $15 and up, carafe of wine $6–7, glass of beer $2–4, whisky $3.50–6, soft drink $1, coffee $1–3.

YMCA/YWCA. Double room with bath, approx $42–52, single room without bath $28–14.

PUBLIC HOLIDAYS

The following public holidays are—with a few exceptions—celebrated nationwide.

New Year's Day	January 1
Martin Luther King Day*	Third Monday in January
Washington's Birthday**	Third Monday in February
Memorial Day*	Last Monday in September
Independence Day	July 4
Labor Day	First Monday in September
Columbus Day***	Second Monday October
Veteran's Day***	November 11
Thanksgiving	Fourth Thursday in November
Christmas	December 25

*   celebrated in most states; on January 15 in a few states
**   celebrated on February 22 in some states (also called
        President's Day or Washington-Lincoln Day)
*** celebrated in most states, on October 12 in some states
        (also called Pioneer's Day, Farmers' Day, Fraternal Day,
        Discoverer's Day)

Lincoln's Birthday (Feb. 12) is widely observed in the northern states, Robert E. Lee's Birthday (Jan. 19) and Confederate Memorial Day (late Apri/early May) in most southern states.

If a holiday falls on a Sunday, banks and most stores close on the following day. There are also long weekends (such as the one following Thanksgiving) when offices are closed for four days. Many restaurants never shut, however, not even at Christmas.

R RADIO AND TELEVISION

You'll almost certainly have radio and television in your hotel room, with a vast choice of programmes. Some television networks broadcast from 6 a.m. until 3 or 4 the next morning; others never go off the air.

American commercial television aims to appeal to the largest possible number. The non-commercial Public Broadcasting Service (PBS) screens music and drama programmes (many of them bought from the BBC) along with its own news and information broadcasts.

There are numerous AM and FM radio stations. Most broadcast pop and country-and-western music, but each large city has at least one classical-music radio station.

RESTAURANTS

In the U.S., there's something for every taste and budget. You can dine in the luxurious surroundings of a fashionable restaurant or eat on the run at an informal lunch counter.

Most restaurants charge more for dinner than for lunch. You can order as little or as much as you want, but sometimes there's a minimum charge. In simple places, you often pay the cashier on your way out, after leaving the tip on the table. See also TIPPING and PRICES.

Breakfast is served from 7 to 10 a.m., lunch between 11 a.m. and 2.30 p.m. and dinner from 5 or 6 to 10.30 p.m. or so. Brunch is featured on Sundays between 11 a.m. and 3 p.m. Reserve a table in advance if you plan to eat in a well-known restaurant.

If you feel hungry at an unusual hour, you'll be able to find a fast-food establishment, diner or coffee shop serving hot food, sandwiches or snacks at almost any time of day or night:

Coffee shops and cafeterias offer sandwiches, hamburgers, salads, simple hot dishes and pastries. They do not serve alcoholic drinks.

Delicatessens (deli), a cross between grocery stores and restaurants (some are just restaurants), are known for their gargantuan sandwiches. Other specialities include salads and hearty soups. Some delicatessens are kosher.

Diners. Originally a sort of coffee shop on the road built in the shape of a railway dining car, some have now become quite elaborate and serve alcohol. But they're still open long (often 24) hours.

"Ethnic" restaurants, a term covering all foreign restaurants—Greek, Italian, Japanese, Chinese, Thai, Vietnamese, Indian, Spanish, Mexican, Middle Eastern, German, Russian, Scandinavian, and so on. There's something for every taste.

Fast-food outlets. You'll see plenty of reminders that you're in the land of McDonald's and Kentucky Fried Chicken.

French restaurants. Approach these with caution, for each excellent one there are another hundred that are mediocre and expensive.

Health-food restaurants and **juice bars.** Every imaginable kind of fruit and vegetable juice is served, plus delicious salads, wholefood and vegetarian specialities. The ingredients are often organic.

Open-air or sidewalk cafés have become very popular in recent years. They serve hamburgers, *quiches, crêpes* and sandwiches, and will usually let you linger over your coffee.

Pizzerias serve a wide variety of pizzas, usually big enough for three people. You can also buy pizza by the slice.

Take-outs are small shops where you can order sandwiches, salads, assorted groceries and drinks to take out and consume elsewhere.

T TIME ZONES AND DATES

The 48 conterminous states of the U.S. are—from east to west— divided into four time zones: Eastern (G.M.T.–5 hours), Central (–6), Mountain (–7) and Pacific (–8). The major part of Alaska is on G.M.T. –9 hours, Hawaii on G.M.T. –10.

Under Daylight Saving Time, observed in all states but Arizona, Hawaii, and parts of Indiana, clocks move ahead one hour the first Sunday in April and turn back again the last Sunday in October.

TIPPING

In general, a service charge is not included in the bill; you are expected to tip the waiter, waitress or bartender about 15% (more in luxury establishments). Cinema or theatre ushers are not tipped, but doormen, cloakroom attendants, etc., should be remunerated—never less than a quarter.

Some further suggestions:

Porter	50¢–$1 per bag (minimum $1)
Hotel maid (not for overnight stay)	$1 per day or $5 per week
Lavatory attendant	50¢
Taxi driver	15%
Bus tour guide	10–15%
Hairdresser/Barber	15%

TOILETS

Americans use the terms "rest room", "powder room", "bathroom" (private) and "ladies" or "men's room" to indicate the toilet. If you encounter a pay-toilet, the usual charge is 25 cents.

TOURIST INFORMATION AGENCIES

For information prior to arrival, contact:
United States Travel Service, American Embassy, PO Box 1EN, London W1A 1EN; tel. 0891 616000
or
Meridian International Center
1630 Crescent Pl., NW, Washington, DC 20009; tel. (202) 939-5566

State tourist departments distribute general information and maps of the state, while local *convention and visitors bureaus* put out free city maps and leaflets on principal tourist attractions.

Travelers Aid Services dispenses just about everything, even—for the traveller genuinely in distress—pocket money. Offices are located in most major cities.

Convention and visitors bureaus in the principal cities:

Atlanta Convention and Visitors Bureau, 233 Peachtree St., NE, Box 2000; tel. (404) 521-6600
Baltimore Office of Promotion and Tourism, 200 West Lombard St., Suite B; tel. (410) 752-8632
Boston. Greater Boston Convention and Visitors Bureau, Prudential Tower, P.O. Box 490, Suite 400; tel. (617) 536-4100
Chicago Convention and Tourism Bureau, 23015 South Lakeshore Dr., tel. (312) 567-8500
Dallas Convention and Visitors Bureau, 1201 Elm, Suite 2000; tel. (214) 746-6700
Denver Metro Convention and Visitors Bureau, 225 West Colfax Ave.; tel (303) 892-1112
Detroit. Metropolitan Detroit Convention and Visitors Bureau, 100 Renaissance Center, Suite 1900; tel. (313) 259-4333
Houston. Greater Houston Convention and Visitors Bureau, 801 Congress Ave.; tel. (713) 227-3100
Las Vegas Convention and Visitors Authority, 3150 Paradise Rd.; tel. (702) 892-0711
Los Angeles. Greater Los Angeles Visitors and Convention Bureau, 633 South Figueroa St., 11th Floor; tel. (213) 689-8822

Miami/Miami Beach. Greater Miami Convention and Visitors Bureau, 701 Brickell Ave., Miami, FL; tel. (305) 539-3000

New Orleans. New Orleans Metropolitan Convention and Visitors Bureau, 529 St Anne's St.; tel. (504) 566-5011

New York Convention and Visitors Bureau, 2 Columbus Circle; tel. (212) 397-8222

Philadelphia Convention and Visitors Bureau, Suite 2020, 1515 Market St.; tel. (215) 636-3300. For information on local happenings phone (800) 537-7676.

Phoenix and Valley of the Sun Convention and Visitors Bureau, 1 Arizona Center, 400 E. Van Buren St., Suite 600; tel. (602) 254-6500

Salt Lake City Valley Convention and Visitors Bureau, 180 South West Temple; tel. (801) 521-2822

San Antonio Convention and Visitors Bureau, P.O. Box 2277; tel. (210) 270-8700

San Diego Visitors Bureau, 11 Horton Plaza; tel. (619) 236-1212

San Francisco Visitor Information Center, 900 Market St., Lower Level, Hallidie Plaza. Dial (415) 391-2000 for information and 391-2001 for a recorded summary of the day's events.

Santa Fe Convention and Visitors Bureau, Sweeney Center, W. Marcy; tel. (505) 984-6760

Seattle King County Convention and Visitors Bureau, 8th and Pike Sts.; tel. (206) 461-5840

Washington, DC Convention and Visitors Association, 1212 New York Avenue, NW, tel. (202) 789-7007; 1455 Pennsylvania Avenue, NW, tel. (202) 789-7038 or (202) 789-7000.

W WEIGHTS AND MEASURES

The United States is one of the last countries in the world to resist the metric system. As yet there is no official changeover programme. Some British and Canadian visitors will be happy to go back to the good old days of feet and inches.

Milk and fruit juice can be bought by the quart or half-gallon, but wine and spirits now come in litre bottles. Food products usually have the weight marked in ounces and pounds as well as in grammes.

There are some slight differences between British and American measures, for instance:

1 U.S. gallon = .833 British Imp. gallon = 3.8 litres
1 U.S. quart = .833 British Imp. quart = .9 litres

Conversion charts

Length

cm	0	5	10	15	20	25	30
inches	0	2	4	6	8	10	12

metres	0	1 m	2 m
ft./yd.	0	1 ft	1 yd.	2 yd.

Distance

km	0	1	2	3	4	5	6	8	10	12	14	16
miles	0	½	1	1½	2	3	4	5	6	7	8	9	10

Weight

grams	0	100	200	300	400	500	600	700	800	900	1 kg
ounces	0	4	8	12	1 lb.	20	24	28	2 lb.

Clothing sizes: dresses, blouses, knitwear

U.S.A.	8	10	12	14	16
Great Britain	10/32	12/34	14/36	16/38	18/40

Note: Men's suits and shirts (collar sizes) are the same in the U.S. and Great Britain.

SPEAKING A DIFFERENT LANGUAGE

Even English speakers take time to adjust to the American accent, which varies from region to region. In addition, certain words have different meanings for Americans and British. This list will help you to avoid confusion.

U.S.	*British*
admission	entry fee
apartment	flat
bathroom	toilet
bill	banknote
billfold	wallet
candy	sweet
check	bill (restaurant)
chips	potato crisps
collect call	reverse-charge call
comfort station	public lavatory
cookie	biscuit
cracker	biscuit
dead end	cul-de-sac
detour	diversion
diaper	nappy
divided highway	dual carriageway
eggplant	aubergine
elevator	lift
fall	autumn
faucet	tap
first floor	ground floor
flashlight	torch
French fries	potato chips
garters	suspenders
gas(oline)	petrol
general delivery	poste restante
generator	dynamo
hood	bonnet
jelly	jam
jumper	pinafore dress
kerosene	paraffin
line	queue

liquor	spirits
mail	post
muffler	silencer
pants	trousers
panty hose	tights
pavement	road surface
person-to-person call	personal call
pocket book	handbag
private school	public school
purse	handbag
railroad	railway
rest room	public convenience
roundtrip ticket	return ticket
second floor	first floor
sidewalk	pavement
stand in line	queue up
straight	neat (drink)
subway	underground
sunny-side up	egg fried on one side
suspenders	braces
tail lights	rear lights
trailer	caravan
truck	lorry
trunk	boot (car)
tuna	tunny
underpass	subway
undershirt	vest
vest	waistcoat
wash up	have a wash
windshield	windscreen
yard	garden

U. S. A.

```
0        200       400 km
0        200       400 miles
```

240

MANHATTAN

0   500   1000 m
0   500   1000 yards

N

Lincoln Tun

NEW JERSEY

Hudson River

North River

Holland Tunnel

West Side Highway

Eleventh

Tenth Avenue

Ninth Ave.

Eighth Avenue

Seventh Avenue

CHELSEA

West 2

General Post O

West 20th St

Madison Sq

Theodore Roosevelt House

Union Square Park

Gramercy

Po Academ Muse

Stuyve

Sq

East

GREENWICH

Cherry Lane

VILLAGE

Washington Square

Fifth Avenue

West Houston Street

Walker Park

Avenue of the Americas

Canal Street

Hudson

West Broadway

Broadway

World Trade Center

W

Trinity Pl.

Church Street

City Hall

Lafayette

Trinity Church

City Hall Park

LITTLE ITALY

Grand

Broadway

St. Mark's-in-the-Bouwerie

Second Avenue

First Avenue

Avenue A

Avenue B

Avenue C

Tompkins Square

N.Y. Stock Exchange

Federal Hall National Memorial

CHINATOWN

Buddhist Temple

Bowery

Delancey Street

Houston

LOWER EAST SIDE

Statue of Liberty

Battery Park

Brooklyn Battery Tunnel

Staten Island

Pearl

St.

Street

Fraunces Tavern

Elevated Highway

South St. Seaport

Madison

East Broadway

Seward Park

Hamilton Fish Park

Avenue D

Franklin D. Roosevelt Dr

Elevated Highway

Grand St

East River

Brooklyn Br.

Manhattan Br.

Corlears Hook Park

Park

Williamsburg Bridge

East

Brooklyn-Queens Expressway

242

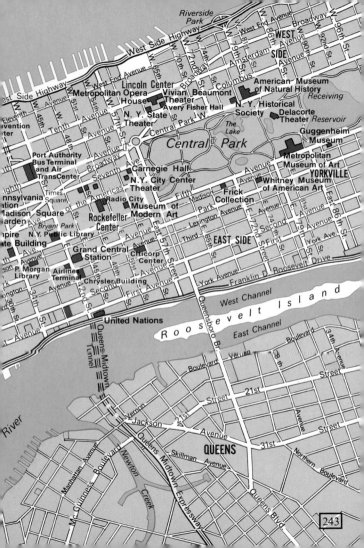

Riverside
Park

West End Avenue
Broadway
W. 96th St.
W. 92nd
Avenue
WEST
SIDE

West Side Highway
W. 72nd
79th St.
Amsterdam
Avenue

W. 65th St.
70th St.
Columbus
American Museum
of Natural History

Eleventh
Avenue
West End Avenue
Lincoln Center
Metropolitan Opera
House
Vivian Beaumont
Theater
Avery Fisher Hall
N.Y. State
Theater
N.Y. Historical
Society
Delacorte
Theater
Receiving
Reservoir

Side Highway
W. 51st
Tenth
Avenue
Central Park W.
The
Lake
Guggenheim
Museum

Convention
Center
Central Park
Metropolitan
Museum of Art
YORKVILLE

Port Authority
Bus Terminal
and Air
TransCenter
Carnegie Hall
N.Y. City Center
Theater
Fifth
Avenue
Whitney Museum
of American Art
East 86th St.

Seventh
Avenue
Broadway
Ave.
Radio City
Museum of
Modern Art
Madison Avenue
Frick
Collection
Second Avenue
York Avenue

Times
Square
of the Americas
Rockefeller
Center
Park
Avenue
E. 72nd Street
First
Avenue

Pennsylvania
Station
Madison Square
Garden
N.Y. Public Library
Lexington Avenue
Third
EAST SIDE

Empire
State Building
Bryant Park
W. 42nd
Grand Central
Station
Citicorp
Center
57th Street
Franklin D. Roosevelt Drive

Madison
Avenue
P. Morgan
Library
Airlines
Terminal
Chrysler Building
Second
Avenue
First Avenue
York Avenue
Roosevelt Drive

Lexington
W. 30th
Avenue
United Nations
York Avenue
Franklin D. Roosevelt Drive
West Channel
Roosevelt Island

River
Queens-Midtown Tunnel
Roosevelt Island
East Channel
Queensboro Br.
Vernon
Boulevard
34th Avenue

21st
Street
Boulevard
Street

McGuinness Boulevard
Manhattan Avenue
Newton
Jackson
21st Street
Queens Midtown Expressway
Avenue
QUEENS
Skillman
Avenue
31st
Avenue
Street
Northern Boulevard

River
Newton Creek
Queens Blvd.

243

BOSTON CENTRE

Boston Inner Harbor

LOGAN ✈

Atlantic Avenue

500 m

500 yards

Museum of / Transportation & Children's Museum

Tea Party Ship

Fort Point

South Station

New Eng. Medical Center

Old North Church

Paul Revere House

Hanover St.

Commercial St.

Salem St.

Parmenter St.

Richmond St.

Endicott St.

John F. Kennedy Bldg.

New City Hall

Faneuil Hall

State St.

Broad St.

Kilby St.

Congress St.

Milk St.

Franklin St.

Summer Street

Washington Street

Beach Street

Kneeland Street

Stuart Street

Harrison Ave.

Washington St.

Shawmut Ave.

Tremont Street

North Station

Boston Inner Harbor

Charlestown Bridge

Massachusetts Dept. of Works

Charles River

Museum of Science

King's Chapel

School Street

Bromfield St.

Winter St.

West St.

Park Street Church

State House

Hart Gray Otis House

Cambridge St.

Suffolk University

State Office Bldg.

Revere St.

Pinckney St.

Mt. Vernon Street

Chestnut Street

Beacon St.

Charles

Boston Common

Washington Mon.

Public Garden

Boylston Street

Arlington

Berkeley Street

Clarendon Avenue Street

Commonwealth

Newbury St.

Boylston St.

Mass. Auditorium

Massachusetts Avenue

Beacon St.

Hereford St.

Gloucester St.

Fairfield St.

Exeter St.

Dartmouth St.

Marlborough

James J. Storrow Memorial Drive

Memorial Drive

Longfellow Bridge

River Basin

Charles

River

Cambridge Parkway

Commercial Avenue

First Street

Torndike St.

Spring Street

Charles St.

Rogers St.

Munroe Street

Binney St.

Porter Street

Fulkerson St.

Sixth St.

Main Street

Ames St.

Amherst St.

Broadway

Portland St.

Binner St.

Vassar St.

Memorial Drive

Harvard Bridge

Massachusetts Avenue

CAMBRIDGE

244

HARVARD UNIVERSITY ↓

Harvard Bridge

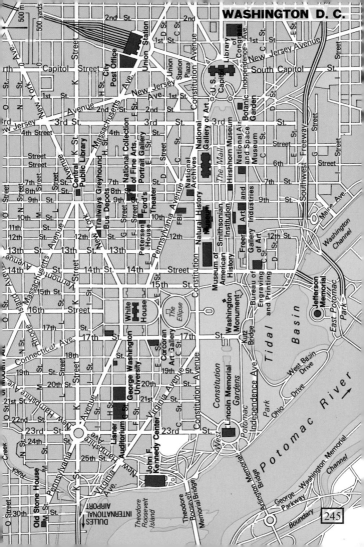

MIAMI AND MIAMI BEACH

Beach Theater of Performing Arts
Lincoln Rd.
South Pointe
Lummus Park
Art Deco District
Collins Ave.
Flagler Memorial
Fisher Island

Venetian Causeway (Toll)
Japanese Teahouse and Garden
Miami Herald
Bayside
MacArthur Causeway
Lummus Island
Port of Miami
Bayfront Park

Virginia Key
Marine Stadium
Planet Ocean
Miami Seaquarium
Causeway (Toll)
Crandon
Key Biscayne
Bill Baggs Cape Florida State Recreation Area

Center for the Arts
N.W. Miami Ave.
14th St.
N.W. 7th Ave.
N.W. 3rd Ave.
S.W. 12th Ave.
Orange Bowl
N.W. 7th St.
N.W. 8th St.
West Flagler
East-West Expressway (Toll)
N.W. 22th
Grapeland Heights Park
East-West Grapeland Expressway
N.W. 7th St.
Dade County Auditorium
Tamiami Trail
West Flagler Street
N.W. 8th St.
S.W. 8th St.
Ludlam Rd.
S.W. 24th St.
S.W. 40th St.
S.W. 57th Ave.
S.W. 67th Ave.

Rickenbacker
South Miami Ave.
Brickell Ave.

Biscayne Bay

3 km
2 miles
METRORAIL
N

Museum of Science and Planetarium
Vizcaya
S.W. 12th St.
S.W. 7th St.
S.W. 3rd Ave.
Highway 1 (Dixie Hwy.)
South Bayshore Dr.
Donner Key
Coconut Grove Exhibition Center
The Barnacle
Coconut Grove
Main Hwy.

S.W. 2nd St.
S.W. 27th
Bird Ave.
Ponce-de-Leon Blvd.
S.W. 42nd
S.W. 37th
S.W. 27th
Le Jeune Road
Magnolia Hwy.
South Dixie Hwy.

Granada Golf Course
Coral Way
Biltmore Hotel
Biltmore Golf Course
Venetian Pool
Bird Road
Coral Gables
University of Miami
Lowe Art Museum
Red Road
Miller Drive
S.W. 56th St.
S.W. 57th Ave.
S.W. 67th Ave.
Sunset Rd.
South Dixie Hwy.
South Miami

Matheson Hammock Park
Fairchild Tropical Gardens
Cutler Road
Snapper Creek Canal
Red Road
North Kendall Drive
S.W. 112th St.
Parrot Jungle
Kendall

MICCOSUKEE INDIAN VILLAGE
NAPLES
Tamiami Canal
West Flagler St.
N.W. 7th St.
41

ORCHID JUNGLE SERPENTARIUM
MONKEY JUNGLE KEY WEST,
HOMESTEAD

247

CHICAGO

W. Oak St.
E. Oak St.
W. Locust St.
E. Delaware Pl.
John Hancock Center
Water Tower
Pearson St.
W. Chicago Ave.
Chicago Ave.
W. Superior St.
W. Erie St.
E. Erie St.
W. Ontario St.
Museum of
Contemporary Art
W. Grand Ave.
E. Grand Ave.
Illinois St.
E. Illinois St.
Wrigley Building
Tribune Tower
W. Kinzie St.
Chicago River
Marina City
E. Wacker Dr.
W. Wacker Dr.
Lake St.
Greyhound Bus Terminal
W. Randolph St.
E. Randolph St.
City Hall
W. Washington St.
E. Washington St.
Madison St.
E. Madison St.
Union Station
Federal Center
W. Adams St.
Lake
W. Jackson Blvd.
E. Adams St.
Chicago
Post Office
Sears Tower
E. Jackson Dr.
THE LOOP
Lincoln Monument
W. Van Buren St.
Art Institute Chicago
Congress Parkway
W. Harrison St.
Harbor
E. Balbo Dr.
Michigan
S. Polk St.
Taylor St.
Central Station
Shedd Aquarium
W. Roosevelt Rd.
E. Roosevelt Rd.
Adler Planetarium
E. 14th St.
Field Museum of
Natural History
E. 16th St.
Soldier Field
W. 16th St.
W. 18th St.
E. 18th St.
E. Cullerton St.
E. 21st St.
W. Cermak Rd.
E. Cermak Rd.
McCormick
E. 23rd Place
E. 24th St.
248
W. 25th Pl.
E. 25th St.

N

CHICAGO-O'HARE
N. Milwaukee Ave.
N. Halsted St.
Chicago River
Branch
N. Orleans St.
N. LaSalle St.
N. Dearborn St.
N. State St.
N. Wabash Ave.
N. Michigan Ave.
N. Rush St.
Kennedy Expwy.
W. Canal St.
S. Wacker Dr.
Franklin St.
LaSalle St.
Clark St.
S. Halsted St.
S. Clinton St.
S. Canal St.
S. Jefferson St.
S. Wells St.
S. Clark St.
S. State St.
S. Wabash Ave.
Columbus Dr.
Lake Shore Dr.
Dan Ryan Expwy.
S. Archer Ave.
S. Dearborn St.
S. Michigan Avenue
S. Indiana Ave.
S. Calumet Ave.
W. Lake Shore Dr.

0   500
0   500

ALCATRAZ, TIBURON

49-Mile Scenic Drive

0   1   2 km

0   1 mile

San Francisco Bay

N

Maritime Museum

Pier 43 1/2   Pier 43

Pier 41

Pier 39

Ghirardelli Square

The Cannery

FISHERMAN'S WHARF

Jefferson St.

North Point Street

Beach Street

Bay Street

North Point Street

Francisco Street

Chestnut Street

Columbus Ave.

Powell St.

Mason St.

Taylor St.

Kearny St.

TELEGRAPH HILL

Coit Tower

Francisco Street

Chestnut Street

Lombard Street

Greenwich Street

Greenwich Street

Filbert Street

Washington Sq.

Union St.

Green St.

RUSSIAN HILL

NORTH BEACH

Vallejo St.

Broadway

Broadway

Pacific Ave.

Cable Car Barn

Jackson Street

Washington Street

Portsmouth Square

Transamerica Pyramid

Ferry Building

NOB HILL

Clay St.

Grace Cathedral

CHINATOWN

Sacramento Street

California Street

Pine Street

Chinatown Gateway

Bush Street

Sutter Street

Sutter Street

Union Square

Geary Street

Geary Street

O'Farrell Street

Ellis Street

Eddy Street

Turk Street

Golden Gate Ave.

Museum of Modern Art

CIVIC CENTER

City Hall

United Nations Plaza

Opera House

Grove St.

Hayes St.

Convention and Visitors Bureau

Old Mint

Greyhound Bus Depot

SOMA

Moscone Convention Ctr.

South Park

Howard Street

Folsom Street

Harrison Street

Bryant Street

Bay Bridge (Toll)

80

First Street

Second Street

TO SAUSALITO

SAN FRANCISCO DOWNTOWN

249

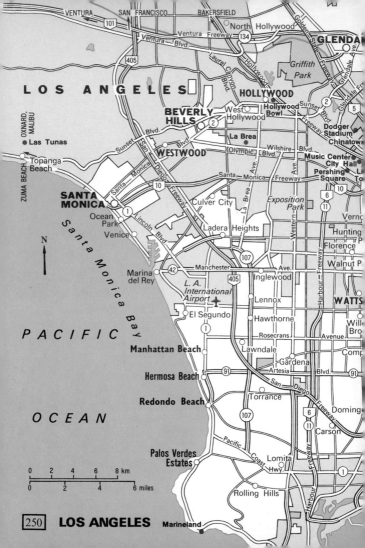

LOS ANGELES

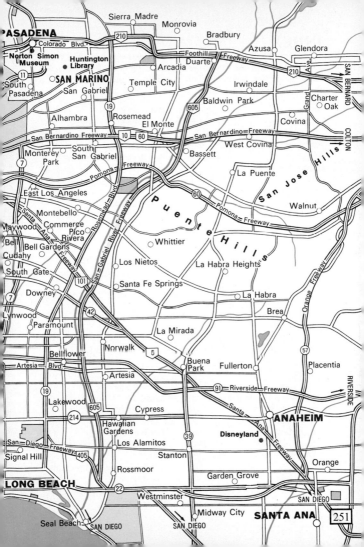

INDEX

An asterisk (*) next to a page number indicates a map reference. Where there is more than one set of page references, the one in bold type refers to the main entry. States listed are in italics. For index to Practical Information, see pages 216–217.

159/606 MUD